CHRISTIANITY and the RELIGIONS OF THE EAST

MODELS FOR A DYNAMIC RELATIONSHIP

Edited by

Richard W. Rousseau, S.J.

VOLUME TWO

MODERN THEOLOGICAL THEMES:
SELECTIONS FROM THE LITERATURE

RIDGE ROW PRESS

University of Scranton Press
Chicago Distribution Center
11030 S. Langley
Chicago IL   60628

Second Printing — April 1987

Ridge Row Press: ISBN 0 940866 01 3

Editorial Office: University of Scranton, Scranton, PA 18510

Business Office: 10 South Main Street, Montrose, PA 18801

Printed in the United States of America

Library of Congress Catalog Card Number 82 80888

CONTENTS

Introduction

First Essay

I t may seem strange to begin a collection of essays on East-West religious relationships with a review of a television series. But it makes sense to do so with Conrad Hyer's review of Ronald Eyre's "The Long Search," because its thirteen episodes not only explore a wide variety of world religions but they also offer a number of incisive and valuable judgments about interreligious attitudes and the paradoxical nature of attempts to bridge the gap between East and West.

In the course of a penetrating and balanced evaluation, Hyers puts his finger on the reason why Eyre's series and books such as this present one are important. He says that most of us, sophisticated though we might be in our own areas of specialization, all to often have only a rudimentary knowledge of other religious traditions, especially Eastern ones. Any book or television program, therefore, that helps us to bring our knowledge of Eastern religious traditions up to a point closer to our normal level of understanding has to be a worthwhile enterprise.

In attempting to summarize Eyre's point of view, Hyers says that he seems to be working from an attitude of religious agnosticism, "a not-knowing beyond all our revelations and illuminations which returns us to the ultimate mystery out of which we have come." According to Eyre, then, each religion is like a mountain, with different shapes and conditions, with each religion offering different climbing "kits." As far as Eyre is concerned the basic question is which kit is best for which mountain. In Hyer's judgment, however, whatever may be the case with Eyre's personal attitude, the facts, the faces, the activities, the symbols and the ideas presented in the course of the programs all combine to give the viewer the opportunity to make a first hand judgment about a number of religious traditions.

In a final caution reminiscent of Talleyrand's "Pas trop de zêle," Hyers warns against unbalanced aggressiveness in this kind of interreligious search. He recommends an atttitude "somewhere between curiosity and need—more than just curious, but less than motivated by consuming need."

Second Essay

In a second essay, "The Yin-Yang Way of Thinking: A Possible Method for Ecumenical Theology," Jung Young Lee of Otterbein College in Ohio draws a provocative contrast between Eastern and Western ways of thinking. The Western mind, he says, operates according to "Either-Or" categories, whereas the Eastern mind uses categories of "Both-And." This

i

Eastern way of thinking appears to him to be preferable for a number of reasons. The Western "Either-Or" way, he says, is responsible for such things as: the development of the absolute dogma of God; the fact that Christianity has great difficulty co-existing with other religions; the suppression of the emotional aspects of life and the pollution of the environment through an alliance of religion with technology. Because of these severe limitations of the Western mind, it is necessary to find a more inclusive way of thinking that can deal with the modern relativistic world view.

For him, the Eastern "Both-And" or "Yin-Yang" way of thinking is such a way. As the Chinese Book of Changes (I Ching) indicates, the concept of change is the key to understanding the universe. And change itself is the interplay of the primary categories of Yin and Yang. Yin-Yang indicates not conflict but complementarity, wholeness rather than partiality. Because it transcends logical categories, it is appropriate as a means of expressing the transcendental divine nature. Even in the West complementary rather than dualistic ways of thinking are gaining in influence. And many Western theologians, directly or indirectly, implicitly or explicitly, are turning to "Both-And" categorizing. The proof of any system of theological analysis is how it deals with such thorny questions as the relation of the transcendent to the immanent, the personality or impersonality of God, the divinity-humanity of Christ, the spirit and matter of man. In all of these the "Yin-Yang" way gives new insights and reorients our thinking from a dualistic to a monistic one. For fruitful theological discussion, therefore, both the "Either-Or" and the "Both-And" ways of theological analysis need to be employed.

Third Essay

In the third essay, "Some Contributions of Hinduism to Christianity," Troy Organ begins by examining the history of Protestant missionary thinking in the 19th and 20th centuries. The Student Volunteers' Motto was an unambiguous "The world for Christ in this Generation." They meant this literally and when it failed, the failure led to some severe reappraisals of missionary work. Among these was the "Report of the Layman's Missionary Inquiry" of 1932, which recommended that missions become cultural exchanges. Another element of change was the gradual realization that every religion, including Christianity, has both a sophisticated tradition and a folk tradition and that when comparisons are being made between traditions, care must be exercised lest a sophisticated tradition in the one be compared to a folk tradition in the other and vice versa.

In the light of all this, Organ presents a brief but broad analysis of sophisticated Hindu religious traditions. He feels that Christians can learn much of value from the following five basic Hindu credal positions: "1. the unity of life; 2. the plurality of ways to salvation; 3. God as a cultural construct; 4. the three forms of God; and, 5. the effort to get behind the God concept." Organ's position is that a serious, sympathetic attempt by Christians to understand these ideas can lead to an improvement in their own Christian commitment.

Fourth Essay

In the fourth essay, "The Bhagavad-Gita as Way-Shower of the Transcendental," John Moffitt, who spent many years in Hindu monastic life in India, analyzes the Gita as one the world's most extraordinary Scriptures. As one of the three canonical books of Vedanta theology, it has been the object of numerous commentaries over the centuries. From all these, he says, it is clear that the Gita is primarily a practical guide to spirituality. The Gita, then, according to Moffitt, presents four ways of communing with the Transcendental: 1. intuitive wisdom (prana-yoga) or an intellectual quest bringing about a direct apprehension of the ultimate; 2. conscious mental concentration (raja-yoga), which is an experiencing of the truth of the Self; 3. devotional self-giving (bhakhti-yoga) to the Supreme in whom all things abide and who fills the universe, and, 4. the way of service in the spirit of worship (karma-yoga). Each of these is appropriate for different temperaments.

The Gita's most original contribution is its synthesis of all these into one overall unity and its emphasis on karma yoga or way of service as the central way open to all. It emphasizes that the presence of God can be felt here in our everyday world as well as in the world of mystical experience and that even mystical experience itself, if it is truly mystical, must also be practical or ethical.

Moffitt then shows some connections between each of these ways and various Christian spiritual traditions. He concludes with a suggestion for further study, one fraught with serious implications, namely that the Gita may be seen as being more than a way-shower to the Transcendental; it may also be a complementary revealer of the Word.

Fifth Essay

After the two preceding essays which indicate that Christianity can learn from Hinduism, Frank Wheeling, in a fifth essay, demonstrates this influence in specific detail. In his analysis entitled "The Trinity and the Structure of Religious Life: An Indian Contribution to Wider Christian Theology," he examines carefully the many interconnections between Hindu religious thought and the Christian doctrine of the Trinity as perceived by Indian Christians. For analogies in understanding the mystery of the Trinity, Indian Christians turn not to the Three Bodies of the Buddha, nor to the Trimurti of Brahman, Vishnu and Shiva, but to the classical teaching of Saccidananda (Sat=Being; Cit=Intelligence; Ananda=bliss). According to Chandra Sen in the late 19th century, the Father is the "I am" of the Godhead, the Son is the "I love" of the Godhead, and the Spirit is the "I save" of the Godhead. The stress is on realized, active truth, expressed in a following of Christ.

A further development within the Christian community itself was the perception of God as Brahman, both without qualities (narguna) and with qualities (saguna). The interweaving of these ideas helped to deepen understanding of the doctrine of the Trinity. Yet the further step into the area of the practical, the existential, the spiritual was probably even more typically Indian and more important. Pannikar has perceived three spiritualities of the Trinity, for example. As Whaling says, "Just as God is transcendent, yet personal, yet immanent, so also we need to worship God in his transcendence, love him in his personhood and realize him in his immanence... These are not three different spiritualities, they are different aspects of the same spirituality, just as there is one triune God."

In conclusion, he shows how Dhanjibhai Fabibhai, a recent Indian thinker, further suggests a quadripartite division of spirituality based on the Bhagavad Gita which adds love to the other three.

Sixth Essay

The next two essays, the sixth and seventh, by John C. Cobb, Jr., the American Process theologian, and Seiichi Yagi, professor at the Tokyo Institute of Technology, appeared originally as part of a dialogue-symposium which included further face-to-face discussion based on initial papers. These are the initial papers, with their original order reversed. Here Dr. Cobb comes first because, speaking as a Christian, his paper sets interreligious dialogue with Buddhism in its historical and theoretical perspective. Yagi, on the other hand, plunges immediately into the theoretical discussion. Though they both deal with the same theme of complementarity between Christianity and Buddhism (that being, in fact, the title of the Cobb essay: "Buddhism and Christianity as Complementary,") each approaches the question from a somewhat different angle, adding to the richness of the dialogue.

Cobb begins by outlining briefly four Christian approaches to understanding the relation of Christianity to Buddhism, and, finding none completely satisfactory, proposes his own. According to Cobb, there are important differences between Christian and Buddhist beliefs, but these differences "need not amount to theoretical contradiction. Both can be true. I believe that both are true."

Using Whiteheadian categories, Cobb supports this contention by analyzing Christian and Buddhist understandings of the self. Salvation of the self in Jesus Christ, he says, is an appropriate response to the nature of reality by Christians and the serenity of the self in Enlightenment is an appropriate response to the nature of reality by Buddhists. "The world needs both universal ways."

The second area explored by Cobb is the doctrine of God. If Christians attend to God's purpose, thereby intensifying personal responsibility focusing on hope, and Buddhists seek realization of ultimate reality as a move towards freedom from personal selfhood, then the difference between Christian and Buddhist ideas of God can be described as not so much a matter of metaphysical truth as two orientations to the totality of what is.

Cobb ends by recommending further careful exploration of the possibilities of complementarity between Buddhism and Christianity because though there may be obvious dangers involved, the enterprise, if properly conducted, can be very enriching for both.

Seventh Essay

Though the subleties of the Eastern philosophico-religious mind can make tough sledding for Westerners, the very seriousness of the analysis in Seiichi Yagi's response to Dr. Cobb, "Buddhism and Christianity," is itself an important contribution to the advance of the Buddhist-Christian dialogue. Yagi also claims that Buddhism and Christianity are complementary. This is so, he says, because Christianity advocates a life in which egoism is overcome and Buddhism advocates a thought process in which the discriminatory intellect is overcome. Since both egoism and the discriminatory intellect can be understood as "contradictory" sides of the transcendent, then Buddhism and Christianity meet in that transcendent in a complementary way. Both Christianity and Buddhism pursue the overcoming of the object-subject dichotomy created by the discriminatory intellect by integrating its realities of mutually related poles.

There are differences, of course, says Yagi, between Christianity and Buddhism. Buddhism, for example, emphasizes the immediacy of life arising out of the overcoming of the discriminatory intellect, which tends to Nirvana. Christianity, on the other hand, in emphasizing faith in God as the transcendent subject, expresses itself as a loving response to that God in the historical here and now, understanding that love as a gift of God to humanity. But egoism and the discriminatory intellect are united and when Christianity overcomes the one and Buddhism the other, they emerge as complementary.

Eighth Essay

In the eighth essay, Kim Maung Din, himself a Christian in Burma, examines "Some Problems and Possibilities for Burmese Christian Theology Today." His study goes beyond the limited context of Burma, however. It engages in the same kind of substantive Buddhist-Christian dialogue just seen above in the Yagi and Cobb essays.

Kim Maung Din's approach is based on the premise that a constructive dialogue between religions cannot take place until each of them has reexamined its own basic ideas in the light of those of the other. If this does not lead necessarily to change, it can at least help to bring about mutual growth and enrichment.

With this possibility of enrichment in mind he examines three basic theological areas: God, Jesus Christ and Man. The most obvious difference between Buddhist and Christian doctrines of God is in their personalistic and non-personalistic views of the godhead. Kim Maung Din suggests that to solve this dilemma we must put aside the Western "Either-Or" categories of thinking and apply the Eastern "Yin-Yang," or "Both-And" ways of thinking (as discussed above in Chapter Two by Jung Young Lee). By doing so, he says, we can learn from Oriental methodology the possibility of describing God as a Person as well as a non-Person, as a Father as well as a non-Father, etc. If communication by prayer with such a non-personality constitutes a problem for Westerners, then perhaps the Oriental method of meditation with the Transcendent is an option to be explored.

With regard to Jesus Christ, he says that it is necessary to avoid confusing "the historical relativity of the Jesus of Nazareth... with the universality of Jesus, the Christ." Emphasis, he says, needs to be placed on the ongoing Incarnation or Immanence of the Kairological Christ in the "now" of history. Christ will remain a stumbling block but only to those who reject the Immanence of the Transcendent (and even there the Yin-Yang method may reject something in one sense while accepting it in another).

Finally there is the question of Man. Here Din focuses mainly on the problem of Sin. The symbolism of original sin itself, he says, needs to be constantly reformulated in the course of its application to varying historical circumstances. Conversion and salvation need further study in this context as well. And finally, there are the economic, political, social and personal crises of our time which need to be faced together for the betterment of a common humanity.

Ninth Essay

In the ninth essay, "Horizons on Christianity's New Dialogue with Buddhism," Paul Knitter (author of a chapter in the first volume of this Series, Interreligious Dialogue: Facing the Next Frontier), encapsulates and summarizes the discussion of the previous three essays while analyzing a wide range of recent theological literature on Buddhist-Christian dialogue.

Knitter proposes that an examination of these authors shows a developing consensus in five major areas: First, the methodology of dialogue: the dialogue with Buddhism must begin with a deep commitment to Christ and move to a "covenant with the East." This covenant, while avoiding facile syncretism, must make use of the principle of "Both-And" rather than "Either-Or." Also it is helpful to experience personally the praxis of another religion, involving one's self in communion as well as communication. Second, God and God Talk: Buddha was not an atheist. He was primarily concerned with transforming rather than understanding the subject. Yet that Buddhist experience of emptiness is a rich kind of emptiness that might not inaccurately be described as the pleroma of God. Closely related to it are such complex questions as the immanence, non-duality and supra-personality of God as well as the dangers of doctrinalism and dualism. Third, The Selfless Self: Christian discussions of the Buddhist doctrine of Anatta/No-Self have been equivocal and misleading because the language has been taken too literally. The true meaning of self in anatta is "the selfless self constantly losing-finding itself in its relations with others." All of which is a corrective for certain Christian emphases on the Fall and excessive individualism. Fourth, Value of this World and Action in It: Buddhism should not be understood as merely world-denying. Rather, Buddhism sees everything is a no-thing that should not be made absolute. Evil in the world has its own reality and there is a need to act against it out of compassion for all beings. This is a correction for Christian activism by grounding it more explicitly and fully in contemplation. Fifth, Jesus and Buddha: Finally, there are many points of convergence between Jesus and Buddha both in their persons and in their works. At the same time, in a corrective for closed exclusivism, they are understood as remaining mutually unique. These five areas of convergence, Knitter concludes, show that Christian conversation with Buddhism can be "clarifying, completing and correcting."

Tenth Essay

Paul Martinson, in the tenth essay, "Wisdom and Love as the Basis for Preaching in Buddhism and Christianity," presents an original mode of comparison between the two religions, namely their preaching. Pauline Sophia and Buddhist Prajna both negate conventional wisdom. For Buddhism the mode of consciousness or right knowing is the principal concern. For Paul it is the mode of conscience or knowing right. Prajna is linked to Karuna or love, and Sophia is linked to Agape. The Prajna-Karuna formula's "As-If" syntax is paralleled by the "So-That" syntax of Christianity's incarnational formula of Sophia-Agape.

Martinson then compares two parables, the first is the Buddhist parable of the Burning House and the second the parable of the Prodigal Son. In a detailed analysis of the preaching modes in these two parables, he shows that Buddhist preaching cleaves consciousness whereas Christian preaching cleaves conscience. He concludes by saying that "Preaching as a mode of religious activity has been of decisive importance for the self-understanding and world effectiveness of both Buddhism and Christianity.... Can we hear our separate preachings?"

Eleventh Essay

In the eleventh essay entitled "Christian Theology in an Asian Setting: the Gospel and Chinese Intellectual Culture," Douglas J. Elwood begins with an exploration of the general principles underlying Western-Eastern dialogue. Thus he examines briefly such modes of interrelating as indigenization-contextualization, dynamic accomodation, critical confrontation and positive transformation as well as the critical Asian principle. Involved in this dialogue are such basic elements as freedom of theological discussion and an appreciation for the nuances between the changeless and the changing. All of which, says Elwood, leads to seeing of Christianity as an Asian faith (for "the first Adam was an Asian and so was the Second") and to the development of Asian-Christian theologies which grow out of their third world cultural roots.

Coming finally to Chinese culture itself, Elwood studies the possibility of a "Confucian Christianity." He feels that such a development would be no more surprising than such other historical forms as Aristotelian or Existentialist Christianity." The goal, he says, is "not to Confucianize Christianity nor to Christianize Confucianism... but a Chinese expression of Christianity."

Looking towards the substance of such a development, Elwood suggests Chinese humanism as a possible bridge. Chinese humanism, he says, stresses the words of Man and Heaven in a positive way as opposed to Western humanism which often expresses a revolt against God. Recent Christian traditions, both Catholic and Protestant, have focused on this new kind of humanism and it does suggest a method for contextualizing Christian thought in Chinese culture. And so he concludes that a Chinese Christian humanism offers great possibilities for the future which should be pursued with confidence and without fear.

Twelfth Essay

Langdon Gilkey in the twelfth essay, "A Covenant with the Chinese," develops a model of interreligious dialogue called "Covenant" in opposition to another model labelled "Mission." By covenant he means the legitimization of the process of synthesis between Gospel and culture. One example would be, of course, the covenant between Hellenism and Christianity. Another would be the covenant between Christianity and Modernity: its science, history, psychiatry, economic and social norms and goals. Unfortunately, says Gilkey, the Church has refused to use this covenant model in dealing with non-Western cultures. So he proposes a brief discussion of how it might be applied to Chinese and, specifically, Maoist culture.

He advances some preliminary cautions: First, that since there are few Chinese Christians, the prospect of developing such a covenant in China is something more for the future than for the present. Second, that imperialism has both political and cultural aspects and even when Christians reject the first they may unconsciously retain the second. Third, that covenants operate on two levels, the cultural and the religious. The religious is a dimension active and implicit in all cultures, no matter how vigorously it may be denied.

How then, he asks, would the West covenant culturally with China? If the West is trying to overcome an emphasis on individual autonomy by rediscovering its communal character, then, he says, it has much to learn from China. China, in turn, has much to learn in working out a balance in this same area. However, developing a covenant between Christianity itself and the religious dimension of Chinese culture is quite another matter, for the results may be both more profound and more problematic. One of the things it might do is creatively reshape the religious dimension of Maoism. It might do this first by trying to make its transcendent dimension clearer thus preventing the denial of Chinese creativity by a new absolute. And, second, by showing that both the inner person and institutions are sinful and in need of transformation. Third, it might do this by indicating that a Christianity that sees its way clear to applying the meaning of the Cross to itself, in culture, in theological formulations and in ecclesiastical might "in favor of the transcendent to which it seeks to witness," will be able to be heard both in China and in the West, thus making a genuine covenant possible.

Thirteenth Essay

The thirteenth and final chapter is the "Statement of the Theological Consultation on Dialogue in Community," issued by a World Council of Churches Consultation in Chaing Mai, Thailand in April, 1977. It makes a fitting summary conclusion for the various essays and points of view expressed in this collection. It begins with an introduction that explains why the theme "Dialogue in Community," was selected. Besides sharing the common heritage of the human community, the Christian community needs to reflect both on how it can relate to the broader community in service and witness and how it can deepen its own commitment to Christ in the process. This discussion needs to be seen, therefore, as related to the total WCC program of involvement in political, economic and social problems.

A general examination is made first of the nature of community as it applies broadly to the human community. There is first the reality of birth, time and place, then there is the sharing of common values, both cultural and religious. Such communities are many and varied and influence each other in many ways. Also all communities have their alienated members. There are many idealogies abroad to reshape communities of which Christians need to be aware. Diversity can be creative, but if it is pushed to absoluteness it can be destructive, something which applies to religious traditions as well.

Second, the Christian community shares in the divisions within the human community. This means that it too has temptations to arrogance and absoluteness which need to be overcome for the Gospel calls us both as individuals and as communities to repentance. There are dangers for Christians, of course, in ecumenical enterprises, such as the danger of syncretism which can either weaken our understanding of Christianity or our appreciation of the integrity of other religions. But forewarned is forearmed and dialogue is too important not to be pursued among religious communities.

In a second part, the Consultation examines the term "Dialogue" in the title "Dialogue in Community." It says that though it too cannot be exactly defined, it is nevertheless to be understood as a fundamental part of Christian service within community, an expression of the love experienced in Jesus Christ. This demands the asking of some basic questions about the place of other faiths in God's activity in history and a "translation" of the Chrisitan message for every time and place.

There are dangers involved, of course, including the dangers of "syncretism" and "ideology" so that mutual caution is necessary: "We welcome the venture of exploratory faith; we warn each other, 'Take Care.' "

First Consensus: Covenant

As with the essays in the first volume of the Modern Theological Themes Series: "Interreligious Dialogue: Facing the Next Frontier," a surprising consensus emerges out of these otherwise unrelated essays.

The major consensus theme of the first book was that if ecumenical efforts among religions are to succeed then "dialogue" must be emphasized rather than "mission." This is repeated here and sharpened somewhat by formulating the dichotomy as "covenant" versus "mission." Cobb, Knitter and Gilkey, for example, all examine in some detail the implications of the word covenant in this ecumenical context. If dialogue implies an exchange of words in conversation, then covenant implies an exchange of attitudes in cultural context. Covenant then goes a step beyond dialogue in the sense that it amplifies the areas of mutual exchange and implies some mutual commitment. As Monika Hellwig argued, in the first volume in this series, in her "Basis and Boundaries for Interfaith Dialogue: A Christian Viewpoint," "A language and model that would seem to be appropriate from the point of view of all three traditions is the biblical notion of covenant or alliance of God with the people." (Interreligious Dialogue, p. 82) Thus the further implication of the word covenant here is that God has made one covenant with all of mankind, the covenant of creation, and that we all share in it in a variety of ways.

Second Consensus: Complementarity

A second major theme of this book is the idea that certain aspects of interreligious relationships can be seen as "complementary." This word is usually defined as the making up, the filling, the supplying of mutual lacks or shortcomings. There is a strong consensus in these essays that some such principle of complementariness is important in evaluating the relationships between Eastern and Western religions.

The discussion of complementariness begins with a basic analytic presupposition, namely that Eastern and Western thought categories are basically different. It is suggested that Western thought operates with "Either-Or" categories, whereas Eastern thought operates with "Both-And" categories. Another contrast is that of the Western "So-That" with the Eastern "As-If." The classic Eastern phrase for the Eastern mode is "Yin-Yang." It is further suggested that this "Yin-Yang" way of thinking is superior to the Western in that it avoids many of the dead-end problems into which Western thought patterns have fallen (the problem of evil, etc.); also that it is a more inclusive way of thinking, capable of dealing with the modern relativistic world view and its ongoing patterns of change; and that since it transcends rigid logical categories, it is better able to deal with the mystery of the Transcendent itself. Furthermore, though they may not be thinking of them as specifically Eastern terms, many Western thinkers have been turning to the use of "Either-Or" categories in their own systems. For all these reasons, then, these terms are seen as much more productive ways to explore the relationship between Christianity and other Eastern religions. One of the great results of such an effort could be the growing realization that East and West stand in a complementary relationship rather than in an oppositional one in both their thought patterns and in their substance. There are dangers in all this, of course, but there are dangers in all interreligious efforts just as there are dangers in not undertaking such efforts at all. The successful results achieved by this approach so far, however, argue for a period of extended experimentation at the very least.

Third Consensus: The Self

A third consensus focuses on the area of the "Self": God as a Self and Man as a Self. There seems to be general agreement that one of the great areas of theoretical or theological disagreement between Eastern and Western religions lies in the understanding of the Self. The first question that arises in this regard is whether or not God is to be considered a Self (or a Person, to use a more Western term). The conventional wisdom is that the Christian God is personal whereas the Eastern God is impersonal. One is a Self the other is a No-Self. For this conventional wisdom to make full sense, however, there has to be some agreement on what constitutes selfhood. And this is precisely where a new consensus is emerging as testified by the essays in this volume: that Eastern and Western concepts of selfhood are not as far apart as they seem at first sight. As a matter of fact, if the Yin-Yang principle which has appeared so frequently in these pages is applied to this problem, then, paradoxical as it may sound at first hearing, it can be said that it is possible to be a Self and a No-Self at the same time. Perhaps this is what many Christian mystics and ascetics have been saying for centuries when they taught that in order for us to be fully what God intends us to be we have to empty ourselves of ourselves. "For anyone who wants to save his life will lose it; but anyone who loses his life for my sake will find it." (Matthew 16:25).

Fourth Consensus: Mutual Learning

A fourth area of consensus is the conviction that Christianity can and must learn from Eastern religious traditions (just as Eastern traditions can and must learn from Christianity). Eastern religions have many insights that will help to sharpen and clarify Western thought, thus strengthening Christianity rather than weakening it. And much the same thing could be said about the process in the other direction.

A New Agenda: Seven Ways

These four remarkable areas of agreement lead to a new theological agenda which tries to work out in specific ways what they have expressed in only general terms. The seven agendas suggested here, then, not only do not preclude the possibility of discovering other agenda items, but each one of them can also be understood as a doorway leading into a many-chambered house rich for further exploration.

1. The contrasting categories of "Either-Or" and "Both-And" need further systematic examination.

2. Christian theologians need to explore in much greater depth such Eastern ideas as: the oneness of life; intuitive wisdom; Saccidananda and the Trinity; spiritualities of God's transcendence; the No-Self and the overcoming of the discriminatory intellect.

3. Western theologians also need to reexamine a number of Western Theological ideas in the light of some of these Eastern insights, for example: the Kairological versus the Historical Christ, the symbolic aspects of original sin and the subtleties contained in the notion of Creation Covenant.

4. Also worth pursuing is the development of a cultural synthesis between Christianity and Eastern culture, the extension of a process that has occurred several times in the history of Christianity the notable example being the early synthesis of Christianity with Greco-Roman culture. If, in later centuries there have been additional minor syntheses such as Aristotelian Christianity or Existentialist Christianity, then why should there be anything surprising about the suggestion of a possible Confucianist Christianity?

5. One word which occurs often in this context of cultural synthesis is humanism. It is suggested that in order to pursue this important goal, the most important vehicle, the one needing the most exploration, is Eastern Humanism, for, it is said, it differs from Western humanism in being open to the Transcendent rather than closed to it.

6. Cultural imperialism is also something that needs to be dealt with by Westerners. For although political imperialism can and has often been overcome by Christian communities, they have not always been so successful in overcoming their cultural imperialism. The development of a greater consciousness of the possibility of cultural imperialism and of the need for its gradual eradication is an important task with much remaining to be done. One way to achieve this would be to apply the theology of the Cross to cultural questions as well as to individualistic ones.

7. Both East and West need to see themselves as communities in dialogue. After all, it is easier to appreciate religious similarities between communities than between individuals since the latter are seen to be arising out of and merging into a common humanity. This dialogue has its own inherent dangers for both sides, but awareness of them will help to overcome them in a process of mutual service.

Conclusion

In conclusion, the Yin-Yang principle of reconciliation of apparent opposites which has figured so frequently in the above discussion makes it easier to understand how it is possible for committed Christians to remain true to their basic religious convictions while at the same time growing in genuine fellowship and religious understanding with their Hindu, Buddhist and Confucianist brothers and sisters.

Richard W. Rousseau, S.J.
University of Scranton

Note: For reasons of accuracy, each author's critical apparatus has been preserved unchanged or with only minor changes.

CHAPTER ONE

"The Long Search"

BY CONRAD HYERS

N OT SINCE Jacob Bronowski's *Ascent of Man* or Kenneth Clark's *Civilisation* has an educational series received so much attention. Consisting of thirteen hour-long programs, *The Long Search* explores contemporary religious forms throughout the world: Protestantism, Roman Catholicism, Romanian Orthodoxy, African Christianity, Judaism, Islam, Hinduism, Buddhism, Chinese and Japanese religions, and a tribal religion in Indonesia. The series concludes with programs on "West Meets East" (in California) and some retrospective "Loose Ends."

Nature of the Series

At first glance one imagines the series to be a combination of Holy Land tourism and the television equivalent of leafing through *The National Geographic*. It is more than this. The creator and host of the series, Ronald Eyre,

Conrad Hyers is Associate Professor of Religion at Gustavus Adolphus College. He holds degrees from Carson-Newman College, Eastern Baptist Theological Seminary, and Princeton Theological Seminary, and is the author of Holy Laughter: Essays on Religion in the Comic Perspective *(1969),* Zen and the Comic Spirit *(1973), and* The Chickadees: A Contemporary Fable *(1974).*

He is here reviewing the television series, The Long Search, *shown on Public Broadcasting System stations during the fall and winter. The shows in the series are now available in videocassettes or 16 m.. films for purchase or rental from Time-Life Multimedia, Time Life Building, Room 32-48, New York, N.Y. 10020.*

Taken from Theology Today, *Vol XXXVI, n.1 April 1979. pp. 78-83. Reprinted by permission of the publisher.*

is not just a tour guide with a running commentary of facts and fancies, but a seeker on a "long search," and he invites the viewer to make the journey with him. The style is "on the spot" and unrehearsed rather than staged or canned, inquiring rather than interpretive or definitive. The cinematography, with its vivid images and juxtapositions, provides a visual journey worthwhile in itself.

Eyre describes his approach as "a series of encounters with men and women who are living their faiths now." And it is a world-wide series of encounters rather than streets of London or San Francisco. The programs are microcosms of the larger world in which we increasingly find ourselves—and for which our educational systems, our churches, and the stereotypes and caricatures offered by our mass media have so poorly prepared us. It is a world where Japanese businessmen meet Iowa farmers, Arab oil producers deal with Georgia bankers, Indian and Tibetan gurus teach American students, Chinese acupuncture becomes as respectable as chiropractics. Zen Buddhism is applied to jogging, and the Tao is related to physics.

There is a welcome existential level to the programs, both for Mr. Eyre and for the viewer. The aim is engagement in "the religious quest." Basic religious questions are being asked: most directly of the variety of people being encountered in these many religious contexts, but, through these questions and answers, of the viewer as well. The programs are therefore not only interesting and educational, but probing and provocative. In some cases they may even be disturbing, as we are suddenly confronted with the bewildering variety of religious forms to which human beings are deeply dedicated, or with a single religious context dramatically different from our own. Eyre, for example, articulates our surprise in discovering that religion for the Chinese has rarely meant *one* religious commitment, but an amalgam of "religions": Confucianism, Taoism, Buddhism, and folk beliefs and practices. Or, he notes how in inquiring about Chinese religion in Taiwan he has not been shown the things he has expected, but rather "people doing quite simple domestic things: placing an incense stick in a pot, paying respects to an elder, balancing flavors in cooking, siting a grave or a house harmoniously, choosing the right moment to start off on a journey, clearing a space, handling objects, bowing." He subsequently discovers other primary associations: gods of longevity, prosperity, and posterity; spring cleaning of ancestral graves; morning exercises *(tai chi chuan);* and ritual uses of tumbling and firecrackers.

In the final program Jacob Needleman asks Eyre whether he is making his inquiries "out of curiosity or need." Eyre's reply indicates that he is somewhere *between* curiosity and need — more than just curious, but less than motivated by consuming need. *The Long Search* is a search, but not a frantic one. Perhaps it does not fit Paul Tillich's criteria for "ultimate concern." The stance is nonetheless a healthy and promising one. Mere curiosity can turn the study of religions into a tour of religious zoos. Desperate need can turn the study of religions into a series of soup-lines for spiritually displaced persons and the religiously unemployed.

Eyre Himself and the Series

Eyre's own background is English Methodism, although he is not a practicing Christian but an agnostic with religious sympathies. This gives the series a special dimension, despite the fact that the search doesn't get much beyond its starting point. Eyre is a modern, western, educated, urban, "post-Christian" individual—a largely secularized person who is nevertheless still asking religious questions and still searching for religious answers. He is intrigued by the persistent vitality of religion, and by the great variety of the religious presence in the modern world. He is not searching for *a* religion, or *the* religion, but searching *out* religion. In this sense he is on a pilgrimage, a quest, a mythic journey, that takes him 150,000 miles to fourteen countries. The image is that of a modern spiritual odyssey.

Eyre is also not, as one might expect, a recognized authority in comparative religion or the philosophy of religion. He is in fact a playwright, stage director, and TV producer who admits to little studied knowledge of any of the world's religions. In some respects this turns out to be an advantage. He is not representing any particular religious persuasion, or identifiable with one—unless his own designation of himself as "a tolerantly agnostic 'lapsed Methodist' " constitutes a religious persuasion. His lack of clear religious definition and his lack of academic training in religious studies give a certain freshness and unpredictability to his language and inquiries. He has questions, not answers or theories. He does not present himself as an authority on the subject, but instead comes into each religious context asking very basic, probing questions—the kinds of questions that the average, educated viewer might well ask. Thus, unlike the Bronowski or Clark series, it is not his role to give a learned interpretation or professional insight to the viewer, but to take the viewer with him to listen as fellow-novices to the interpretations and insights offered by the practitioners themselves. Furthermore, Eyre isn't seeking official answers either, but personal ones. What does this mean for *you?*

Because of these characteristics the series is well-suited for use in church or community study groups and for introductory courses in religion. An accompanying text, also entitled *The Long Search* (Little, Brown and Co., 1978), has been prepared by Ninian Smart, although almost any good introduction to the world religions will do. For study groups a discussion guide has been prepared by Frederic and Mary Ann Brussat of the Cultural Information Service (P.O. Box 92, N.Y. 10016). And for college courses a Miami-Dade Community College faculty team has prepared a "Student's Guide to The Long Search" (William Brown Co., Dubuque, Iowa).

Principles of Selection

There are certain idiosyncracies in Eyre's selection of materials that may initially raise some eyebrows. He does not—and could not—survey the whole of any religious tradition in any systematic or inclusive way. But some of his samplings seem quite arbitrary. The series starts with a program on Protestantism, and the context is Indianapolis, U.S.A., otherwise most noted for its Speedway. In Indianapolis he selects three churches: a fundamentalist Baptist temple, a mainline Methodist church, and a black Baptist tabernacle. One is left with many puzzlements. Why just U.S. Protestantism? Why just these three forms? Why Indianapolis? What can this approach really tell us about the historical roots and concerns and divisions of Protestantism? What Eyre gets out of it in part is that ''Protestantism is an impulse to keep things moving.''

In the program on Orthodoxy, Eyre selects, again surprisingly, the church in Romania, leaving aside any Greek or Russian Orthodox examples. The program on Roman Catholicism moves rather quickly away from Rome and the Vatican to the atypical and marginal desert-cave meditations of a Spanish order, The Little Brothers of Jesus, and to a Catholic family in Leeds. The program on African religions explores the blend of Zulu and Christian beliefs and practices in white-dominated South Africa. The program that is representative of a ''primal'' religion, surviving into the twentieth century, focuses on the Torajas people on the Island of Sulawesi in Indonesia.

Selectivity is an inevitable problem when fishing in so vast a sea. But whatever the principles of selection in the programs, they are often elusive, and perhaps the issue is best ignored. In part Eyre seems to have intentionally chosen the unexpected and avoided any suggestion of a conventional or predictable approach. One has the sense of being an average individual who more or less happens to be somewhere, sees something of a religious nature, and begins inquiring about it.

The treatments of the other religious contexts are not quite so unusual. The segment on Judaism focuses on the problem of being a Jew ''after Auschwitz.'' The meaning of being ''the chosen people of God'' is explored with a rabbi in Jerusalem and a writer in New York who is a survivor of Nazi camps. The segment on Buddhism visits a monastery in the heart of Theravada Buddhism, Sri Lanka, where the basic teachings and practices of orthodox Buddhism are discussed and observed. (There is an especially moving vignette at the end where for two minutes the camera follows a monk doing ''walking meditation'' and practicing ''mindfulness.'') The segment on Hinduism takes up the great Indian paradox of belief in one all-pervading divine reality and worship of what are said to be 330 million gods, by meandering through festivals, pilgrimages to the Holy City of Varanasi, initiation rites, and harvest ceremonies. The segment on Islam does a good job of capturing the simplicity of Muslim belief and practice, and it helps counter popular misconceptions of the Muslim by choosing as representatives an Egyptian couple who are both doctors. The segment on Japanese religions focuses on Zen monastic practice and its pervasive influence on various aspects of Japanese culture, with brief looks at the Buddhism of faith and grace (Pure Land), Shinto, and the modern Soka Gakkai movement. The next-to-the-last program deals with the difficult problem of what happens when west really meets east on a relatively equal footing, and where the peculiar developments and contributions of each are taken seriously. The site is California, where for good or ill almost anything, and any combination of ingredients, may be found. Actually west and east have been meeting and influencing each other for more than 4000 years. We are simply not aware of the degree to which the west has assimilated elements from the east and vice versa. But the process has been speeded up dramatically in this century, and other cultures and religions are "next door" by virtue of economic interdependence and jet travel, if not more and more literally next door. Whether or not California is a desirable or encouraging anticipation of the future, it is a clear instance of the problem and promise of accelerated cultural interchange. Eyre explores a variety of groups and programs, including attempts at interrelating science and mysticism, biofeedback and meditation, ecology and a wholistic religious philosophy. Whether or not one sees any of the California solutions as the wave of the future, increased interaction between cultures and their religious heritages *is* the wave of the future. Putting our heads back in the sands of isolation, or continuing to pat ourselves on the back with renewed assurances of cultural and religious superiority, will hardly be adequate bases for meeting that future.

Religious Agnosticism

If one is hoping for simple, clear-cut answers to all the questions raised by the series, the final program will be quite disappointing. There is a flashback to a Zulu holy man's distinction between God as he is in himself and images of God which the holy man has drawn in a book. All finite images are symbols that point beyond themselves, but can never capture or contain that to which they point. Eyre recalls the great concern, especially in Judaism and Islam, over idolatry. He recalls a similar concern in Hinduism, which, despite its 330 million gods, affirms the ultimate level of godhood which is beyond all finite name and form, nameless and unspeakable. He reiterates the desire, witnessed in the walking meditation of Theravada Buddhism and the sitting meditation of Zen Buddhism, to go beyond words, images, categories of the mind. We are then taken to the library of Dr. Howard Thurman, former Dean of the Chapel at Boston University, who talks about the contagion of religious experience which then tends to get bottled up and labelled in particular creeds and practices and dogmas in an effort to preserve it and defend it. There is an intriguing consensus in all this, however it is expressed, which finds a kind of religious unity, not in any common affirmation or attitude or even experience, but rather in the awareness of and response to an ultimate *mysterium*, which is beyond all picturability, and which no metaphors and myths can fully contain or exhaust. Any claim to do so would stand in contradiction with both the ultimacy and the mystery with which we wrestle.

This seems to be Eyre's conclusion. It is not agnosticism as such, but a *religious* agnosticism, a not-knowing beyond all our revelations and illuminations which returns us to the ultimate mystery out of which they have come. Eyre adds something else: a suggestion prompted by mountain-climbing. We find ourselves at the base of different mountains: some tropical, some icy, some gradual, some sheer-walled. Different religions offer different "climbing kits" for different mountains. The question, then, for Eyre is not which climbing kit is best, but which is best for a particular mountain. This image will no doubt prove to be the most controversial point among many controversial points in the series. To this Eyre would probably respond, as he does throughout the series, "How would *you* describe these relationships?" He does this, in a way, in the final scene of the series which, instead of bringing everything to some grand finale orchestrated from the top of the highest mountain, shows Eyre lighting a fire beneath a teakettle in his kitchen!

Assessment

If one were to give an overview assessment of the series, it would be that Eyre gives the impression throughout of having only recently discovered and reflected upon the great variety of religious forms on planet Earth. This, coupled with his lack of expertise in the field of religious studies and interfaith relations, often gives an elementary, and sometimes naïve, character to the questions being asked and the answers being given. This is also the strength of the series because this is the level of most viewers' questions. Eyre is not intimidating, and in fact quite charming and homey. But that this type of host and program should have been produced by the same BBC which had produced Kenneth Clark's *Civilisation* suggests something of the longer search most westerners have yet to go through in dealing in a sophisticated and knowledgeable way with the variety of religious forms that are very much a part of the twentieth century.

We may graduate students from our high schools and universities with advanced knowledge in any number of academic areas, based on years of graded study and carefully developed curricula. But when it comes to religious traditions—whether our own or those of other cultures—few graduates have more than third grade equivalency. Most have virtually no knowledge of other religions at all. The fact that in the 1970s it is possible for a crew from one of the west's finest broadcasting companies, employing some of the most respected producers and directors, and using the most advanced film technology, to travel to fourteen countries asking the most rudimentary questions about what people believe and why they believe it, is itself an example of our contemporary problem. If nothing else, the programs underline how ill-prepared we are to comprehend and function in a rapidly shrinking world.

CHAPTER TWO

The Yin-Yang Way of Thinking
A Possible Method for Ecumenical Theology

BY JUNG YOUNG LEE

The basic issue and related problems

The dominant issue in the history of Christian thought is neither the problem of the divine reality nor that of human belief but the Western way of thinking, that is, thinking in terms of "either/or." This was deeply rooted in the Graeco-Roman view of the world, which became the general framework for theological thinking in the West from the beginning of Christianity. Its origins may go back to the Persian religion, Zoroastrianism, whose basic characteristic is the ultimate dichotomy between the opposing forces of Ormazd, the spirit of good, and Ahriman, the spirit of evil. It was also directly enshrined in Aristotelian logic, which became the foundation of the "Western" way of thinking. Some obvious examples in the West are easily noticeable to Easterners. We in the West think that what is not good must be evil, and what is not evil must be good; what is not wrong must be right, and what is not right must be wrong. But it is also possible that what is wrong may be neither right nor wrong, and what is not right may be both right and wrong at the same time. This Aristotelian conception however excludes the validity of the middle. The axiom of the "excluded middle", which is based on dualistic absolutism, is quite alien to

Professor J. Y. Lee is Assistant Professor of Religion and Philosophy in Otterbein College, Westerville, Ohio. This essay is taken from The International Review of Mission, *Vol. 289, 1971, pp 363-370 and reprinted here by permission of the publisher.*

what the Christian faith presupposes and has created some of the serious problems that Christianity has to deal with in our generation.

First of all, the either/or way of theological thinking in the West not only promoted but shaped the absolute dogma of God. The God of dogma is not God at all. The God who is absolutized by human words is less than the God of Christianity. That is why Emil Brunner rightly points out, even though he himself was led into the same mistake, that the formation of the doctrine of the Trinity was an intellectual indulgence of the early Church./1/ The doctrine of the Trinity became the norm to test the validity of the divine nature. Thus the doctrine became the judge of the divine. The Word of God became the servant of human words. The absolutization of human words is very characteristic of the either/or way of thinking, and the Western emphasis on the Absolute Reason, from which even the Divine cannot escape, is primarily derived from it. Thus God has been made an idol of intellectual display.

Secondly, the either/or way of theological thinking is responsible for the predicament of Christianity in the world of to-day. Christianity seems unable to co-exist with the different religions of the world. Its isolation from other religions in Japan, in India, in China and other countries where major world religions are dominant is chiefly caused by the absolute claim of man-made dogmas, based on the either/or category of thinking. This category does not provide any room for the possibility of reconciliation and compromise with different forms of belief. Accordingly, Christianity has no choice but *either* to accept *or* reject them totally. That is why Christian missions in the past stressed conversion rather than cultivation, and total commitment rather than mutual dialogue. Buddhism, for example, existed very successfully alongside other religions in China, Japan and South-East Asia for many centuries, because of its middle-way approach to other religions. Yet Christianity either dominates others or is isolated from them. The exclusive character of either/or thinking made the inclusive exclusive.

Thirdly, the either/or way of thinking has made scientific technology possible. Thus Christianity is allied with technology to reject the nonrational aspects of human life. It suppressed occult phenomena and devalued the emotional aspects of religious life. Mysticism did not thrive in the life of the Western Church. The Western Church considered the exploration of psychic matters as the works of the devil. Her rejection of them is based on the absolute style of either/or thinking, which allows no room for mysticism. Thus Christianity in the West, and especially Protestantism, failed to meet the needs of the whole man whose nature includes mystic elements, and this failure is responsible for youth turning away from the Church and seeking to satisfy its spiritual needs in Eastern mysticism.

Finally, the either/or style of theological thought has contributed towards the pollution of our environment. It created the dichotomy and conflict between man and nature, between body and spirit. Man must *either* conquer

10

nature *or* nature will conquer him. *Either* the spirit overcomes the body *or* the body will overcome the spirit. In this kind of relationship we can expect nothing but conflict and war. Man gradually overcomes nature through the use of scientific technology but he never conquers it completely. Ultimately neither of them survives. The conquest of nature is ultimately the conquest of himself. Thus, by this way of thinking, the opposites never come together into an harmonious and peaceful co-existence.

The Task Before Us

Our task should not be the total elimination of the either/or way of thinking, but the limitation of its function in theological enterprise. Its total elimination might result in the complete renunciation of our theological work. Thus we can summarize our task as two-fold: the limitation of the function of the either/or way of thinking in theology, and the search for the most inclusive category of thinking to complement it.

a) the limitation of the either/or way of thinking

The limitation of the either/or way of thinking is essential in theology, because of its tendency to absolutize. The divine nature cannot be absolutized by human thinking. Moreover, the absolute category is no longer compatible with the contemporary understanding of the world. Our way of thinking is relative to our understanding of the world, because we think through the use of world-imagery. The way of thinking in New Testament times, for example, was based on the world viewed as a three-storied structure. The traditional Western view of the world, to which we are still accustomed, is the Euclidean notion of the world, in which both time and space are infinitely extended. Even Newtonian physics did not offer any radically new world view. The absolute categories of space and time were still maintained. However, the contemporary world view which Einsteinian physics describes, is radically different from the traditional Western world-view. According to this contemporary view, everything is relative, including time and space. Since everything is relative, the absolute category of either/or thinking is out of harmony with the contemporary world view. Just as Newtonian physics which presupposes the absolute categories of both time and space, functions well in ordinary mechanics, so the either/or style of thinking can deal with ordinary human situations, with penultimate matters. But, just as the former is unable to deal with the wholeness of the universe, theology, which deals with the ultimate concerns of our life, cannot be effectively expressed in either/or categories. Therefore, this must be limited to penultimate matters only and is useful for the method of analysis and discrimination.

b) the search for an inclusive category of thinking

We have to find the most inclusive category of thinking which can be based on the relativistic world view. And since this relativistic world view, which contemporary physics attempts to describe, has been known to the Eastern people for a long time, it is reasonable to seek the symbol of relativistic thinking in the East. The world view to which Indian people are accustomed is certainly relativistic and inclusive. However, the concept of Maya has been often viewed negatively by Christians since it seems to reject the reality of the world. Thus it may arouse suspicion in some Christians if we take the symbol of thinking from the world view of India. However, the way in which the Chinese people have been thinking for many centuries is not only relativistic but is also compatible with the Christian idea of the world. In other words, the Chinese world view is positive and affirmative, just as the Christian world view is. It is then the Chinese world view which can help us to find the symbol of thinking that is most inclusive.

If Christian theology is to be universal in its orientation, it does not make any difference whether the symbol of thinking is taken from China or from the West as long as it satisfies the frame of reference through which Christian truth is conveyed. Furthermore, the Eastern symbol is much more practical than the Western to establish a point of contact between Christianity and other world religions, which have their origins in the East. Through this point of contact a Christian dialogue with world religions is possible. Thus the use of an Eastern category of thinking can be helpful not only for the development of ecumenical theology but for the mutual co-existence of Christianity with other religions in a creative process of becoming.

c) the yin-yang symbolism as a possible category of theological thinking

One of the most profound treatments of cosmology in China is found in the Book of Change or the *I Ching*, /2/ which is one of the oldest books in China. Since this book was accepted by both Taoism and Confucianism and became the focal point of the intellectual movement in Neo-Confucian philosophy in the later years, the cosmic view of this book is normative for the Chinese people. The Book of Change views the world as the flux of change, which was reaffirmed by Confucius. He stood by a river one day and said, "like this river, everything is flowing on ceaselessly, day and night" (Analects 9:16). The concept of change then becomes the key to the understanding of the universe. Because of change everything is relative. Time and space are not absolute but relative, for everything including themselves is changing ceaselessly. Time and space are not *a priori* categories of all other forms of existence. Thus the general theory of relativity, which presupposes change, is in conformity with the Chinese view of the world. Since a relativistic world presupposes change, change can become the symbol of the basic categories of all things in the world.

The category of change, according to the Book of Change, is the interplay of *yin* and *yang*, which are the primary categories of all other categories of existence in the world. The idea of *yin-yang* may have a deeper historical root than any other concept in China. It is almost impossible to trace back the origin of this idea, even though the technical use of these terms may come from sometime during the Han dynasty. The concept of *yin* originally came from the imagery of shadow, while that of *yang* from brightness. *Yin* then came to signify female, receptive, passive, cold, etc., and *yang* male, creative, active, warm, etc. *Yin* represents everything that is not *yang,* and *yang* what is not *yin.* Thus in an ultimate analysis everything, whether spiritual or material and temporal or spatial, can be categorized by the symbol of *yin* and *yang* interplay. The symbol of *yin* and *yang* is then the primordial category of everything that exists in the world. The characteristic nature of this symbol is not the conflict but the complementarity of opposites. It is the category of wholeness rather than of partiality. It is the category of becoming rather than of being. It is the transcendental category of expression, because it transcends the logical and analytical categories of our rational thinking. It is therefore possible to express the divine nature which transcends every dichotomy and conflict of opposites. The characteristic of transcendence is expressed in the complementarity of opposites. *Yin* presupposes the necessity of *yang,* and *yang* cannot exist without *yin.* The one requires the other. Thus *yin-yang* thinking is a way of both/and thinking, which includes the possibility of either/or thinking. The latter is effective in dealing with penultimate matters, as the former is with ultimate concerns. Since theology is concerned with the ultimate, theological thinking must be in terms of both/and.

The both/and category of thinking, which is based on the *yin-yang* symbolism, is characteristic not only of the Chinese but also of the Indian way of thinking. As Betty Heinmann pointed out, "The West thinks in *aut-aut,* the disjunctive either-or." India, on the other hand, visualizes a continuous stream of interrelated moments of *sive-sive,* the "this as well as that", in an endless series of changes and transformation."/3/ The relativistic world view of India certainly provides this category of both/and thinking which seems to be the general characteristic of Eastern people, and must be adopted by theology.

Scientifically also, the contemporary world view forces the West to think more and more in complementary terms. For example, scientists today do not believe either the wave theory or the quantum theory of light but accept both of them at the same time. In our living the stress of contextualism tends to avoid ethical absolutes. Thus the both/and category of thinking seems to have a universal orientation. If Christian theology also has a universal implication, I believe that it is to be expressed in this universal category of both/and thinking.

There is a growing interest among theologians in the possible use of the *yin-yang* category of thinking in theology. For example, Wilfred C. Smith of Harvard University says, "What I myself see in the *yang-yin* symbol with regard to this matter, if I may be allowed this personal note, is not an image that would reduce Christian truth to a part of some larger whole. Rather, I find it a circle for embracing Christian truth itself... In this, the image says to me, as in all ultimate matters, truth lies not in an either/or, but in a both/and.''/4/ Nels Ferré not only realizes the advantage of using this complementary category of thinking in theology but suggests that this is the only possible category. He says, "There is here no place for paradox, excluded middle, *totum simul* or *Alles auf einmal*. What we need is a contrapletal logic.''/5/ Ferré recognizes that the idea of contrapletal logic was already used by Ramanuja in *Vedarthasamgraha,* one of the most profound treatises in Indian literature. He says also ''A prime example has been the Chinese use of *yin* and *yang*. Two realities like day and night or light and darkness are contradictory in one dimension and yet fulfilling of each other within their place in nature and man's experience.''/6/ The growing interest in the use of the both/and category of thinking by Western theologians will have a profound implication as an impetus for the creation of universal theology.

The implication of the *yin-yang* category for theological thinking

Since the *yin-yang* way of thinking transcends human reasoning, its application to theology not only clarifies some paradoxical issues but provides fresh interpretations of divine attributes. It can, for example, illuminate such concepts as the nature of divine transcendence and immanence, God as personal, Jesus as the Christ, or the relation of body and spirit.

The West, using either/or categories of thought, finds it difficult to express the divine transcendence and immanence together. For the *yin-yang* way of thinking it is no trouble at all to think that God is *both* transcendent *and* immanent at the same time. He cannot be *either* transcendent *or* immanent. The God of transcendence is *also* the God of immanence.

Similarly, in the West we ask the question, "Is God personal or impersonal?" But God, who transcends all categories cannot be a personal God *only*. God who is only personal is a limited God. The God of creation is not only the God of personal beings but of impersonal beings as well. To make God personal is to limit him. Thus the use of the *yin-yang* category provides a new understanding of the divine nature.

Further, Jesus as the Christ, as both God and man, cannot really be understood in terms of either/or. How can man also be God? In the West we have to speak in terms of paradox or mystery in order to justify the reality of Christ. However, in *yin-yang* terms, he can be thought of as both God and man at the same time. In him God is not separated from man nor man from God. They are in complementary relationship. He is God because of man: he is man because of God.

Finally, one of the classical dilemmas in theological thinking is the relationship between the spirit and the body (or matter). According to Judaeo-Christian teaching, they are one and inseparable. Our spirit is also our body and our body is also spirit. Nevertheless, because Western thinkers have been pre-occupied with making distinctions, they have thought in terms of dualistic entities, of dichotomy between the spirit and the body. The *yin-yang* way of thinking clarifies the theological meaning of man and reorientates our thinking from a dualistic to a monistic view of the world. It thus renders a great service to the renewed understanding of Christian theology as well as to a universalistic outlook of the Christian message to the world.

Conclusion

The use of this transcendental category of thinking has been shown not only to solve controversial issues in theology but often to bring to light new meaning and fresh understanding of theological issues. The *yin-yang* way of thinking applies to ultimate matters which either/or thinking fails to deal with, just as the latter deals with penultimate matters which the former fails to do. We need both the *yin-yang* and the either/or ways of thinking to carry out successfully the theological task. Christian theology becomes universal only when the either/or category is de-absolutized, and it becomes significant only when the *yin-yang* category allows the creativity of either/or thinking. The effective method of theological thinking is possible when both *yin-yang* and either/or categories complement one another./7/

Footnotes

/1/   See his The Christian Doctrine of God: *Dogmatics Vol. 1. Philadelphia: Westminster Press*, 1950, p. 226.
/2/   *For full explanation see my* The Principle of Changes: Understanding the I Ching, *New York: University Books, 1971.*
/3/   *Betty Heinmann*, Facets of Indian Thought, *London: George Allen and Unwin, 1964, p. 168.*
/4/   *Wilfred Cantwell Smith*, The Faith of Other Men, *New York: The New American Library, 1963, p. 74.*
/5/   *Nels F. S. Ferré*, The Universal World: A Theology for a Universal Faith, *Philadelphia: The Westminster Press, 1969, p. 80.*
/6/   Ibid., p. 100.
/7/   *The* yin-yang way *of thought is applied as a theological method in my book,* The I: A Christian Concept of Man, *New York: Philosophical Library.*

CHAPTER THREE

Some Contributions of Hinduism
to Christianity

BY TROY ORGAN

T he Protestant missionary enterprise in Asia began in the nineteenth
century. The high point in Christian foreign missions, both Protestant and Catholic, was reached in 1928, when total outlay for
foreign missions was $90,000,000. The Student Volunteer Movement,
which began in 1886, enlisted thousands of young people in England,
Canada, and the United States for foreign missionary service. Its early motto
was "The world for Christ in this generation." At the 1935 meeting of the
Student Volunteers in Indianapolis, John R. Mott said, "It should be clear
today, as it always was in the early days of the movement, that the evangeli-
zation of the world in this generation did not mean the conversion of the
world in a generation. . . . It does mean that it is the duty of each generation
of Christians to bring the knowledge of Christ to its own generation." We
who attended that convention were not pleased to hear the old gentleman
deny the dreams of his youth. The Volunteers of the late nineteenth century
meant what they said. They were going to convert the world to Christ in their

*Dr. Troy Organ has been teaching philosophy at Ohio University since 1954. He has made
four trips to India for long periods of study. His publications in Indian Studies include the
following books:* The Self in Indian Philosophy *(Mouton, 1964),* The Hindu Quest for the
Perfection of Man *(Ohio University Press, 1970),* Hinduism, Its Historical Development
(Barron, 1974), and Western Approaches to Eastern Philosophy *(Ohio University Press,
1975). He is at present Distinguished Professor Emeritus of Philosophy. From* Religion in
Life, *Winter, 1978. Copyright © 1978 by Abingdon Press. Reprinted by permission of the
publisher and author.*

own generation. But at the 1935 convention many of us felt we were attending a wake. We were eulogizing past hopes which seemed quaint and unrealistic.

Meanwhile two other factors were reshaping thinking about foreign missions. One was the Layman's Missionary Inquiry. Seven denominations in the United States joined in the late 1920s and the early 1930s in an extended study of foreign missions in Asia. The members of the Layman's Commission made intensive studies of Christian missions in India, Japan, China, and Burma. The report of these studies appeared in a carefully written book entitled *Re-thinking Missions* (1932) and in seven supplementary volumes. The commission decided that the day of foreign mission as it had been practiced was over, and recommended that two-way missions replace one-way missions. Missions should become cultural exchanges. For every missionary sent from the West by a Christian church, provision should be made for bringing a missionary from the East. Exchanging, sharing, and even blending of ideas, values, and practices should replace the efforts to convert Asiatics to Christianity.

The second factor which was reshaping thinking about foreign missions was a reaction to a certain style of foreign missionary propaganda. This was the presenting of the non-Christian world in the worst possible light. Katherine Mayo's *Mother India* (1927) is a classic example of such propaganda. Patently biased studies encouraged rebuttal, and it was not long before Hindus began writing books in reply. One of the best was Dhan Gopal Mukharji's *A Son of Mother India Answers* (1928). The Hindus could point to a plethora of unsavory events in the history of Christianity: religious wars, inquisitions, the burning of witches, slavery, heresy hunts, demon possession, adoration of relics, snake cults, and many more. This form of argument — our good and wise ways contrasted with your evil and foolish ways — was possible for both Hindus and Christians. But good came out of this propaganda. Some became aware that all religions contain two elements: a sophisticated tradition and a folk tradition. Sociologists and anthropologists had known this for years, but the average layman had not thought of the two elements in his own religion. In Christianity there is the profound theology of Origen, Augustine, Aquinas, Luther, and Calvin. This form of Christianity is capsulated in creeds. But there is also a folk tradition. An instance of the folk tradition is what emerges at Christmastime. Some call it "manger theology." The Advent is cluttered with angels, a miraculous star, a blue-eyed blond baby, talking animals, Santa Claus, holly wreaths, a decorated tree, candles, stockings, fireplaces, a red-nosed reindeer, etc. In Christianity there are sophisticated hymns like "Our God, Our Help in Ages Past" and "Holy, Holy, Holy." But Christianity also has folk-level sentimentalities like "In the Garden" and gruesome horrors like "There Is a Fountain Filled with Blood." In Hinduism there is the metaphysics of the Upanishads, the inspired poetry of the Vedas, the great

18

epics — the *Ramayana* and the *Mahabharata* — and the lofty speculations of philosophers like Shankara, Ramanuja, and Aurobindo. At the folk level can be found cow adoration, snake worship, child marriage, widow immolation, and untouchability.

These two conceptions — foreign missions as cultural exchange and the recognition of both a sophisticated tradition and a folk tradition in religions — were changing the thinking of some Christians about foreign missions. Christians still sang "we, whose souls are lighted with wisdom from on high" must take "the lamp of life" to "the heathen (who) in his blindness bows down to wood and stone," but some were beginning to have difficulties with the ideas expressed in the great missionary hymns. Through the 1930s the foreign missionary enterprise was conducted officially in the accustomed manner. Missionaries were still sent to the foreign field to convert the heathen. But disturbing events were taking place: some Christian missionaries were being converted by the heathen! William Adam, a minister with the Carey Mission at Serampore, deserted his fellow missionaries to join a Hindu cult, the Brahmo Samaj. The other missionaries at Serampore denounced Adam, calling him "the second fallen Adam." Dwight Goddard had been sent to China to convert the heathen Buddhists; but Goddard became a Buddhist, returned to the United States, established a printing press at Thetford, Vermont, published a collection of Buddhist writings which he called *The Buddhist Bible* (1932), and devoted the rest of his life to promoting Buddhism in the United States. Alan Watts deserted his work as a missionary of the Episcopal Church in Japan to become an author, teacher, and lecturer on the Buddhist way. Three Anglican missionaries — Charlie Andrews, Leonard Elmhirst, and William Pearson — left their posts in India to join Rabindranath Tagore in his ashram at Shantiniketan.

Two experiences I have had in India illustrate the newer attitude toward non-Christian religions. One day in 1959 I was talking to a retired Methodist missionary about the work of the Christian churches in India, and he finally said that he was proud that he had never asked a Hindu to become a Christian. Later a Hindu friend told me that this missionary had done much good in India, and that he hoped the churches would send out more people like him. The second experience was a conversation with the librarian of St. Xavier's College in Calcutta. This Jesuit from Belgium said he and his colleagues had developed such favorable attitudes toward Hinduism that they would not let their friends in Belgium know, as "they would never understand."

The seven Protestant denominations which subsidized the Layman's Missionary Inquiry made a serious mistake in not following the recommendation to change foreign missions to exchange missions. Cultural borrowings do take place. They ought to be recognized. Martin Luther King derived his principal instrument for the integration of blacks and whites — nonviolent civil disobedience — from Mahatma Gandhi, and Gandhi said he got many of his insights from Kropotkin, Kingsley, Tolstoy, Thoreau, Ruskin, and the Sermon on the Mount.

In 1971 an article of mine entitled "A Cosmological Christology" was published in *The Christian Century* (November 3, 1971) in which I argued that Christians must cease holding that redemption is exclusively linked with Jesus the Christ. I wrote that Jesus is one of the many witnesses to universal and eternal redemptiveness. I was surprised by the hate mail my article triggered. Many Christians have not yet risen to the marvelous statement of Vatican II: "This (i.e., the hope of salvation) holds true not only for Christians, but for all men of good will in whose hearts grace works in an unseen way. For, since Christ died for all men, and since the ultimate vocation of man is in fact one and divine, we ought to believe that the Holy Spirit in a manner known only to God offers to every man the possibility of being associated with this paschal mystery."

I now submit that, if not as Western Christians then as Americans whose nation was founded with decent respect for the opinions of mankind, we ought to be open to insights from Asian cultures. In addition there is the matter of the survival of human civilization itself. Our Western civilization is in an unhealthy condition. The list of our illnesses is frightening: increase in criminal behavior, breaking up of the family, destruction of our life-support systems, pollution of our natural environment, possibility of a nuclear war, etc. To this list should be added the relative impotence of political and religious leaders. While the early students of Oriental thought sometimes claimed that light from the East would solve Western problems, modern Orientalists are less optimistic. René Guénon in *East and West* (1941) argued that the relation between East and West should be association rather than assimilation. Heinrich Zimmer began his *Philosophies of India* (1950) with the claim that the West now faces a time of decision-making which India reached centuries earlier: "We of the Occident are about to arrive at a crossroads that was reached by the thinkers of India some 700 years before Christ. This is the real reason why we become both vexed and stimulated, uneasy yet interested, when confronted with the concepts and images of Oriental wisdom."

In my opinion the Protestant churches made a mistake in not following the advice of the Layman's Commission to alter the pattern of foreign missions. If the churches were even at this late date to put into practice the recommendation of the 1932 study, what could Christians expect to receive from Hinduism? I shall suggest five possible contributions. I do not say these are the only contributions of Hinduism, but I do claim that these five from the sophisticated tradition within Hinduism might be adapted into Christianity. The five are: (1) the unity of all life, (2) the plurality of ways to salvation, (3) God as a cultural construct, (4) the three forms of God, and (5) the effort to get behind the God concept.

Some Contributions of Hinduism to Christianity

THE UNITY OF LIFE

B. G. Gokhale in *Ancient India* (1952) says that India is responsible for having introduced five values into Asian culture: the unity of all life, a love for the ultimate and the universal, tolerance, cooperation, and pacifism. Gokhale does not state, but he might, that the first value is basic and the other four are derivative. The animating principle according to Hinduism is the *jiva*. It is the *jiva* which transmigrates from body to body in the life-death cycle. The term *jiva* is translated as soul, or spirit, or self. The *jivas* of plants, animals, and humans are essentially the same. Hence, that which was human in one incarnation may be a lower animal or a plant in the next. The belief in a spirit which occupies another body after the death of the present body is not a common view among Western people. Both immortality and transmigration are held largely on faith. As one of my Hindu friends once said, the question is which is less absurd. Far more important than either faith in immortality or faith in transmigration is the Hindu conviction the *jivas* constitute a unity. The *jiva* is the individual self, but according to the view of many forms of sophisticated Hinduism individuality is not very important. Individuality is an appearance rather than a reality. Individuality is like the convergent rails we see when looking down a railroad track. Convergence is how the parallel rails appear to us. Parallel rails under certain conditions must take on convergence in order to be parallel rails. In similar fashion the individual selves which we appear to be are the necessary pluralistic manifestations of a unitary Self. The reality of this Self is oneness. This is the *Atman,* the universal Self, the real Self. The *jiva* is the individual self, the phenomenal self. *Atman* is Brahman; i.e., the real Self is the Totality. Sigmund Freud referred to the happy condition "in which object-libido and ego-libido cannot be distinguished," a state of "limitless narcissism."

If our real Self is one, then here is a justification for the Golden Rule. Christianity says I should treat my neighbor as myself. But why? Because Jesus so requires? Because people who act like this reap a nice reward? Hinduism gives a reason. I should treat my neighbor as myself because my neighbor is my self. Belief in the *Atman* means I will not harm others. This is the virtue of *ahimsa,* of avoiding injury to others, of willingness to let others live. *Karuna* (intelligent charity), *amitri* (active doing good), and *daya* (tender sympathy) also flow from the *Atman* doctrine. Belief in the unity of all life determines Hindus to show consideration for life in all its manifestations. Many are vegetarians because they cannot square the eating of animal flesh with this doctrine. They practice what Albert Schweitzer regarded as the fundamental moral virtue — reverence for life. Judaism and Christianity, on the other hand, hold that man has power and authority over plants and animals. The result has been fatal to hundreds of species. Can we reverse this aggressive attitude? Peter and Jean Medawar have recently written, "The unity of nature is not a slogan but a principle to the truth of which all natural processes bear witness. The lesson has been learned too late to save some living creatures, but there may just be time to save the rest of us."/1/ Christians stand condemned for what has been done to buffalo grass, the passenger pigeon, the wolf, and the American Indian. Hinduism reminds us that life is a unit such that the life we save is our own.

PLURAL WAYS TO SALVATION

In Hinduism a way to salvation is called a *marga*. Originally the term meant a path made by an animal. Then it meant the path a hunter follows who is tracking down an animal. Finally it came to denote any path an individual takes to lead to a desired goal. The *margas* are the approved paths which a Hindu may select in order to bring him to the goal of *atmanvidya*, full knowledge of the true Self. There are four paths in Hinduism. Each is reliable if one stays with it. Because of its belief in the efficacy of each *marga*, Hinduism has been freed from the internal quarrels which have defaced Christianity, such as the quarrels among mystics, moralists, rationalists, authoritarians, fundamentalists, modernists, social activists, contemplatives, and traditionalists. Hindus are offered the way of thought *(jnana marga)*, the way of devotion *(bhakti marga)*, the way of works *(karma marga)*, and the way of physical and psychological disciplines *(yoga marga)*. The choice is up to the individual Hindu, although according to Hindu belief the choice will be conditioned by the *karma* accrued by the *jiva* from past incarnations.

What must I do to be saved? What can I do to be saved? This has puzzled and bothered Christians. Unfortunately, the answers given are usually authoritative and exclude other alternatives. Luther said through faith; the church of his day said through works; Calvin said through thought; Wesley said through prayer; Fox said through mysticism; Woolman said through social service; and others recommend asceticism, silence, ecstasy, contemplation, etc. Many good and simple Christians have said, "Just believe in Jesus." Others said, "Believe in God, keep the Ten Commandments, and obey the Golden Rule." In my rural boyhood community it was, "Don't swear. Don't play cards. Don't smoke. Don't drink. Do go to church on Sunday. And never work on Sunday — except for doing the farm chores and preparing a huge Sunday meal!"

The tolerance shown by Hindus supporting different *margas* is an object lesson for Christians. I know a temple in India which is a Hindu temple when approached from the west and a Buddhist temple when approached from the east. Another has the architecture of a Hindu temple, or a Muslim mosque, or a Christian church as it is viewed from different directions. At the temple of Nataraj, the dancing Shiva, in Chidambaram, Vishnu priests are allowed to operate no more than fifty feet from the center of the temple. This is the equivalent of giving Billy Graham a pulpit in the Vatican.

GOD AS A CULTURAL CONSTRUCT

Paul Tillich once said that so much evil has been done in the name of God, and people have so abused the concept, that he advised at least one generation to avoid the use of the term. Hindus take their God — or gods — far less seriously than do Christians. Each Hindu has a right to his *ishta devata*, his chosen deity. He may choose to worship a local village god; he may choose one of the forms of the godhead, specifically Shiva or Vishnu; he may choose to worship one of the nine incarnations of Vishnu; or he may choose to worship no god at all. *Ishta devata* means the right to select any god for worship and also the right to reject all gods. I recall visiting the home of a university professor where the husband was a member of the Brahmo Samaj, the wife worshipped Krishna, and the son was a follower of Sri Aurobindo. They saw nothing unusual about this arrangement.

Hindus do not seem to need a Rudolf Bultmann to teach them to de-mythologize. A villager does not think it strange that his village worships one god and village five miles away worships another. The notion of sending a delegation from his village to induce the people of the other village to change gods does not enter his mind. The God concept is recognized as a cultural creation. I as a Christian have been welcome at Hindu services, and on one occasion I helped lead a Christmas service in a Hindu temple.

Hindus seem able to distinguish between the god created by human imagination and what the created god stands for. In the final analysis gods are appearances. They are symbols for reality. The stories about the gods tell us what we need to know, and they are not descriptions of how things are. When a Hindu showed me through the Mylapore temple in South Madras, he told me that the temple was located on the spot where Parvati once appeared in the form of a peacock. "But you don't believe that," I said in an inquiring tone. "Well, so we believe," he replied. He did not say this was what actually happened in time and space, but he wanted me to realize that he as an educated Hindu believed that in some fashion what we know as "God" is manifested among men. He was able to use the language of mythology without becoming sidetracked by a question on the factuality of the myth.

THE THREE FORMS OF GOD

The Hindu *Trimurti* is often called the Hindu Trinity. This is a serious mistake. *Trimurti* means three forms. Deity is manifested in creation (Brahma), preservation (Vishnu), and destruction (Shiva). The Christian Trinity is surely the most puzzling of all Christian doctrines. Augustine, who wrote the definitive statement on the doctrine, concluded that we say God is three persons and one essence not to express what God is, but to say something about God./2/ Many have claimed that it is impossible to discuss the Trinity without committing either the error of denying the oneness of God or the error of denying the unique individuality of the three members of the Trinity. Thus it is an admirable instrument for ferreting out heretics! In

Hinduism, Brahma is a mythological representation of the activity of creating, Vishnu a mythological representation of the activity of preserving, and Shiva a mythological representation of the activity of destroying. The *Trimurti* has a definite advantage over the Trinity in that each member is recognized as a creation of the human imagination to stand for a cosmic activity. The *Trimurti* is *maya* (appearance), not *sat* (reality). Another advantage is that destruction is incorporated into the godhead. We in Judaism and Christianity have a real problem here. We have appropriated from Zoroastrianism a cosmic figure which we call Satan or the Devil to explain destruction. Destruction for us is not part of the godhead. Destruction and death ought not to be, yet they are. Only the last dozen or so years have we begun to incorporate death into our philosophy of life. The Hindus — especially those in the sophisticated tradition — have known this for centuries. Shiva is as much god as is Brahma and Vishnu. Carl Jung argued that we ought to have a Quadrinity rather than a Trinity: creation, redemption, presence, and destruction. Theodicy, the vindication of the justice of evil in the world, is still an undeveloped area in Christian theology. A careful study of the *Trimurti* might help.

THE EFFORT TO GET BEHIND THE GOD CONCEPT

The fifth possible contribution of Hinduism has been anticipated in some of the ideas I have already expressed. The Hindus, especially in their sophisticated tradition as contrasted to their folk tradition, make a distinction between the conception of God and what the conception is about, a distinction between god as a mythological-theological construct and what the construct denotes. This distinction has been made by a few Christians. For example, Eckhart said we must separate *Gott* and *Gottheit*. The former is an idea of man; the latter is the reality which the idea represents. Tillich in *The Courage to Be* said we must go from God to what he called "God beyond God." Later he used such terms as "the Ground of Being" and "Being itself." (Tillich once told me in private conversation that his favorite philosopher was Parmenides.) But it was Augustine who best stated the issue: "If we say eternal, immortal, incorruptible, unchangeable, living, wise, powerful, beautiful, righteous, good, blessed, spirit; only the last of this list as it were seems to signify substance, but the rest to signify qualities of that substance; but it is not so in that ineffable and simple nature. For whatever seems to be predicated therein according to quality, is to be understood according to substance or essence. For far be it from us to predicate spirit of God according to substance, and good according to quality; but both according to substance."/3/ Augustine described God as *esse ipsum, verum ipsum, bonum ipsum* (being itself, truth itself, goodness itself). To express what he called this "ineffable and simple nature" hyphens can be placed between the six words to show the integration of being-truth-goodness. Conceptions of God are efforts to symbolize the unsymbolizable. The Christian God, said Augustine, is no spirit, no person, no being, not even a god. Rather the term "God" symbolizes eternity, immortality, incorruptibility, unchangeableness, life, wisdom, power, beauty, righteousness, goodness, blessedness, and spirituality. God is not a substance with these qualities. Rather these which appear as qualities are the substance of God.

Where does Hinduism fit into this? According to Hinduism the Total Environment, the Absolute, the Totality, the All, is Brahman. Brahman is the Unity which cannot be the object of knowing. To "know" Brahman would require a separation of knower and known. But there is no such separation in Brahman. Brahman can be "known" only by falsifying Brahman, i.e., by making Brahman an object of knowledge. This reduces Brahman from reality to appearance. Brahman must be pluralized in order to be Totality, but this pluralization is the necessary appearance of reality, not reality itself. Brahman appears as Brahma, as Vishnu, and as Shiva. They are the forms of Brahman's appearance. The *Trimurti* is the manner by which finite minds can think about, talk about, and image Brahman. This apparent Brahman is called Saguna Brahman, the Brahman with attributes. It must not be confused with Nirguna Brahman, the Brahman without attributes.

The conception of Brahman sounds like a pantheism, and some have so regarded it. For example, the English philosopher F. C. S. Schiller in an essay entitled "From Plato to Protagoras" wrote:

It is easy enough for thought to fuse the multitude of discrepant deities. . .into one vast power which pervades the universe. This process is typically shown in the evolution of Hindu thought. And pantheism is not only easy, but also specious. . . . Whoever conceives religion as nothing more than an emotional appreciation of the unity of the universe may rest content with pantheism, and even derive from its obliteration of all differences the most delirious satisfaction. Whoever demands more, such as, e.g., a moral order and a guiding and sympathizing personality, will ultimately fail to get it from any theory which equates God with the totality of being./4/

Schiller's charge, I believe, can be made against Paul Tillich. Tillich spoke of "the Ground of Being" and of "Being itself." He also spoke of "Ultimate Concern." But he never to my satisfaction brought being and value into a synthesis. This is not the case in Hinduism. Brahman is described as *Satchitananda*. This is a composite term formed by running together the Sanskrit words for being *(sat)*, for consciousness *(chit)*, and for value *(ananda)*. Brahman is not a being which is, which is conscious, and which possesses value. Rather Brahman is the integration of being, consciousness, and value. Brahman is being-itself-consciousness-itself-value-itself. And this is how Augustine understood the Christian God.

Hinduism can help improve our Christianity. It can aid us in the discovery of the depths in our own religion. It can remind us that nowhere has God left himself without witness. John Dunne, the innovative Roman Catholic theologian, has recently expressed his confidence: "By passing through what I call 'sympathetic understanding' of other religions, one can appropriate those insights and return to one's own. In this way, all the basic spiritual experiences of humankind can somehow be reenacted in our own lives."/5/ The Christian has everything to gain and nothing to lose in this sympathetic understanding.

FOOTNOTES

/1/   "Revisiting the Facts of Life," *Harpers, Feb., 1977, p. 59.*
/2/   De Trinitate, *V, 9, 10.*
/3/   Ibid., *XV, 5.*
/4/   Studies in Humanism *(1906). p. 26.*
/5/   Psychology Today, *Jan., 1978, p. 48.*

CHAPTER FOUR

The Bhagavad Gita
as Way-Shower
to The Transcendental

By JOHN MOFFITT

Anyone who knows even slightly the Hindu Bhagavad Gita, "Song of the Lord," recognizes that is not a work of mere abstract theology or speculative philosophy. It is a practical guide, whose aim is to show spiritual seekers to commune with what today we like to call the Transcendental. We shall make no mistake in calling it one of the world's most extraordinary scriptures. The Gita, which may be dated about 250 B.C., not only illuminates the teachings of the ancient Upanishads, from which it quotes, but carries them forward in a grand synthesis—a synthesis once more superbly illustrated in the nineteenth century, twenty-one hundred years after its first announcement, in the life experience and influence of the modern saint Ramakrishna./1/

Those who have studied the religion of the Hindus know how important a scripture it has always been for them: it is one of the three canonical books that form the bedrock of the Vedanta theology—the other two being the Upanishads themselves and the extremely terse aphorisms based on them

John Moffitt was born in Harrisburg, PA. He graduated from Princeton University in 1928 (A.B. in English) and the Curtis Institute of Music in 1932. (Diploma in Musical Composition). He spent twenty five years as probationer, monastic novice and monk of the Ramakrishna Order of India. He returned to Christianity in 1964 and became copy editor and poetry editor of America magazine. He is still serving as Poetry editor and now lives in Virginia.

From 1939 to 1964 he helped edit the translation and original works on Hinduism of Swami Nikhilananda of the Ramakrishna-Vivekananda Center of New York. (In the Gospel of Sri Ramakrishna he put all translations of hymns and devotional songs into English verse). He has

27

Christianity and the Religions of the East

known as the Vedanta Sutras. Various prestigious medieval theologians, those whom we may call Hindu "scholastic philosophers," have tried in their commentaries on it to demonstrate that the Gita upholds one or another particular system of mystical theology. Yet even they would surely have had to grant that it is first and foremost a practical guide to spirituality. Since, however, there is not always consistency of meaning in certain of the important terms it uses—e.g., yoga, Atman, Brahman—there has always been and always will be a place for commentaries to explain them and it.

Perhaps the most striking characteristic of this yoga-shastra, this scripture on the communion of the individual soul with the Universal Soul, is its psychological approach to self-unfoldment. I refer to the fact that the Gita takes into account several different basic types of human character and offers disciplines suited to persons possessing the temperaments that go with them—disciplines all seen as ways to attain one and the same transcendental vision. "In whatever way men approach me," says the Lord Krishna, "so I reward them; for it is my path that men follow in all things."/2/ This verse applies not only to the manner in which men approach God, whether with a hidden motive or with motiveless love, but also to the specific *ways* by which they approach him. Implicit in the Gita is the doctrine that the Lord Krishna is to be found at the end of all these ways or yogas.

What are these ways? The Gita suggests four disciplines by which one may achieve communion, through grace, with the Transcendental. They are the way of intuitive wisdom (jnana-yoga) for the predominantly intellectual; the way of consciously practiced mental concentration (raja-yoga) for the meditative; the way of devotional self-giving (bhakti-yoga) for the predominantly emotional; and the way of service in the spirit of worship (karma-yoga) for the active. The Gita never separates these yogas into mutually exclusive paths after the fashion of sectarian theologists. But for the sake of clarity I shall identify the nature and aims fo the first three of them somewhat as they have been presented by the theologians. I wish to call special

published four volumes of poetry: This Narrow World *(Dodd, Mead, 1958),* The Living Seed *(Harcourt, 1962),* Adam's Choice *(Golden Quill, 1967),* Escape of the Leopard *(Harcourt, 1974). A fifth volume,* Signal Message, *is scheduled for publication by Golden Quill Press in late Spring, 1982. A further collection,* This One Instant, *is in preparation.*

He edited A New Charter for Monasticism, *the proceedings of the Meeting of Monastic Superiors in the Far East, held by the Benedictine Organization A.I.M. at Bangkok in 1968, during which Thomas Merton died; contributed an introduction and (as "expert on Hinduism") a paper on "Varieties of Contemporary Hindu Monasticism," and a background piece "Christianity Confronts Hinduism," later published in* Theological Studies *(June, 1969). He wrote* Journey to Gorakhpur: An Encounter With Christ Beyond Christianity *(Holt, 1972). Also has an unpublished work,* The Road to Now, *which may appear later this year or in 1983. He helped edit* Zen Comments on the Mumonkan, *by the Rinzai Zen Master Zenkei Shibayama (Harper and Row, 1974). And, from 1966 to the present, has written many articles on interreligious ecumenism.*

Taken from Theological Studies, *38, June, 1977, 316-331, Reprinted by permission of the publisher and author.*

attention to the last of these ways, the yoga of active service, as a medium for commuting with the Transcendental; for it is the Gita's unique contribution to Hindu spirituality. But first let us consider the ways of intuitive wisdom and mental concentration and devotion, since the real meaning of the fourth yoga may be grasped when we have understood the other three taken separately. The synthesis found in the Gita consists in its showing that, for most men and women, what is embodied in the paths of jnana and bhakti by way of revelation and discipline, and by raja-yoga as a matter of equally strenuous mental control, is embodied by the fourth, karma-yoga, in a method of living out those disciplines in everyday life.

Way Of Intuitive Wisdom

The way of intuitive wisdom, in its classic formulation, involves an intellectual search leading to intuitive apprehension of ultimate reality. It concerns itself with the nature of the Godhead, the soul, and the world, together with disciplines for opening oneself to the truth. Its original statement is found in the Upanishads, where the Vedic seers have affirmed the identity of Brahman, the reality underlying the physical world, and Atman, the reality underlying the individual self or soul.

Early in the second chapter of the Gita, "The Way of Ultimate Reality," Krishna tells the warrior Arjuna, his disciple, about the nature of reality: "The unreal never truly is. The Real never ceases to be...That by which all this [universe] is pervaded know to be imperishable. None can destroy that which is immutable."/3/ Significantly, Krishna begins his discourse by referring to the Self in man, the Atman or true person spoken of in the Upanishads as *sat* or the Real. Implicit here is the idea that the reality of Atman is a matter for immediate experience by each one of us. Our experience of it at present is, except occasionally, little more than a matter of faith: though it is the nearest of the near, our attention is turned for the most part away from it. But that it *can* become a matter of almost continuous experience through the help of intelligent thinking, coupled with self-discipline, is here taken for granted. As we see from the text quoted, reality is what never changes; but it must be remembered that *asat*, the "unreal," is not something illusory or nonexistent; rather it is simply whatever is subject to change. And the real Self is said to be the witness of the constant changes both in the body and mind in which it dwells and in the whole outer world.

It is only much later in the scripture, in chapters 7 and 9, that the complementary doctrine of Brahman is spelled out. But what is described in those chapters must remain at first totally a matter of faith; we have no direct experience of the reality underlying the physical world and so have to rely upon revelation for our knowledge of it. "Earth, water, fire, air, ether, mind, reason, and ego: such is the eight-fold division of my nature," Krishna declares. "This is my lower nature. But, different from it, know my higher nature—the indwelling spirit by which the universe is sustained."/4/

"By me, in my unmanifest form, all things in the universe are pervaded. All beings exist in me, but I do not exist in them"/5/ The idea here is, as the theologian Shankara points out in his commentary on the Gita,/6/ that Brahman is incorporeal and hence, though all exists in him, he is not in his true nature connected with any object.

It is in expounding passages such as these, dealing with Atman and with Brahman, that the commentators of the various schools exercise their ingenuity in setting forth their views about the reality underlying the individual self and underlying the cosmos. The absolute nondualist Shankara/7/ holds that the individual self and the world are in actuality nondifferent from Brahman. The modal nondualist Ramanuja/8/ holds that the self and the world are parts of the whole comprised by Brahman. Madhva, a thoroughgoing dualist,/9/ holds that the self and the world are separate from Brahman, though eternally related to yim. The three views are not necessarily incompatible—something the commentators refuse to see. They may all be taken to represent valid, though differing, spiritual experience. When a person identifies himself with the physical body and the ego-self (as most of us do), he will experience himself to be different from ultimate reality, which he sees as "personal." When, again, he identifies himself with the Atman known in intellectual ecstasy, and loses the sense of separate selfhood, he will, in recollecting that experience, hold the world to be insubstantial and himself to be nondifferent from ultimate reality, which he sees as "impersonal." When, finally, he enjoys the immediate sense of the divine presence during the state of everyday awareness, he will then find his relationship to ultimate reality, which he sees as transpersonal, to be one of ineffable difference *and* nondifference. It is when these three views are adhered to as matters of intellectual persuasion or devotional faith, and an attempt is made to apply them to a scripture such as the Gita as a whole, that disagreements arise among theologians (and their followers).

The question of practical disciplines for opening oneself to the Transcendental through the path of intuitive wisdom is another matter, and here there need be no argument. The disciplines recommended by the Gita are taken up at the end of chapter 2.

This celebrated passage/10/ offers an extended description of the "man of steady wisdom," the enlightened soul fully conscious of his or her relationship (as Atman) with Brahman or ultimate reality. It states, in substance, that to become enlightened one must have cast off all desires, including the desire for happiness; as a result, one will have become free from attachment, fear, and anger, and unperturbed by adversity. One must have learned not to rejoice when obtaining good or vexed when obtaining evil. Through mental control, one must have acquired the power to withdraw the senses from attention to sense objects and even from the taste for them, and to remain intent on the Lord Krishna (i.e., Brahman himself). Thus one becomes free from all the fruits of attachment; desire, anger (at not obtaining what is desired), delusion, failure to recall the lessons of scripture and of the teacher as well as of experience, and loss of discrimination about what is real and what unreal. Only then will one succeed in practicing contemplation on the nature of the Self (the divine spark in a man or woman), and being free of the sense of possessiveness, attain peace and, in the hour of death, liberation from ignorance of the truth.

Just before this passage several verses have explained the proper attitude toward active work of all kinds, which I shall touch on later but which may be taken as part of the discipline here as well. "Neither let your motive be the fruit of action, not let yourself be attached to nonaction," says Krishna./11/ One should remain evenminded in success and in failure, casting off all attachment to their fruits. Those who learn to perform action with evenness of mind, freed from the fetters of rebirth (caused by desire and action with a motive), go beyond relative good and evil and attain liberation from ignorance. In a way, we may see the remainder of the Gita as explaining how we can perfect all these disciplines outlined at the end of chapter 2; for many of the chapters following this one describe in detail the implications of the disciplines we have just considered.

Way Of Mental Concentration

In touching on the way of conscious practice of mental concentration, most to our purpose is chapter 6, "The Way of Meditation," which seems like a commentary on the contemplation spoken of near the end of chapter 2. The aim of this way, as outlined in the Gita, is not so much to encourage intellectual belief in ultimate reality as to help the individual man or woman *experience* the truth of the Self. Here are the most succinctly stated teachings about preparation for mental concentration and conscious practice of it to be found in any scripture of its kind-teachings further spelled out in Patanjali's well-known and far more detailed treatise on control of mind known as the Yoga Sutras./12/ For those who seek practical means to commune with the Transcendental through the intellectual or the devotional path, this chapter can be an extremely useful supplementary guide.

"Let a man be lifed up by his own self; let him not lower himself; for he himself is his friend, and he himself is his enemy," Krishna warns./13/ In these words we hear the voice not of faith but of ripe experience. Effort is called for on the part of the aspirant if divine grace is to find a way to enter his or her life. For those who want to learn meditation, Krishna suggests the following disciplines./14/ One should retire into solitude and live alone, and after having conquered restlessness of mind and body, try always to concentrate the mind on the chosen ideal. The meditation seat should be firm, neither too high nor too low, and should be placed in cleanly surroundings. Sitting in this seat, one should restrain the activities of mind and senses and bring one's thoughts to a point, holding body, neck, and head erect and still, without looking about. Keeping a vow of sexual continence (those involved here are presumably monks), serene of heart and therefore free from fear, and always thinking of the Lord Krishna as ultimate reality, one should practice union with him. One should follow a sort of middle path, being temperate in one's food and recreation, temperate in exertion at work, temperate in sleep and waking.

One's mind, concentrating on the Atman or Self, should be like a "lamp in a windless place," unflickering./15/ When it wanders, one should restore it again and again, undaunted, to the search for the Self. Thus one attains contact with Brahman, which is exceeding bliss. The supreme yogi, says Krishna, is he who, seeing Krishna everywhere and everything in him, "looks on the pleasure and pain of all being as he looks on them in himself."/16/ This verse amounts to the golden rule of Hinduism.

It should be noted that in this sixth chapter the terms Atman or Self, Brahman, and Krishna are used almost interchangeably to refer to the spiritual ideal.

Way of Devotional Self-Giving

In chapters 8, 9, and 10, Krishna prepares the devotional aspirant for the revelation of his Universal Form to take place in chapter 11. There, as Swami Nikhilananda has pointed out in his commentary, the warrior Arjuna through the grace of Krishna obtains a staggering, indeed terrifying, vision of the totality of the Godhead. As he puts it, "In an ineffable oneness are revealed all the facets of the Godhead—spirit and matter, being and becoming, infinite and finite, past and future."/17/ In wonder the disciple cries out: "Infinite One, Lord of gods, Abode of the universe, thou art the Imperishable, Being and nonbeing, and that which is the Supreme. Thou art the first of gods, the ancient Soul; thou art the Supreme Resting-Place of the universe; thou art the Knower, and that which is to be known, and the Ultimate Goal. And by thee is the world pervaded, O thou of infinite form."/18/ Here is direct evidence to Arjuna of the all-encompassing presence of God, seen by him as the Lord Krishna. But the vision is more than he can bear. We are made to understand that the mystical experience of the Universal Form is not meant for men and women in general. Krishna then shows himself in his usual form, benign and unterrifying. And in the chapters that follow, from 12 onward, the Brahman of the Upanishads is presented as a reality with whom we can have a personal relationship.

The way of devotional self-giving or bhakti-yoga is concerned, like that of intuitive wisdom, with the nature of the Godhead, the soul, and the world, and with the question of how to experience the divine presence. Throughout this scripture diverse suggestions are given about how to approach God. Clearly, he may be approached as a man. "Though I am unborn and eternal, and though I am the Lord of all beings, yet, subjugating my material nature, I accept birth through my maya./19/ Whenever there is a decline of righteousness and a rise of unrighteousness, I incarnate myself. For the protection of the good, for the destruction of the wicked, and for the establishment of righteousness, I am born in every age.'' /20/ Despite a great deal of misapprehension on the part of both Hindus and Christians about the exact meaning of the others' term ''incarnation,'' I believe that we must grant that in the avatara or ''descent'' of Vishnu, as seen from the human point of view, there is quite as much of a taking on of human nature as in a soul's being born as a man or woman. The basic difference between the two is that the avatara, unlike the human soul, is not under the control of the human nature, and thus is incapable of sin.

As we have seen, Krishna tells Arjuna that God rewards men in whatever way they approach him. In chapter 8 it is said that the Supreme Person, in whom all beings abide and who pervades the whole universe, may be attained by whole-souled devotion directed to him alone./21/ Moreover, to those who worship him, never harboring any other thought and always devoted to him, the Lord ''brings what they need and preserves what they already possess.''/22/ Even those who, with faith, worship other gods, worship him alone, though in a wrong way/23/— a teaching close to the Christian doctrine of ''implicit faith,'' through which the sincere believer in any faith is said to be worshiping the Beloved (that is, Christ) though by another name and without knowing perfectly who he is.

Two of the most telling verses on the devotional approach to God are found in chapter 9: ''Whoever offers me, with devotion, a leaf, a flower, a fruit, or water—that I accept, the pious offering of the pure in heart. Whatever you do, whatever you eat, whatever you offer in sacrifice, whatever you give away, and whatever you practice in the form of austerities—do it as an offering to me.''/24/

Chapter 12, ''The Way of Devotion,'' deals exclusively with this path. Very explicitly, Krishna suggests disciplines for the devotee or bhakta: he should fix his mind on God alone; if at first he cannot fix his mind on God steadily, he should draw the mind again and again from other objects and try to keep it fixed on him; if he cannot manage that, he should seek to devote himself to service of the Lord (as in chanting the Lord's names and glories, listening to others chanting them, observing fasts and other austerities, or making offerings of food, flowers, and other objects of ritualistic worship). If he is unable to perform even this sort of service, then, taking refuge in the Lord, he should strive to be self-controlled and simply surrender the fruit of each of his actions to him./25/

Summing up, Krishna says: ''He who never hates any being and is friendly and compassionate to all, who is free from the feelings of 'I' and 'mine' and even-minded in pain and pleasure, who is forebearing, ever content, and steady in contemplation, who is self-controlled and possessed of firm conviction, and who has consecrated his mind and understanding to me—dear to me is the one who is thus devoted to me.''/26/ Krishna has already assured Arjuna: ''Those who consecrate all their actions to me, regarding me as the Supreme Goal, and who worship me, meditating on me with single-minded concentration—to them, whose minds are thus absorbed in me, verily I become ere long the Savior from the death-fraught ocean of the world.''/27/

Way Of Service

The three disciplines we have discussed as means for communing with the Transcendental—intuitive wisdom, mental concentration, and devotion—may be practiced separately or along with one another, depending on the temperament of the individual worshiper. But in the fourth discipline, service through active work, we find in the Gita a fusion (for the average man or woman) of the paths of jnana and bhakti, in that through karma-yoga the intellectual and emotional disciplines are to be employed harmoniously in the everyday world. (It is possible, of course, for an agnostic or even an atheist to practice karma-yoga, in which case he would work selflessly for the work's sake alone. But in the present context we are speaking of aspirants who believe in a transcendent-immanent reality that overarches and undergirds the physical universe and the individual soul.)

In chapter 2, as we saw, the Gita gives a concise statement of the gist of this yoga. ''To action alone are you entitled,'' says Krishna, ''never to its fruit.''/28/ One is not to be attached to the results of what one does; nor, on the contrary, is one for that reason to give up activity and become inert. But, endowed with evenness of mind, one should cast off in his very life both good deeds *and* bad deeds done with a selfish motive, performing simply whatever duties one's place in life requires one to perform./29/ Here Krishna makes one of his best-known statements: ''Karma-yoga is skill in action.''/30/ And this is what one is asked to strive for. Thus everyday life becomes a challenge and, if the challenge is met, an adventure in fulfillment.

Chapter 3, ''The Way of Action,'' deals specifically with this yoga. This way is not inferior, for the average man or woman, to the way of an all-renouncing monk. ''Not by merely abstaining from action does a man reach the state of actionlessness,''/31/ Krishna tells Arjuna, ''nor by mere renunciation does he arrive at perfection.''/32/ Everyone is forced to act, in one way or another, because of impulses born of past desires and deeds; and one who restrains the organs of action/33/ but continues to dwell on sense objects with the mind is a conscious or unconscious hypocrite./34/ The way to act without being bound is to do work as sacrifice, that is, as worship without selfish desire for gain./35/ The man who does his work as sacrifice, and therefore without attachment, attains the Highest Goal./36/

Like the ordinary person, the man of enlightenment, too, performs work, though he has no object to gain from it—just as Krishna himself, Lord of the universe, constantly works./37/ But the ordinary person may determine what is best to do by taking into account his or her own dharma or personal duty, the inner law that shapes the whole character. ''Better is one's own dharma, though imperfectly performed,'' warns Krishna, ''than the dharma of another, well performed.''/38/

In chapter 4 Krishna once again speaks profound words about the nature and realization of one whose attachment to work is gone. Such a person sees ''inaction in action, and action in inaction.''/39/ Swami Vivekananda, a prophet of modern Hinduism, in his series of lectures entitled ''Karma-Yoga,'' gives what amounts to a commentary on this verse: ''The ideal man is he who in the midst of the greatest silence and solitude finds the intensest activity, and in the midst of the intensest activity the silence and solitude of the desert... That is the ideal of karma-yoga, and if you have attained to that, you have really learned the secret of work.''/40/ For such a person, as the Gita states in one of its most expressive verses, ''God is the process of the sacrificial offering, God is the offering itself, and it is God who pours the offering into the sacrificial fire, which also is God. God alone is attained by him who sees God in all action.''/41/ The implication here is that he sees God *in* everything, and this because he sees that nothing can exist apart from God. Indeed, his day-to-day life itself becomes for him a process of sacrificial offering.

In the Bhagavad Gita, Krishna shows time and again that all the faculties of the human person are to be utilized as means of communing with the Transcendental. The paths of intuitive wisdom and devotional self-giving, though for the contemplative monk they have their own sets of rigorous disciplines, are for the average man or woman matters of faith rather than of direct experience. Through either of them separately, or both of them in concert, with the help of the methods of the path of conscious mental control (which itself may be pursued independently), the mystic arrives at the break-through that gives him an immediate vision of the indivisible Atman-Brahman, ultimate reality as differentiated from the world of becoming. But, as Krishna states clearly in chapter 5 and by implication elsewhere, it is also possible for the average man or woman to reach the goal attained by the truly mature mystic/42/—and that without going through the mystic's heroic struggle and shattering transegoistic experience.

For the mystic, if he is to be called a mature mystic, must *return* to the ''relative world'' and realize the transcendental, now and here, in everyday living. If he cannot, he remains an immature mystic—immature in that he cherishes the belief that his own particular vision of God, conditioned in its expression though it must be by his own cultural heritage, alone is true and accurate, and others' vision of him is false, and in addition that the world of becoming is ultimately lacking in substance. This is not a mature view; for what must never be forgotten is that God is not only transcendent but also immanent. True, it is said by Krishna in the Gita: ''Whatever glorious or beautiful or mighty being exists anywhere, know that it has sprung from but a spark of my splendor...With a single fragment of myself I support the whole universe.''/43/ God far transcends the world of his creation. But it is also said: "He who sees the Supreme Lord abiding alike in all beings, and not perishing when they perish—verily, he alone sees."/44/ Hence, when we think of this scripture as showing a way to the transcendental, we must remember that the gate at its far end is not a one-way affair. The Transcendental does not merely transcend. Contrary to the popular saying, there *is* a round-trip ticket to nirvana. What is more, most of us have no need of one.

It is *through* the creation that most of us shall eventually see the Lord. The majority of men and women can never expect to experience anything in this life beyond the relative world. But all the statements about action in the Gita indicate that, through work selflessly performed for the sake of the Lord (or even for its own sake), the average man or woman can achieve a realization of ultimate reality, in this life, as immanent in the creation.

To some, such as the late R. C. Zaehner, the Gita's method shows that, in good Christian fashion, Krishna leads us from the "impersonal" to the "personal" view of God, and puts the personal, that is to say, himself as total embodiment of Vishnu, "above" the so-called impersonal Atman-Brahman. This would be a correct assessment if one could be certain that we may look on the Brahman envisioned in chapter 2 as being utterly without attributes rather than merely indescribable. Yet that is to make Brahman something entirely negative—in its own way as much of an object (in being a *denial* of objective qualities) as any anthropomorphic concept of deity. And Krishna, be it noted, always speaks of Brahman as "me." When we come to realize through devoted work of service to God or humanity, or through any other discipline inducing selflessness, that personality is something far more profound and mysterious than the individual uniqueness of the ego-self, we shall perhaps be able to see that the goal reached by the so-called impersonalists and by the so-called personalists—as Ramakrishna untiringly pointed out in the last century from the evidence of his own experience, and as the Gita so often affirms—is one and the same.

And this is what Krishna means when in chapter 18 of the Gita he says: "Abandon all dharmas/45/ and come to me alone for shelter. I will deliver you from all sins; do not grieve."/46/ For the "me" he refers to here is simply the Ultimate Person, who is one with what we have been referring to as the Transcendental—just as the "I" is when Jesus Christ says to his questioners: "Truly, truly, I say to you, before Abraham was, I am."/47/

· What all this seems to show is that the divine presence can be realized here in the relative world as well as in the world of mystical experience. As it was announced in the Upanishads some centuries earlier: "That [transcendent reality] is full; this [conditioned reality] is full. This fulness has been projected from that fulness."/48/ Hence, for all but perhaps the profound mystic, whatever is not to be realized in sense experience (purified of personal bias) is simply a *form of thought.* Thus, even the terms "transcendent" and "immanent" are meaningless for the person fully awake to the divine presence. Krishna's final exhortation to his disciple Arjuna to "aban-

36

don all dharmas'' and come to him alone for shelter is tantamount to saying: "Give up at last all mere duties seen as something of absolute value in themselves, even the specific disciplines of the four yogas, and realize God's immediate presence within your purified person, in direct experience."

Before undertaking any study of the Bhagavad Gita, a Christian may justifiably ask to know more about the relationship of its way of approaching the Transcendental to specifically Christian spirituality. This is not the place for a detailed examination of all the similarities and dissimilarities of Hinduism and Christianity. I have already noted, casually, a few parallels in the course of the discussion. But I wish to focus here on specific instances of similarities in practical matters. As for dissimilarities, until we have first understood the meaning of the points where the two religions closely approach each other, we cannot hope to appreciate the meaning of those instances where they diverge. It may not be out of place, however, to mention one that perhaps everyone who reads the Gita will notice. Whereas in Christianity full communion with the Transcendental is believed to be possible only after death, it would appear on the evidence of scripture and saints alike that in Hinduism it is possible in the present life. Yet even here one must guard against the quick assumption that this dissimilarity indicates a contradiction. On further inquiry, one may find that the term connotes in the two contexts not contradictory but complementary dimensions of the spiritual life—the one based on revelation and faith, the other on practice and experience.

Of all the similarities in the practical sphere, surely the most striking parallel between Hinduism and Christianity is to be found in the four ways of communing with the Transcendental that we have been considering. For whatever we may understand that term to convey, each of the ways forms a strand not only in the Hindu but also in the Christian spiritual fabric. It is true that in India, in the centuries following the third century B.C., the four ways became far more specialized than in the Gita, where they are harmonized by Krishna himself into a unity much as they are in Christianity. But this fact, though apparently an occasion of difference, in actuality enables a Christian aspirant to appreciate the qualities of the various strands of the Christian fabric more intelligently./49/ Again, in individual Hindu saints' lives there has often been an interweaving of two or more of these strands. Yet it is in the nineteenth century that one finds the ideal of the Gita *fully* realized—in the life and teaching of the saint Ramakrishna.

In the light of our previous discussion of the four ways as found in the Gita, where are their counterparts to be identified in the Christian tradition? The answer to this question is that all four ways are either hinted at or clearly represented in the sayings of Jesus and the apostles, and later in the writings of the outstanding mystics and thinkers of the Church. The way of intuitive wisdom, for example, which represents an intellectual search eventually yielding intuitive apprehension of ultimate reality, in its Christian formulation bears witness to the one nature of God, to his indivisible unity (or, as Hindus would say, nonduality), and to his dwelling in the depths of the human soul as the "true light" that enlightens every man and woman./50/ In some of the statements of St. Paul and St. John, as well as of mystics like Pseudo-Dionysius, Meister Eckhart, St. Catherine of Genoa, and St. John of the Cross, to mention but a few, it speaks of a relationship of the soul to God so intimate as to make it seem—as in the Hindu nondualist schools—all but indistinguishable or indeed essentially indistinguishable from him. The Old Testament revelation "Then God said, 'Let us make man in our image, after our likeness,' "/51/ and Jesus' declaration "I and the Father are one,"/52/ both point in this same direction.

The way of mental concentration, which in its Hindu version aims at helping the individual through conscious control of mind to experience the truth of the Self, is seldom as explicitly spelled out in Christian teaching as in Hindu. Yet it is implicit in the teaching of Jesus that "unless a grain of wheat falls into the earth and dies, it remains alone; but if it dies it bears much fruit."/53/ And its message that "death," that emptying of self-will, is impossible without rigorous spiritual discipline, is echoed not only in St. Paul's "I have been crucified with Christ,"/54/ but in the writings of St. John of the Cross, St. Ignatius Loyola, and St. Francis de Sales, and in manuals of spiritual practice by later spiritual directors.

Again, the way of devotional self-giving concerns itself with the nature of God as person, with the soul's relation to him, and with how the soul may experience the divine presence by making use of its capacity for emotion. Its Christian expression bears witness to the three Persons of the Godhead, to God's love for the human soul as its Creator, a love so perfect that he sent his only Son that men and women might inherit eternal life, and to the obligation of his children to love one another. One of its clearest expressions is found, of course, in Jesus' command "As the Father has loved me, so have I loved you; abide in my love."/55/ But since it forms, along with the way of service, the very basis of practical Christianity, the devotional way may be identified in the sayings of the apostles and the writings of all the Church Fathers and saints and spiritual guides who followed them.

Finally, the way of service teaches the active person that it is his right only to perform his work well, serving the Lord through his fellow humans, and to expect no reward for what he does. In Christian tradition, as the means by which Jesus' command to love one's neighbor in put into practice, it permeates the entire teaching of the Church outside the sphere of mysticism (where, however, it may be presumed that the striving of contemplatives is also to be carried out without selfish aim). Quite as explicitly as ever in the Gita, Jesus himself laid out the basic requirements for faithful following of this way. "As you did it to one of the least of these my brethren," he told his followers, "you did it to me."/56/ And "When you give alms, do not let your left hand know what your right is doing."/57/

38

The Bhagavad Gita and the Transcendental

It is clear, I think, from these examples (which could be indefinitely multiplied) that a real relationship exists between the Hindu and Christian ways of approaching the Transcendental. The Bhagavad Gita as a practical guide would thus seem to have a special importance for Christians as a means of helping them appreciate in greater depth the implications of what their own best mentors have been trying to tell them. Insofar as its disciplines do not conflict with the best disciplines of Christianity, perhaps it would seem not of great importance to try to find out what is the authority responsible for them. And yet, if we could finally determine that one and the same inspiration is speaking through all of them, the task of those entrusted with carrying on a conversation with other religions would be immensely lightened. This is not a hopeless undertaking; for, as we recall, the aspect of experience through spiritual practice is not the only aspect of religion. There is also the aspect of revelation itself. And the Bhagavad Gita as a scripture, as a true document of the human spirit, derives its importance from more than the similarities it bears to Christian doctrine in the matter of ways to commune with the Transcendental.

It is beyond the scope of this paper to examine the Gita as revelation; for that purpose we should have to study in detail the nature of the Lord Krishna as there revealed. Suffice it to say that if Krishna is understood, as the Gita understands him, as the mystery at the heart of the universe, the ultimate basis of matter and of the ever-creative law of cause and effect, and at the same time as the mystery at the heart of the human person, source of the never-ceasing flow of thought and feeling, the Gita may one day be seen as more than a way-shower to the Transcendental. It may be seen as well as a revealing by the Word who was from the beginning of another dimension of the divine, a dimension complementary to that revealed in the New Testament. For it involves, beyond the four ways to commune with the Transcendental that it sets forth, a witnessing/58/ to the sacramental nature of the physical and psychological universes, of this whole world of becoming in which all of us, whether we know it or not, are making our way to the transforming vision of a God who lives with us—beyond the transcendent and the immanent—now and here.

FOOTNOTES

/1/ *Ramakrishna Paramahamsa (A.D. 1836-86) is held by many to be, along with his most important disciple, Vivekananda, the prime mover in the revitalization of Hinduism in the nineteenth century. By practicing the spiritual disciplines of the various denominations of Hinduism, he satisfied himself that all faiths, if sincerely followed, led to communion with God. He himself was almost continuously aware of the divine presence in later life, and he inspired Vivekananda to found the now well-known Ramakrishna Mission, whose twofold ideal is realization of God and service to humanity, especially the poor, the starving, the sick, the illiterate.*

/2/ *Bhagavad Gita 4, 11. Quotations from the Bhagavad Gita in this article are (sometimes adapted) from* The Bhagavad Gita, *translated from the Sanskrit, with notes, comments, and introduction by Swami Nikhilananda (New York: Ramakrishna-Vivekananda Center, 1944).*

Christianity and the Religions of the East

The textual explanations in this volume follow in the main the commentary of Shankara, the ninth-century nondualistic theologian.

/3/   *Ibid. 2, 16-17.*

/4/   *Ibid. 7, 4-5. Differing from both the Upanishads and later theologians, the Bhagavad Gita devotes itself preponderantly to Atman in its expounding of the way of intuitive wisdom.*

/5/   *Ibid. 9, 4.*

/6/   *P. 216. In dealing with intuitive wisdom, my interpretation leans to the approach of be nondualist Shankara; for I consider his interpretation of the Upanishadic texts clearly relating to this path the most faithful.*

/7/   *Perhaps the greatest exponent on Nondualistic (Advaita) Vedanta theology, Shankara is said to have lived from A.D. 788 to 820.*

/8/   *The traditional dates for Ramanuja, the leading exponent of Modal (Visishtadvaita) Vedanta theology, are A.D. 1017 to 1137.*

/9/   *The most important exponent of Dualistic (Dvaita) Vedanta theology, Madhva is said to have lived from A.D. 1199 to 1276.*

/10/   *Bhagavad Gita 2, 54-72.*

/11/   *Ibid. 2, 47.*

/12/   *Most of the text of the Yoga Sutras was probably in existence in the second century B.C.*

/13/   *Bhagavad Gita 6, 5.*

/14/   *Ibid. 6, 10-28.*

/15/   *Ibid. 6, 19.*

/16/   *Ibid. 6, 32.*

/17/   *Swami Nikhilananda (n. 2 above 268, commentary on B.G. 11, 48.*

/18/   *Bhagavad Gita 11, 37-38.*

/19/   *The word "maya" here refers to the Lord's creative power of "veiling" his true nature and "projecting" the multiplicity of the relative world.*

/20/   *Bhagavad Gita 4, 6-8.*

/21/   *Ibid. 8, 22.*

/22/   *Ibid. 9, 22. The phrase given in the test as "never harboring any other thought" may also be translated as "mediating on their identity with me." The former is a modal nondualist or dualistic interpretation, the latter a nondualist.*

/23/   *Ibid. 9, 23.*

/24/   *Ibid. 9, 26-27. The word "me" in these two verses refers to Krishna as the Lord.*

/25/   *Ibid. 12, 8-11.*

/26/   *Ibid. 12, 13-14.*

/27/   *Ibid. 12, 6-7. In dealing with devotional self-giving, my interpretation leans to the approach of the modal nondualist Ramanuja; for I consider his interpretation of the Gita texts clearly relating to this path the most faithful.*

/28/   *Ibid. 2, 47.*

/29/   *Ibid. 2, 49-50.*

/30/   *Ibid. 2, 50.*

/31/   *The "actionlessness" referred to here indicates a state of freedom from egoistic action, not abstention from all activity.*

/32/   *Bhagavad Gita 3, 4.*

/33/   *The "organs of action" are the hands, feet, vocal organ, genitals, and excretory organ.*

/34/   *Bhagavad Gita 3, 5-6.*

/35/   *Ibid. 3, 9. As the commentator Shankara points out, there are various types of sacrifice: sacrifice to the gods, in the form of offerings and ritualistic worship; sacrifice to Brahman, through teaching and reciting scripture; sacrifice for human beings, in feeding the poor and homeless and treating guests as God; sacrifice for creatures, through feeding the lower animals; sacrifice for the ancestors, by making offerings for the peace of their souls. See Swami Nikhilananda, commentary on B.G. 3, 13, p. 100.*

/36/   *Ibid. 3, 19.*

/37/   *Ibid. 3, 20-22.*

/38/   *Ibid. 3, 35.*

/39/   *Ibid. 4, 18.*

/40/   *Vivekananda: The Yogas and Other Works (New York: Ramakrishna-Vivekananda Center, 1953) 461. Vivekananda was born in 1863 and died in 1902.*

The Bhagavad Gita and the Transcendental

/41/ *Bhagavad Gita 4, 24. The word here translated as "God" is "Brahman" in the original. This verse should not be interpreted as being pantheistic.*

/42/ *Ibid. 5, 5.*

/43/ *Ibid. 10, 41-42.*

/44/ *Ibid. 13, 27.*

/45/ *The word "dharma" may be understood here to imply not only all individual duties or all disciplines of the four ways we have encountered in the Gita, but righteous actions in general performed with a selfish end in view.*

/46/ *Bhagavad Gita 18, 66. The meaning here would appear to be that communion with ultimate reality is not to be won through performance of any sort of duty with the notion that one can oneself attain it through such means. Salvation, or liberation from ignorance, consists in one's having been emptied of the ego-self and having realized that it is the Transcendental (i.e., the Lord Krishna) who lives in one. The nondualist Shankara's commentary on this verse (see Swami Nikhilananda 368-69) is usually held to rule out all activity as a means to salvation. In this view, it is to be obtained only through Self-knowledge. It appears to some, however, that actions performed without the egoistic notion of being the doer are not here ruled out as a means–so long as one has thrown oneself on the mercy of Krishna and acts in the faith that one is simply an instrument of the Lord. This sort of activity leads to the state of "actionlessness" referred to earlier (B.G. 3, 4; see n. 31 above), which the Gita states is not to be attained by mere abstention from action. A reassessment of the nondualist Shankara's position in the light of Ramakrishna's doctrine of the mature mystic, experiencing the state beyond ecstasy, is badly needed.*

/47/ *Jn 8:58.*

/48/ *Isha Upanishad, Invocation; Brihadaranyaka Upanishad, Invocation; 5, 1, 5.*

/49/ *For an interpretation of the way of intuitive wisdom as a separate way, Shankara's approach is perhaps the most representative; Ramanuja and Madhva both interpret the way of devotional self-giving authoritatively, the former with a modal nondualist slant, the latter with a purely dualist. For a classic interpretation of the way of mental control, the Western student may best consult Patanjali's Yoga Sutras. The only thorough presentation of the way of service outside the Gita is to be found in Swami Vivekananda's Karma-Yoga, which is included in* Vivekananada: The Yogas and Other Works *(see n. 40 above) along with popularized versions of the other three ways. Though the Gita, as is now thought, may be placed at about 250 B.C., perhaps there were already differentiations of the four ways almost as distinct as those that occurred later; else why should Krishna be seeking to integrate them? It is possible also that the only one thus differentiated was the way of mental control, and that Krishna, like Christians from the time of the apostles onward, merely saw the others as harmonious strands of one already complete sanatana dharma or "eternal religion." See nn, 7, 8, and 9 above, for the first three theologians mentioned.*

/50/ *Jn 1:9.*

/51/ *Gen 1:26.*

/52/ *Jn 10:30.*

/53/ *Jn 12:24.*

/54/ *Gal 2:20.*

/55/ *Jn 15:9.*

/56/ *Mt 25:40.*

/57/ *Mt 6:3.*

/58/ *Cf. Bhagavad Gita 3, 22-24; 4, 6-8; 7, 4-12, 24-26; 9, 4-10, 17-18; 10, 8, 20, 42; 13, 12-17; 14, 26-27.*

CHAPTER FIVE

The Trinity and the Structure of Religious Life: An Indian Contribution to Wider Christian Theology

BY FRANK WHALING

I ndian Christian theology has begun to make a significant contribution to total Christian theology in a number of ways. One of these ways is to look at the doctrine of the Trinity again not merely in terms of the Godhead itself but also in terms of the religious life resulting from the fact that Christians think of God in terms of a Trinity.

Indian Christians have done their main work against the background of a culture primarily influenced by Hindu ideas. It is true that there are almost seventy million Muslims in present-day India, not to mention hundreds of millions more Muslims if we think of the whole sub-continent including Bangla Desh and Pakistan. However, Indian Muslims did not begin to respond significantly to the challenge of Christian and western thought until the foundation of what is now Aligarh Muslim University in 1870, and the mutual interaction between Christian and Muslim thought has been slight.

Dr. Frank Whaling served as a Methodist minister at the Birmingham Central Hall, England (1960-1962), as a Methodist missionary in Faizabad and Banaras in North India (1962-1966), and at Eastbourne, Sussex (1966-1969). He is presently a member of the largest British divinity faculty at New College in the University of Edinburgh where he is coordinator of the Edinburgh University Religious Studies degrees and Religious Studies Unit. He is also chairman of the Scottish Working Party on Religions of the World in Education, codirector of the Edinburgh/ Farmington Project in Religious Studies, and a member of the Shap Working Party, as well as a member of the New York International Center for Integrative Studies.
Dr. Whaling has published a number of articles in journals such as Sikh Sanskar, Indian

By contrast, Raja Ram Mohan Roy was attracted by Christian ideas at the end of the eighteenth century. He has been called the "father of the Indian Renaissance" and he and his Hindu successors were profoundly influenced by Christian ideas./1/ It is virtually impossible adequately to understand modern Hindu thought without taking seriously the effect upon it of Christian and western views. We are now beginning to realize that the converse is also the case. Indian Christian theologians have been influenced by the Hindu background within which they were thinking, living, and writing./2/ In attempting to communicate the Gospel within this background, in attempting to express Christian truths in Indian terms, in attempting to conceptualise the Gospel in ways that would make sense to the thought-world of India, Indian Christians have begun to make exciting new contributions to world theology. In this paper we are concerned with the contribution they have made in regard to the Trinity and the religious life arising from an Indian Christian view of the Trinity. A number of Indian Christian theologians have lent their talents to this new theological work and rather than concentrate upon one of them we will interpret the views of a number of these thinkers in order to gain an integral picture.

Western Christians have tended to isolate the doctrine of the Trinity from the rest of Christian doctrine and indeed from the practical living of the Christian life itself. Indeed the very word "theology" does not figure in the New Testament and when it did begin to be used in the Patristic period it was sometimes isolated to refer solely to the doctrine of the Trinity. Another word namely "oikonomia" was used for doctrines of salvation and so on, and "theologia" was restricted among some of the Fathers to the doctine of God in himself as a Trinity./3/ This is not to say that the doctrine of the Trinity was not important or that it was completely isolated from other doctrine or from life. I am, however, suggesting that it was not fully bound up with wider doctrine and with life. This is not the case as far as Indian Christian theology is concerned. Indian theologians have made contributions to the doctrine of the Trinity and at the same time to practical theology as well. The two are bound together, and we must look at both.

In the first place it is worth making the obvious comment that the concept of the Trinity is important to them. As far as they are concerned God is not merely Christ, although he is certainly that; he is Father, Son, and Holy Spirit. They do not restrict God to Christ by indulging in a form of

Journal of Philosophy, Forum, Scottish Journal of Theology, Irish Theological Quarterly, Journal of Religious Studies, *and* Journal of Religious Education. *He has written or edited a number of present or forthcoming books including* An Approach to Dialogue: Hinduism and Christianity; The Development of the Religious Significance of Rama in North India; Contemporary Approaches to the Study of Religion; Christian Theology and World Religions; Contemporary Issues in Religious Education in Britain and the United States; *and* Think Globally or Perish.

This essay is reprinted from The Scottish Journal of Theology, 32, 1974 pp. 354-364 by permission of the publisher and the author.

Christolatry. They recognise that the trinitarian nature of God is vital to Christian belief and life.

In the second place we may say that there is little possibility of Christian notions of the Trinity being aided either in theory or in practice by Christian contact with Jewish or Muslim world views insofar as they deny the concept of the Trinity. The same applies to Theravāda Buddhist, Confucian, and Taoist thought which equally have no doctrine of the Trinity. Mahāyāna Buddhist views of the Three Bodies of the Buddha seem to have superficial similarity to the Trinity with their reference to the Buddha in his historical aspect, in his glorified aspect, and in his cosmic aspect. However, this seeming resemblance turns out on closer examination to be a radical difference. Within the Hindu context Mathothu has written as a Christian upon the Hindu concept of the *trimūrti*, the trinity of personal deities, namely Brahmā the Creator, Visnu the Preserver, and Siva the Destroyer./4/ However, there seems to be little affinity between the *trimūrti* and the Christian Trinity./5/ More promising ground exists within Indian thought in the concept of *Brahman*, Ultimate Reality, as capable of being expressed in a triune way, as also in the idea that Brahman is both without qualities (*nirguna*) and with qualities (*saguna*). Indian Christians have availed themselves of these concepts in order to give deeper meaning to the doctrine of the Trinity. Let us examine briefly how they have done this.

Classical Hindu thought had suggested that the Absolute, Brahman, could be thought of as *Saccidānanda*, that is, *Sat, Cit,* and *Ānanda*./6/ These three terms mean Being, Intelligence, and Bliss. They provided for Indian Christian thinkers not merely an opportunity to present Christ to Hindus in their own thought-patterns but also the possibility of using these terms to deepen the meaning of the Trinity for Christians. For Being could refer to God in his ineffable aspect, Intelligence could refer to Christ as the Logos, and Bliss could refer to the Holy Spirit who is the Giver of Joy. Equally Being could refer to the inwardness of the Christian life whereby we are alone with God, Intelligence could refer to the intelligent personal relationship between the Christian and God, and Bliss could refer to the communion of the saints. Further Being could signify God in his unmanifest aspect, Intelligence could signify God in his incarnate aspect, and Bliss could signify God in his immanent aspect. Moreover Being could be linked with a spirituality of transcendence, Intelligence with a spirituality of personalism, and Bliss with a spirituality of immanence. There is a distant similarity between some of this type of thinking and the work of some of the early Fathers such as St. Augustine who had thought of the Trinity in terms of the analogy of being, knowledge, and love. However, the difference is that Indian Christian thought has placed more stress upon the experiential and practical outworkings of the doctrine of the Trinity rather than concentrating upon the doctrine for its own sake. In this it has been aided by the traditional Indian perception that truth must not be merely intellectually formulated but

actually lived. Indeed the Sanskrit word *Sat* means both Being and Truth./7/
In order to follow God who is Absolute Truth we must live the truth as well
as express the truth in theological terms.

An early example of this kind of theology lies in Keshab Chandra Sen,
who lived from 1838 to 1884. In his *Acknowledged Christ of the Hindu
Renaissance* M. M. Thomas has shown how a number of Indians responded
to the Gospel in significant ways without actually becoming Christians, and
prominent among them was Sen./8/ Indeed one of the most remarkable
developments in the whole history of Christian theology may well be the
theological contribution made by these Indian thinkers who never techni-
cally became Christians. Sen went further in theological reflection on the
Trinity than had Rām Mohan Roy who had been unitarian in his
approach./9/ In a paper of 1882 Sen spoke of "That Marvellous Mystery—
the Trinity"./10/ He pointed out that the Trinity and *Saccidānanda* were
similar notions of who the Godhead is. The Father, he said, is the Creator,
the still God, the "I am" of the Godhead, who is Force, the True, and *Sat*.
The Son, he said, is the Example, the journeying God, the "I love" of the
Godhead, who is Wisdom, the Good, and *Cit*. The Holy Spirit, he said, is
the sanctifier, the returning God, the "I save" of the Godhead, who is
Holiness, the Beautiful, and *Ānanda*. According to Sen, the Trinity can be
seen to operate through the analogy of an equal Triangle whose summit is the
Father, one side represents the descent of the Son to earth, the base is Christ
at work in the regeneration of mankind, and the other side represents the
Holy Spirit taking regenerated mankind back up to the Father. Sen did not
remain at the level of intellectual dogmas or theological models. He despised
the West for doing just that. The Christ who had descended to earth, he
pointed out, had made His abode in Asia, and any doctrine of the Trinity in
terms of *Saccidānanda* must lead on to living encounter with God in Christ
or it would be worthless. Sen typifies the Indian stress upon theological truth
as something that must be realised within and lived without. Truth is not
merely abstract intellectual theories, it is following the example of the divine
humanity of Christ in our outward lives, and it is "being in God" as "Christ
is in the Father" in our inward lives, through the prompting of the Spirit.

Keshab Chandra Sen opened up a number of the themes that were to be
developed by Indian Christians themselves. Before we examine this development in more detail let us pause in order to glance at the second
adaptation of Indian thought made by Indian Christians. In addition to giving
Christian content and form to the concept of *Saccidananda*, they also
pressed into service the important Indian idea that God as *Brahman* (Ultimate Reality) is both without qualities (*nirguna*) and with qualities
(*saguna*). As *nirguna* he cannot be known in himself for he is beyond this
phenomenal world and transcends what can be positively known; however,
as *saguna* he does show himself to the world as having qualities and form in
the shape of a personal God (*Iśvara*). In adapting this strand of Indian

thought Indian Christians have had to avoid various traps, notably the *Advaita Vedanta* notion that Brahman is basically impersonal and that his personal *saguna* form is of secondary importance./11/ Given that these traps have been successfully bypassed, Indian Christians have begun to teach the wider church new insights into the meaning of the Trinity. As *nirguna Brahman*, God is greater than anything that can be conceived. He is not reduced to the level of anthropomorphism or even human analogies. He can never be pinned down; he can never be adequately conceptualised; He cannot be known in himself; there are areas of God's being beyond the personalism we see in Christ. And yet *Brahman* is also *saguna*. He is the personal *Iśvara* as well as the ultimate *Brahman*. He is the Creator as well as the One beyond creation. He is immanent as well as transcendent. He is accessible as well as remote, Indian Christians such as Brahmabandhab Upadhyaya,/12/ Panikkar, and others have shown how the first Person of the Trinity can be conceived of as *Brahman*, God without qualities, and the second Person of the Trinity can be seen as *Iśvara*, God with qualities. Christ makes the invisible God visible, and gives personhood to the un-manifest God. The working out of the meaning of the first two persons of the Trinity in terms of *nirguna* and *saguna Brahman* has been subtly done by Indian Christians in different ways. There is the material here for a new formulation of the doctrine in the thought-forms of India.

Now let us turn to the practical applications of the Trinity to the religious life on the part of Indian Christians. Notable in this venture has been Panikkar's *Trinity in World Religions* but others have contributed as well. /13/ The main thrust of this work has been to relate the Trinity to the three religious ways outlined in the *Bhagavad Gita*, the ways (or *yogas*) of knowledge, devotion, and works (*jñana, bhakti*, and *karma*). In the bal-anced Christian life these ways are related, not exclusive, in the same way that the persons of the Trinity are related and one. And yet they are not the same either, although used by one particular individual. According to Panikkar the spirituality depending on *karma* is related to God the Father, the spirituality depending on *bhakti* is related to God the Son, and the spirituality depending on *jñana* is related to God the Holy Spirit. For Panikkar these three types of spirituality are built into *all* religious traditions, as is a triune notion of God. It may be that this implied claim is inaccurate and that this theory works in regard to Christianity and Indian thought. Nevertheless, and in a sense for this very reason, this idea can be helpful in Christian theology. God the Father is transcendent, beyond our sight, in light inaccessible, Wholly Other, unknowable in himself. We can form mental images of God, but they point beyond themselves to One whom we cannot comprehend. We can only obey him, and stand in silence before the Absolute. We can offer him the service of our *karma* (ritual works) and we can adore him in silence through the images we make to represent him. We serve him and approach him with awe through the spirituality of *karma*. And so the spirituality associated with the first Person of the Trinity is that of *karma*, the service that we offer in obedience to God's holy otherness and the ritual adoration with which we respond to his majestic awe.

God the Son is associated with the spirituality of *bhakti* which involves our personal love for God. Christ shows above all the personhood of God. He can be seen as a Person is a way that would not be true of God the Father or God the Holy Spirit. Panikkar points out that the early church notion that God is in three "Persons" can restrict the fullness of God's being by limiting him to human analogies. Christ is the Personhood of God, He is the Lord, He is *Īśvara*. He is the link with God whom we know not so much in himself but through the Lord. He is the "Thou" whereby we know the Absolute whom he mediates. We know him through the spirituality of love, devotion, and prayerful relationship. According to Panikkar the Lord is present in all religious traditions whether known or unknown. He is fully shown through the medium of the church but he is present, though perhaps unknown, in other traditions. Others are therefore "saved" by Christ who uses their tradition as normal channels to lead them to God. At this point Panikkar is universalising the western notion of Christ so that he can be visualised in non-western and non-Greek categories. And yet this Lord, this Logos, who cannot be confined to human boundaries is the Divine Person to whom we respond in love and prayer and devotion. He is the Lord of *bhakti* with whom we enjoy an I-Thou relationship.

God the Holy Spirit is associated with the spirituality of intuitive inwardness. He is immanent. He is not Other, he is not Person, he is not One with whom we enter into relationship — He is One whom we realise in the depths of our being. He is the Ground of our being beyond our outward self and we realise him inwardly through silence, through inwardness, through union of our own deepest self with the Spirit of God. We are now in the realm of mysticism and inward realisation, not that of devotion or that of adoration of transcendent majesty. We are in the realm of the Spirit.

I have summarised a lot of intricate ideas rather quickly in highlighting this important concept of the "three spiritualities of the Trinity". This Indian Christian theological reflection is important for general theology in various subtle respects. It is also helpful in more direct ways. For part of the battle in the western world lies in the area of spirituality rather than in the realm of ideas. The western church has tended to stress the conceptual, the ethical, and the organisational aspects of religion rather than the experiential. The popular success of certain eastern movements almost surely lies in their stress upon the inward elements of religious life. The Christian church in its past history has not been lacking in deep spirituality but this feature is not conspicuously present at the moment. It is likely that it may be revived by the stimulus given by Indian Christians and others who have been influenced by other religious groups who *have* given a central stress to inward spirituality./14/ Indeed the strength of the Indian Christian reflection on the

Trinity is this. In addition to dwelling upon the difference in unity within the godhead, it has also stressed the difference in unity within Christian spirituality. It has made the point that ritual worship of God, loving devotion to God, and inward realisation of God are related aspects of an integral spirituality which finds concrete expression in service for God in the world. All of these different aspects of spirituality are bound up together. Just as God is transcendent, yet personal, yet immanent, so also we need to worship God in his transcendence, love him in his personhood, and realise him in his immanence. At the end of the day these are not three different spiritualities, they are different aspects of the same spirituality just as there is one triune God. This would appear to be an important contribution to Christian theology which, in its western garb, has tended to stress the role of Christ rather than that of the Trinity and the role of involvement rather than that of spirituality in the wider sense.

A recent Indian Christian thinker Dhanjibhai Fakirbhai has added an important element to this debate about the spiritualities of the Trinity. He has given a deeper Indian structure to this type of theology by expressing it in poetic and dialogue form./15/ Whereas Panikkar utilised the theological method common in Indian philosophy, namely commentary on key verses of sacred texts, Fakirbhai uses the dialogue method found in the *Bhagavad Gita*. Both these methods are Indian and important for future theological developments on a world scale. The dogmatic tome may have become standard in western theological work elsewhere. However, Fakirbhai is also significant for the added dimension he gives to the content of trinitarian spirituality. For him the centre of Christian theology lies in the conviction that God is Love. God is *Saccidananda* and the spiritualities of *karma*, *bhakti*, and *jñana* are relevant for the Christian. But overarching *Saccidananda* and these three spiritualities is Love. God is above all Love and to follow him is above all to love. ''So it is,'' he says, ''that the complete *yoga* of Action, Worship and Knowledge (*karma*, *bhakti* and *jñana*) is attained through the Way of Love (*prema yoga*).'' Fakirbhai adds to the discussion in two ways. In the first place, Panikkar tends to limit *karma* to ritual and sacrifice which is one of its Sanskrit meanings whereas Fakirbhai stresses the meaning of *karma* as service or action. A crucial element of involvement is added to Panikkar's view of spirituality. In the second place, Fakirbhai stresses the role of love as the key factor. In fact he is not going as far beyond Panikkar as appears to be the case because Panikkar had made *bhakti* and the Lord his key link and he had done this because loving devotion was central to the Trinity and to spirituality. Fakirbhai weakens the meaning of *bhakti* to ''worship'' instead of ''loving devotion'' and introduces the word *prema* to denote ''love'' in a stronger sense than is implied in *bhakti*./16/ Nevertheless they are not far apart in asserting that the Personhood of Christ is central to the Trinity and that personal devotion is important in any authentic Christian spirituality. In the third place, and here I

49

interpret the theological and existential quest of Indian Christian theology, Fakirbhai is indicating that in fact there are four kinds of spirituality arising out of trinitarian theology, namely those of worship, action, love, and knowledge. Fakirbhai makes love the controlling factor; other Indian Christians would make one of the other three predominant; and yet these four elements tend to appear in one form or another. In their understandable desire to enable their theology to arise out of the Christian doctrine of the Trinity and the three *yogas* of the *Bhagavad Gita*, Indian Christians have felt in duty bound to speak in terms of three spiritualities whereas in practice they have alluded to four. It is fascinating to reflect that the *Bhagavad Gita* also cites three ways of spirituality (knowledge, love, and action) but also uses the word *karma* in two senses, namely those of action and ritual; to that extent the *Bhagavad Gita* is also alluding to four types of spirituality while mentioning only three in a formal sense.

This whole development is tremendously important for wider Christian theology and life. Different churches at different times have emphasised one or perhaps more than one of these ways. Sometimes churches of individual Christians have stressed the primacy of worship, regular attendance at the public celebration of preaching and the sacraments. At other times they have stressed the centrality of loving God in Christ — he is the Friend whom we love as well as the Master whom we worship, and by commitment to him personally we enter into a devotional relationship with him. This relationship may be a quiet one as in the case of *bhakti* or it may be an emotional one as in the case of *prema,* the point is that it is a devotional relationship. At other times Christians have stressed the need for action, service, and involvement in the world. /17/ This has been the springboard for the expansion of Christian hospitals, schools, and welfare services. Especially in the case of America this sort of activism has been encouraged as being not only integral to but central to the Christian life. At other times, more rarely and mainly in the past, Christians have stressed the need for a strong inner life of meditation and contemplation and inwardness on the supposition that the Kingdom of God is within as well as without and that constant practice of the presence of God is crucial to the Christian life. Indian Christians are in the process of pointing out to us that all four ways are integral to the full Christian life. They do not exclude but include each other. They are not separate but related. They are all necessary. If any one of them is missing then the fullness of the Christian life is not there. This is a lesson that the Church may learn in our time to her great benefit in so many places and in so many ways. This intuition about the integral nature of the Christian life has been derived from a dual source, on the one hand Indian thought, especially the *Bhagavad Gita*, and more importantly on the other hand the doctrine of the Trinity. Indian Christian theologians are showing us that we are called upon as Christians to live in this way because God the Trinity mirrors this integral life in his own nature.

The Trinity and the Structure of Religious Life

Footnotes

/1/   A good summary of modern Hindu thought is to be found in D. S. Sarma, Hinduism Through The Ages (Bombay, 1973). M. M. Thomas, The Acknowledged Christ of the Indian Renaissance (SCM, London, 1969), details the Christian influence upon the Hindu reformers.

/2/   Robin Boyd, An Introduction to Indian Christian Theology (CLS, Madras, 1975), intimates this, as do the various publications of the Christian Institute for the Study of Religion and Society, Bangalore.

/3/   As the medieval period developed theologia came to refer to all Christian doctrinal formulations, not just that of the Trinity.

/4/   K. Mathothu, The Development of the Concept of Trimūrti in Hinduism (Palai Kerala, 1974).

/5/   There are a number of reasons for this claim. Two important reasons are that the Goddess Sakti came to replace Brahma the Creator as an effective focus of later Hindu devotion; also that the three personal deities were seen as separate manifestations rather than as strictly trinitarian.

/6/   Saccidananda is the union in Sanskrit of the three words sat, cit, and ananda.

/7/   It is interesting to note that the Arabic language too has not so radically divorced the meaning of the words Being and Truth.

/8/   Sen was a leader of the Brahmo Samaj; he had a deep attraction to Christ; he was also influenced in later life by the Hindu mystic Ramakrishna.

/9/   Ram Mohan Roy engaged in dialogue with Marshman, one of the Serampore missionaries, and he converted another, Adam, to unitarian Christianity.

/10/   Keshab Chandra Sen, Keshab Chandra Sen's Lectures in India (Cassell, London, 1909).

/11/   As formulated by the followers of the great Indian philosopher Śankara, Advaita posits two levels of truth, the empirical and the higher levels. A leap of realisation is required to pass from one to the other, and they are discontinuous.

/12/   Brahmabandhab Upadhyaya (1861-1907), a Bengali Brahmin, was baptised in 1891.

/13/   R. Panikkar, The Trinity and World Religions (CLS, Madras, 1970).

/14/   The rise of the notions of Christian Yoga and Christian Zen is evidence of this

/15/   D. Fakirbhai, Kristopanishad (CISRS, 1965); and The Philosophy of Love (ISPCK, Delhi, 1966).

/16/   The bhakti of the earlier devotional movements influenced by Ramanuja was moderate and restrained; some of the later devotional movements were more ecstatic in nature and prema indicates a more emotional content in the devotional attitude.

/17/   The modern stress upon secular Christianity would be an example of this.

CHAPTER SIX

Buddhism and Christianity as Complementary

BY JOHN B. COBB, JR.

Methodological Questions

Christians believe that God is the God of all and that in Jesus Christ God effected in principle the salvation of all. This universalistic conviction has forced Christian thinkers to reflect about the meaning of movements other than Christianity especially when they have some apparent power and goodness in themselves. The study of cultures and religious Ways other than Christianity is a theological imperative for Christians.

In the last two centuries the cultures and religious Ways of Asia have become increasingly important for Western intellectuals, and in the last two decades they have taken on importance for millions of ordinary Western Christians. The reality of Asian Ways is no longer known only through reading and travel. They have penetrated Western culture and life and offer a vital alternative for serious-minded Westerners. In this situation the urgency of theological reflection is enhanced. Western Christians can be grateful that

Dr John B. Cobb, Jr., author of several well known theological works, is Ingraham Professor of Theology at the School of Theology at Claremont, California and Avery Professor in the Claremont Graduate School. He is also Director of the Center for Process Studies. This essay was part of a dialogue conversation with Dr Seiichi Yagi whose essay follows. Dr Cobb's essay is taken from the North East Asian Journal of Theology, *n. 20-21, 1978, pp. 19-30. It is reprinted here by permission of the publisher.*

Eastern Christians have been involved in these questions for generations. Japan is now the world center for the encounter of Buddhism by Christians.

The experience of the early church is instructive for us as we face our new situation. In the New Testament itself the religious Ways of the Gentiles are viewed primarily as idolatrous. We should not be contemptuous of this treatment, for of course the practise of the masses of Gentiles *was* idolatrous. But the New Testament writers themselves were influenced by Platonic and Stoic modes of thought and expression, and as the thinkers of the early church encountered the work of the philosophers in its purity, they could not dismiss Greek thought simply as idolatrous.

The church's struggle to come to terms with philosophy still continues. Within Protestantism there have been many who see the appeal to philosophic reason as itself a sophisticated and dangerous idolatry. Nevertheless, viewing Christian history overall, we must say that Christians decided that one could be both a Christian and a philosopher. Furthermore, Greek philosophy entered constitutively into the structure of Christian thought throughout the Middle Ages; and during most of the modern period as well, theology and philosophy have been deeply intertwined.

When Christians encounter the great Oriental religious Ways they face different challenges, which are yet analogous. These new challenges have evoked analogous responses. Despite notable exceptions, prior to World War I the dominant response was to view Asian religious Ways as idolatrous. As in the case of the New Testament, there was some justification. Even today as tourists visit Buddhist temples in Southeast Asia or Japan, much of what they observe is, at least superficially, idolatrous or superstitious.

However, as Christian thinkers during this period became aware of the profound philosophy, the meditational practices, and the personal faith present in these Ways, they could no longer dismiss them as merely idolatrous or superstitious. Serious theological reflection on their meaning has become imperative. It is still in its early stages. I will list four approaches to the understanding of the relation of Christianity to Buddhism, none of which I find satisfactory. I will then make my own proposals.

First, some Christians concentrate on the similarities with Buddhism. Buddhism can be seen as a partner which shares the same essential convictions and experience. Differences are then viewed as matters of cultural accretion, language, imagery, and emphasis. Discussion consists in discovering how the other tradition identifies and describes central elements experienced in one's own. This was Tillich's approach when he visited Kyoto.

Second, some Christians who have been more impressed by the differences have accepted the image of many paths up the same mountain. Although the Ways are quite different, it is thought that they are all means of achieving salvation. Even if salvation is conceived differently, it is held that in fact it is one and the same for all. This view is popular among followers of some Oriental Ways, especially in India.

Third, some Christians who hold fast to the universal meaning of Jesus Christ view the several paths not as attaining salvation but as diverse preparations for the Gospel. Just as the Judaism of the Old Testament prepared the Jews for the Gospel, so also Hellenistic culture prepared the Gentiles, and Oriental Ways prepared the peoples of the East. The uniqueness of Jesus Christ is then to be expressed in the diverse cultures and languages of humankind rather than to be bound finally to Judaism. Roman Catholic theology, especially since Vatican II, has leaned in this direction.

Fourth, when the differences between Christian and Buddhist teaching are still more fully appreciated, some Christians come to the conclusion that they are irreconcilably opposed. In their view, if Christian teaching about God and the soul is correct, then Buddhist teaching must be erroneous insofar as it differs. However attractive are the achievements of Buddhism in art, culture, and personal life, the Christian response must be to try to correct its errors and convert Buddhists to the truth. This has been the dominant view of Christian missions in the past even when there was considerable appreciation of Buddhism.

I want to defend a fifth position. This agrees with the stress on differences between Christianity and Buddhism, both in their beliefs and in their goals. But it holds that these differences need not amount to theoretical contradictions. Both can be true. *I* believe that both *are* true. In this case we have much to learn from each other about features of reality and types of experience little developed in our own traditions.

For this position to be correct, reality must be more complex than either tradition, by itself, has recognized. It is very clear that in Western Buddhist scholarship in general, at least until quite recently, the questions that have been asked of the Buddhist texts have been questions that could be understood and answered already in Western experience. Nirvana has been understood either as this-worldly or other-worldly, and these categories were understood in the sense they had gained in the West. If Nirvana was other-worldly, then it was either literal extinction or else mystical union with God. If it was this-worldly, then it could only be some form of moral excellence or psychological fulfillment. The scholarly students of Buddhism alternated among these views.

Some Western philosophers have been able to think through to categories that transcended Western common sense and in doing so to come closer to grasping Buddhist thought and experience. Friedrich Schopenhauer is an example. Despite his lack of scholarship he understood Nirvana better than did the Buddhologists. He could do so because his own philosophical imagination brought him to conceive of the radical extinction of the will as the door to a wholly different mode of being.

In the twentieth century Martin Heidegger offers an effective way for the

Western mind to approach Buddhism because he also penetrates to a mode of experience radically new for the West and approaching the experience of Buddhist enlightenment. Indeed, Heidegger may well be the most Buddhist thinker the West has produced. His later work provides an important basis for Western understanding of Buddhism.

Schopenhauer and Heidegger illustrate how philosophical thought can break through the established categories of the Western mind and open it to an understanding of Buddhism. They do not, however, support my thesis of the distinct truths of Buddhism and Christianity. For them, if the truths are different, this would be because one penetrates less deeply than the other. Divergences must express different levels of apprehension of one truth. I am arguing, in contrast, that Christianity and Buddhism lie on different lines of development that cannot be compared as more superficial and deeper.

I am closer to another philosopher, F.S.C. Northrop. In *The Meeting of East and West* he describes their relation as complementary. This requires a concept of reality that allows the mind to move in two different directions from its primary experience. Northrop describes the common starting point as the differentiated aesthetic continuum. From it the West moves to attention to the differentiating forms; the East, to the underlying undifferentiated continuum.

I do not find the details of Northrop's analysis either adequate or convincing, but I am grateful for the basic model. Northrop sees East and West as profoundly different, but he holds that the truths they realize and treasure are complementary rather than contradictory. He is able to do this, again, because of his philosophical vision, each encompassed dimensions of reality poorly articulated in the West.

Northrop was a student of Alfred North Whitehead, and his work shows Whitehead's influence. However, he intentionally simplified Whitehead's philosophy and accepted only limited aspects of it. It is my belief that a richer use of Whitehead's conceptuality can allow a more varied grasp of alternative Eastern views and a deeper penetration into Buddhism while retaining the idea that they complement one another. Whitehead's own view was that Christianity and Buddhism represent the culmination of Western and Eastern religious developments, that both are in decline, and that neither can regain its vitality except as enriched through the other. I share his conviction and I am trying to use his general perspective in order to show how Christianity can be enriched through its contact with Buddhism.

The Self in Buddhism and Christianity

One major point of apparent conflict between Christianity and Buddhism is about the self. Christianity emphasized the self, whereas Buddhism declares it an illusion from which we are to be freed. There is no doubt that between most Christian formulations and most Buddhist ones there are strict contradictions. My question is whether the contradictory statements are necessary to the contending parties.

It *is* essential to Buddhism to deny that there is, metaphysically speaking, such an entity as a persisting self. Any doctrine of a self-existent, self-contained entity of this sort must be refused. If Christian doctrine requires affirmation of a substantial or transcendental self, then there is irresolvable metaphysical contradiction between Christianity and Buddhism. However, it is by no means evident that Biblical thinking involves either substantialist or transcendental views. On the contrary, they appear foreign to the Biblical frame of mind. There is, certainly, some notion of what we would call a personal self, but the hypostatization of this self developed only through interaction with Greek philosophy, and much of what is most strictly contradictory to Buddhism began with Descartes.

On the Buddhist side, it is clear that the denial of the self is not a denial that in ordinary experience there is a strong connectedness among successive experiences of a single person. In this sense the factuality of a personal self is far from denied, it is presupposed in the idea of *karma*. What is denied is that this special connection between these experiences is metaphysically given or that there is a common subject to whom they occur. And what is proposed is that full realization that ideas of a metaphysical unity or of an underlying subject are illusions can break the factual bondage of present to past and future.

There is no reason for Christians to deny the accuracy of the Buddhist analysis. Nevertheless, Christians affirm that there is positive value in the personal ordering of selfhood from which Buddhists seek liberation. The issue for Christians is complex. The personal self is to be ''denied'' or even ''crucified.'' But denial and crucifixion are not means of obliteration. They presuppose a strong self which then sacrifices its purposes and desires so that God's will may be done. Denial and crucifixion assume continuity through time and personal responsibility for past and future. Ethical norms play a central role. All of this very different from what Buddhism means by the realization of no-self.

My view as a Whiteheadian is that Christian and Buddhist doctrines about the universal nature of reality need not differ. There need be no logical contradiction. Buddhism and Christianity should each be able to understand intellectually the structure of existence advocated by the other and partly realized by it. Each should be able to see also the important human values attained in the other's structure, and each should be ready to learn more about these from those who more fully realize them. All this can be said without minimizing the profound differences. Indeed, it is precisely because Buddhism differs so profoundly from Christianity that Christians have so much to learn from it.

This entails that the enlightenment Buddhists seek is quite different from the salvation with which Christians are concerned. This is turn is in apparent conflict with many Christian formulations of the claim of universality. Certainly the claim of universality must be reconceived in a pluralistic world. Nevertheless, such reconception should not be abandonment. Jesus Christ is uniquely bound up with what Christians mean by salvation. This salvation is relevant and available to all. But it differs from and is only remotely related to what Buddhists call enlightenment, a condition which is also relevant and available to all. It is entirely appropriate that Christians witness to the joy of salvation through faith in Jesus Christ. It is entirely appropriate also that Buddhists witness to the serenity that is achieved in enlightenment. The world needs both universal Ways. For either, in its present form, to displace the other would be a profound loss.

The Doctrine of God in Buddhism and Christianity

A second area in which Buddhism and Christianity appear to contradict each other centers around the Christian doctrine of God. Buddhism denies the existence or reality of what Christian theology generally has called God. There are at least three features of most Christian teaching about God that clearly evoke Buddhist negation.

Most Christian thinking presents God, analogous to the personal self, as substantial or transcendental. Indeed, God is often conceived as the purest instance of substance, completely self-contained, and needing nothing else so as to exist. Buddhism insists that whatever is is relational through and through, interdependent with everything else. Confronted with this insistence, Christians must ask themselves whether they have truly been faithful to their own Scriptures and experience in depicting God as beyond all real relations or relativity. I believe we have not, and that the encounter with Buddhism can be an occasion for freeing our concept of God from the absolutist straightjacket.

Most Christians have also laid stress on God's radical transcendence. Here again a Buddhist may have to say ''No!'' If transcendence means beyond relations and relativity, then we have already seen that Buddhists properly reject this. If it connotes a spatial sense of above and beyond the physical world, it is either simply naive or else bound up with a dualism that the Buddhist rightly opposes. There cannot be a being of a fundamentally different order or type from the remainder of what is.

But there are other meanings of transcendence which Buddhists need not reject. If transcendence means vast qualitative superiority, then most Buddhists recognize this in Gautama and other Buddhas when these are compared with themselves. There is a sense in which the enlightened state transcends ordinary experience and in which reality transcends our concepts of it. The encounter with Buddhism presses Christians to reconsider what we have meant by God's transcendence. When we do so, we find that the Biblical sense of God's transcendence is qualitative and that our doctrine of God can avoid those types of transcendence which Buddhists legitimately reject.

Most theologians, in the third place, have also identified God with ''ultimate reality.'' To do so attributes to ultimate reality characteristics incompatible with the Buddhist understanding of Nothingness or Emptiness. It is true that there has been the negative way in Christianity, and that some mystics have spoken of the Divine Nothingness in ways that suggest affinities with Buddhism. But when the meaning of Emptiness for Buddhists is fully appreciated, we must agree that it would be deeply misleading to name this God. Buddhist Emptiness is not the God of the Christian scriptures.

Here again we Christians are forced to rethink our theological habits. If ultimate reality is Emptiness, and if Emptiness is not the Biblical God, then does the Biblical God have no reality at all? Or is it possible that the Bible does not present God as ultimate reality in the metaphysical sense? If we look open-mindedly for the Biblical idea of the metaphysical ultimate, might we not find it in the chaos or nothingness from which God created the world? Was, perhaps, the theological identification of God with ultimate reality or Being Itself a mistake?

That there is a tension betweeen the metaphysical ultimate—the God of the philosophers—and the ultimate of faith—the God of Abraham, Isaac, and Jacob—has long been realized by Christians. Emil Brunner noted the difference and opted for the God of Abraham, Isaac, and Jacob. Paul Tillich noted the difference and affirmed Being Itself as the God beyond the Biblical God.

The encounter with Buddhism suggests that when Being Itself is fully understood and experienced it resolves itself into the Nothingness of dependent origination. It not only differs from the Biblical God but also lacks those characteristics of Being Itself that have enabled Westerners to think of Being as God. It thus makes clear that to speak of God at all should be to speak of the Biblical God rather than of Being Itself as ultimate reality. If Buddhist analysis correct, then the Biblical God must be a manifestation of ultimate reality as dependent origination.

The idea of God or Gods as manifestations of ultimate reality is an old one. Hinduism affirms it emphatically, and Buddhist thought at least allows it. But Christians have resisted this way of understanding God. The tendency to imply that God is one manifestation among others, dispensable to the initiate, is quite unacceptable to Christian theology. If it is recognized that God is not ultimate reality as such, then God must be seen as the one, everlasting and ultimate embodiment of ultimate reality, essential for the occurrence of whatever else may be. Although such a universal manifestation of dependent origination is not envisaged in Buddhist doctrine, I believe there is no contradiction involved and that Christian faith will benefit from clarifying itself in this way.

Alfred North Whitehead's philosophy moves us a considerable distance in this direction. He distinguishes creativity, his name for ultimate reality, from God. His account of creativity - the many coalescing into a new one which is then a part of the many which coalesce again - is remarkably similar to some formulations of *pratityasamutpada*. God is the primordial, unique, and everlasting instantiation of creativity. Since creativity is everlasting, God did not exist before all creatures, but God plays an essential and constitutive role in the coming to be of each new creature.

If, then, we can affirm both Buddhist Emptiness and the Christian God, the difference between Buddhism and Christianity is not a matter of metaphysical truth but of two orientations to the totality of what is. Both orientations have been present in both Buddhism and Christianity. Yet we may recognize a polarity in the dominant traditions, the former exploring the meaning and value of the realization of ultimate reality, the latter exploring the meaning and value of faith in God.

This duality of directions corresponds to the duality we have noted previously between strengthening the contingent personal self and its extinction. To seek the realization of ultimate reality as *pratityasamutpada* is to move toward freedom from personal selfhood. To attend to God and God's purposes in the world orients one to the future and to the new possibilities of the present in a way that evokes the exercise of will, intensifies personal responsibility, and focuses on hope. This leads to the strengthening of personal selfhood.

The Risks and Rewards of Such Dialogue

The position which I am defending is that Buddhism and Christianity are both true, that both embody and express possible and real life orientations and perceptions of reality. Yet it seems that existentially they preclude each other. To be a Buddhist is to participate in one kind of existence and to seek one kind of perfection. To be a Christian is to participate in quite a different structure.

Even if we are left with this insuperable duality, our encounter is profitable. I have suggested ways in which Christian thought can be stimulated and corrected through the meeting. For Christians there is also intrinsic value in expanding our understanding of the rich varieties of experiences and realities. It is a gain also if we can express our truth to Buddhists in ways that do not seem immediately false.

Nevertheless, the admission that there is a form of beautiful and admirable experience that is forever closed to the Christian can not but be personally painful. It is also theologically distressing. It would mean that in fact Jesus Christ is not, as we have affirmed, relevant to the Buddhist, for Buddhist enlightenment would preclude any possibility of the salvation offered in Jesus.

My hope is that this is not the final word for the Christian in relation to Buddhism. Christians have in the past appropriated complementary truth and practice from other movements. The extent to which the results distort or enrich is always to be critically judged in each concrete case, but I am fully convinced of the importance of the venture. Success is most likely when the danger is fully appreciated and when we are quite aware of what we are doing. In relation to Buddhism the adventure has begun.

It is important that we recognize that to live deeply into Buddhist experience will upset established forms of Christian existence. We cannot simply add a few superficial elements of Buddhism to our present form of Christianity. Also we cannot expect to judge the outcome of an effective relation to Buddhism by the norms we hold before we enter into the relation. Those norms must also be subject to change through the encounter. We cannot enter the relation as Christians unless we are called into it by Christ. But if we are called into it by Christ, as I believe, then we must trust him and not the beliefs and ideas which we now identify with him. The risk is great, but is is the risk of faith itself.

CHAPTER SEVEN

Buddhism and Christianity

Thesis

Egoism and discriminating intellect *(funbetsu;* for meaning, see below) are united in their roots. Christianity testifies to the life in which egoism is overcome, whereas Buddhism knows the thinking which has overcome the discriminating intellect. In this sense Christianity and Buddhism complement each other in the breaking down of the union between egoism and discriminating intellect.

Egoism

Egoism is the mode of life in which the self, ignoring its original relationship with the transcendent and with other selves, pictures up the state of the self which seems desirable to itself. It endeavors to realize this picture and to press it not only on others, but also on the reality itself, i.e., it not only attempts to rule over others and to have them acknowledge the realization of the picture, but it interprets the reality so, that the very reality, according to its interpretation, justifies this realization. For instance, the egoist who

Seiichi Yagi, after studies at Tokyo University, did graduate work in theology at Göttingen University in Germany. In 1965 he became professor of German language and literature at the Tokyo Institute of Technology where he is at present. (182 Chofu-shi, Jindaiji-machi 1856-21, Tokyo, Japan). He is working in three fields: New Testament Theology, Comparative Religion and Philosophy of Religion. He has lectured on these at Tokyo University, International Christian University and Hanazono University (Zen Buddhist-Kyoto). Since 1970 he has been a Director of the "Japan Society of Christian Studies" and "Japan Society of New Testament cannot endure any authority above him will deny the existence of God as the ruler. On the other hand the egoist who seeks his security dependent upon the mighty person will invent God as his patron. Thus the egoist produces illusions constantly. In order to realize the desired state of the self, the egoist must first of all make his existence secure. For this purpose he seeks wealth and property. In the second place he must know where in the structure of reality he is located. He seeks to have useful knowledge of the empirical reality, so that his self-realization may become possible. In the third place he wants power because he needs it for his self-realization. In the fourth place the state of the self, which he wants to realize, must have the content desirable to himself. It consists not only in the fulfillment of its desires but it must seem brilliant to himself and others as something worthy of admiration.

It is not necessarily egoistic for a person to make his existence secure, to develop his possibilities and to produce brilliant achievements. These can be the results of the realization of an authentic existence, the results which it did not seek intentionally. The egoism consists in the fact that a person wants these results intentionally and apart from his relation to others. And the egoist, when he attains his desired self-realization, gazes at his own brilliant figure and *unuboreru* (falls in love with himself), just as Narcissus of the Greek myth who, having seen his own beautiful figure reflected on the water, fell in love with himself until he became the flower called narcissus. Here it becomes clear that the egoist objectifies himself and gazes at his objectified figure, concentrating all his interest upon it.

Discriminating Intellect

Thus out of the behavior of the egoist we can read his understanding of the self; according to him he is what he is only by and through himself. He objectifies himself uniting the objectified self with the picture of himself and takes the objectified self for his true self which should be realized. The egoism has two sides: the self-realization and the self-understanding. And the way in which the egoist understands himself is that he takes the objectified, pictured self for his true self which is realized and maintained only by and through himself. This way of understanding is fundamentally the same as the way of thinking in which the descriminating intellect grasps reality.

The discriminating intellect is the intellect which works as follows. It objectifies reality as beings and regards their self-identical contents as their essence and expresses it by distinct words. It tends to grasp the self-identity of beings. Therefore the typical form of its expression is: "S is P." The

Studies.'' Among his works are Shinyaku Shisōno Seiritsu, Tokyo, Shinkyō Shuppansha, 1963 (Doctoral Dissertation) (The Formation of New Testament Thought); Kiristoto Jesu, Tokyo, Kōdansha, 1969 (Christ and Jesus); Bukkyōto Kirisutokyono Setten, Kyoto, Hōzōkan, 1975 (The Contact Points between Buddhism and Christianity). Taken from the North East Asian Journal of Theology, n. 20-21, 1978, pp. 1-18. Reprinted by permission of the publisher and author.

realm in which the distinct, unambiguous language is valid lies in the commonness in our communal life. The language used in the communal life must be understood in the same way by all members of the community. When we transmit the information about objective beings, this information must be distinct. Thus in the language which is used in the communal life and which is valid in its commonness the conception must be defined in an objective and distinct way and the sentence must be free from contradiction. The principles which guarantee the self-identity of the concepts and the distinctness of the sentence are the three principles of formal logic, i.e., the principle of identity ("A is A"), the principle of contradiction ("A is not non-A"), and the principle of excluded middle ("There is nothing which is neither A nor non-A"). The language of the common, communal life must be formulated in accordance with these principles. Now these principles are those of the discriminating intellect and its expression, not those of the structure of reality. But we regard these principles as the expression of reality itself because we are born into the world where the language of the discriminating intellect is dominant. What structure would be presupposed then by this language, if it were unconditionally valid as the expression of the structure of reality? We can see a typical reality? We can see a typical instance in the atomism of natural science during the past centuries. According to the atomistic thinking, reality can be analyzed into fundamental, objective and self-identical entities which exist as what they are by and through themselves; that is to say, the atom is thought to be substance. The diversity of the empirical world is explained then from the various combinations of atoms. The changes in the empirical world are understood as the results of the meeting and parting of atoms. Now there are laws in the world of change which remain constant. There are constant, self-identical relations between changing quantities. Therefore we can expect certain results under certain conditions. Now the premise of such thinking is the so-called "principle of sufficient reason" in formal logic, which is sometimes regarded as its fourth principle. If we interpret this principle as the expression of the identity in the changes, it is included in the property of the discriminating intellect which seeks identity. The principle of sufficient reason is also valid in personal relations; human acts can be interpreted as causal, especially in the realm of law and economy. Now it is clear that the language of law and economy must be clear and distinct. So we can consider the language of law and economy as typical of the discriminating intellect together with the language of science.

Thus the discriminating intellect works as follows: it separates object from subject, analyzes the reality into entities and explains the diversity of the objective reality from the combination of the substantial entities, and the changes from the causal point of view. Now what happens when we understand ourselves with the discriminating intellect? Then we objectify ourselves separating one's self from another; we regard the objectified self as true self which exists only through itself. When it applies the causal thinking to human relationships, it can make use of personal relations for the purpose of its self-realization. It is clear now, that this way of thinking can be united with egoism and egoistic self-realization. The discriminating intellect as such is by no means egoism. But egoism comes to exist with the help of the discriminating intellect.

Christian Love

Love overcomes the way of egoistic self-realization in which one pictures up the state of his being desirable to himself and strives to realize it forcing others to acknowledge it. This love, i.e., *agape,* is not created by the human self. It is the work, the expression, of life itself determined through the fundamental structure of human existence. On the other hand, the fundamental structure of human existence is revealed in love. It comes to light when we love each other in *agape* and, in this sense, it is not brought to light by virtue of the objective cognition. We cannot confirm love of others towards us through objective observation. When we love we understand what love is and at the same time we understand the nature of the human self which becomes what it should be as the subject and object of love. This way of knowledge is called self-awareness. Self-awareness is not the cognition in which the self objectifies itself and observes it. In this case the content of the self as the non-objectifiable subject does not become manifest to the subject. Self-awareness is the modus of cognition in which the subject becomes ''revealed'' to itself; the content of the subject is experienced and revealed when it acts as subject, just as we understand what freedom is when we act as a free subject. But in the case of love the understanding of love is not mere self-awareness but at the same time believing knowledge. He who loves becomes aware of the fact that love does not issue from the self as such, but from the depth which transcends the self (I John 4:7 ff). But we cannot observe as an objective fact how love comes from the transcendent. Therefore we believe and know that love is given to humanity from the transcendent. It comes from the depth, which is even deeper than the fundamental structure of human existence, though the work of love is conditioned by this structure.

The nature of human existence becomes manifest in love; it comes to light in the self-awareness as believing knowledge. The self is then not what it is only through itself. I am I in relation to Thou (''Im Anfang ist Beziehung.'' M. Buber). In this sense the self is not a substantial entity which exists by and through itself. It is rather a pole. Generally speaking, the pole is what it is only in relation to other poles. Just as is the case in the two poles of a magnet, a pole is different from, even opposed to, the other in nature, yet one cannot exist apart from the other. In love it becomes clear that the human self is a pole in personal relation.

The self is in its nature not something that depends on the others or rules

Buddhism and Christianity

over them unilaterally. It is a free subject as the subject of self-determination. In this sense the "principle of sufficient reason" is not absolutely valid for the act of the subject because its decision is not determined by any power alien to it. Thus there is discontinuity between human subjects, yet freedom becomes event in the relation of love. On the other hand, freedom is expressed as and in love. Thus humanity is free in love and loves in freedom.

In speaking about love, we might introduce the category of *emeth*. *Emeth* is a Hebrew word which is generally translated as "truth" and "faithfulness". *Emeth* is something that becomes event in the historical reality by the work of God and through the free act of humanity. It is something that, so to speak, under pressure from God, wants to realize itself, something that will find formation in history, though it may be invisible now. It has the power to realize itself; therefore, we can expect its realization, and we can participate in it. Now love itself and the human community in which love prevails are both *emeth*. He who loves knows and believes that the work of God is the ground of love and sees the realization of the will of God in the formation of the community of love. He has the vision of its realization and participates in it. The act of love thus becomes event by the work of the transcendent and through the free decision of the man who participates in it. Now the subject of the decision is, because the latter is the act of a person in historical reality here and now, at the same time the subject of the discriminating intellect. Love makes use of it, and the discriminating intellect becomes the work of love. This order cannot be reversed. When we consider the structure of the religious self, we must make clear that the very self is the expression of the work of God and at the same time the subject of the discriminating intellect. In so far as it is the subject of the discriminating intellect, it is always possible for it to have the egoistic care for itself which may be brought forth by the discriminating intellect, though the self in its deepest nature is the expression of the work of God.

Integration

The relationship between the poles we call "integration". The typical instance of integration is the community of the saints as the "body of Christ." Generally speaking, integration is the system which consists of plural individuals. Each of them is independent; it does not depend on the others, nor is it ruled over by them unilaterally. But on the other hand, none of them can be what it is apart from others. Each has its being mediated by, and in relation to, the others. Namely, the individual in integration is, according to our term, a pole. And these poles are united as a whole into one system. Such system we call integration.

As an analogy of integration we might take music. Music consists of many sounds each of which has its own individuality. Yet each sound is what it is in relation to the whole and to other sounds, namely, each tone of the sound is determined in this relation. The sounds make up one system. Because the musical sound is thus what it is in relation to others and to the whole, each sound conceives, reflects the others and the whole in it. If we do not perceive this mutual implication and expression, we do not understand the music. Now the integrated system which consists of poles has has structure, and the role of the structure consists in the maintenance of the self-identity of the integration. The structure is the constancy of the relation between the poles and between the pole and the whole. Thus the structure is the identity maintaining aspect of the integration. Now we call that aspect in the integrated system which is valid for all its members alike "unity." For example, the structure of the integrated system can remain unchanged even though its members have changed. It is not bound to specific members of the community. Now the structure of human community must be maintained on the consensus of its members. Thus the structure belongs, generally speaking, to the unity of the integrated system. In the integrated community the unity is seen not only in the structure, but also in common belief and common evaluation. At the root, the discriminating intellect and its language play in the community the most important role as the principle of unity. The unity can oppose individuality. The unity can restrict, even deny the freedom of the individuals. But the unity has its *raison d'être* in integration as the principle of its self-identity. If the very nature of integration is misunderstood, if its unity — the discriminating intellect which grasps the self-identity of the matter tends to this misunderstanding — so that the unity oppresses the freedom of the individuals, if in this way the over-estimated unity distorts the integration, the individuals must liberate themselves from the unity and form a new integration on the ground of the work of God. A typical instance of this process can be seen in the event in which the individuals who were liberated from the oppression of the casuistic law of Judaism — at their head stands Jesus — formed a new people of God as the Christian Church.

This integration is something *emeth*. The integration is formed and maintained by the individuals who act under the pressure of the work of God through their free decision. In terms of integration, love is the integration of two poles.

On the basis of the pressure towards integration which comes from the depth we can speak of God. Namely, God works towards integration. And when we speak of the work in general terms, we can discriminate in it three constituents: the subject of the work, the content of the work and the transmittance of the work. It is also true in the case of integration: the ultimate subject of the work towards integration is God; the content of the work, namely the principle which determines the mode of being of individuals towards integration, is Christ as *logos* and *eikon* of God. What transmits this content into the historical reality is the Holy Spirit. Thus on the basis of the work of the trinitarian God the integration of human beings is realized.

Therefore, personal integration is called the "Body of Christ," the temple of the Holy Spirit. In other words, the integrated community in the historical reality is "Christ who became flesh."

In speaking of integration we can express the transcendent with the analogy of the "field". The field is, generally speaking, the space in which individual beings receive the power which makes them poles and integrates them. In the field of gravity the heavenly bodies are "integrated" to form a system such as the solar system. Life can be interpreted as the field in which the material beings are "integrated" to a living body. We can regard also the human heart as a kind of field in which, e.g., the sounds are "integrated" to music. In this case music is the expression of the human heart, and therefore we understand the heart as the power to integrate the material beings to the art. On the other hand, it is the human heart which perceives integration in the material beings and understands it as the expression of the human heart. Now in the case of the community of persons, we can regard the transcendent as the field in which human beings receive the power so as to become poles and are integrated into "the Body of Christ." But it is not right to think of the field as something that transcends physical space, as if the former holds the latter, because then the former is no longer transcendent enough. We must regard each person as the contact point with the whole transcendent field, so that each person is the "temple of the Holy Spirit" and at the same time the church as a whole is the "Body of Christ." In this way it can be said that God is omnipresent and He has His center everywhere.

We understand what integration is not by the discriminating intellect but by the believing knowledge which is at the same time subjective self-awareness. Not he who observes but he who loves understands what personal integration is. In the integrated system the pole is what it is in mutual mediation, and therefore each pole reflects and contains other poles in itself. It exists as it is not by virtue of itself but on the ground of the work of the transcendent which denies the direct, egoistic mode of willing to be and to become itself. Therefore, in the relationship of integration the principles of formal logic lose their unconditional validity as the expression of the real structure, because the pole is not something self-identical and integration is not a mere collection of substantial, therefore distinctly analyzable entities. Then the language with which we speak of integration is not the same as the language of the discriminating intellect. In the language of integration the concepts cannot be defined in an objective way, and the sentences carry contradictions within themselves (cf. Gal. 2:20). Here the "direct transmission" (Kierkegaard) of the objective information about God, man and the historical reality is impossible. If we regard the Bible as a whole as objective information about God and the salvation of man, we misunderstand its nature, so that it loses its authority in our modern "scientific" age.

Christianity and the Religions of the East

Enlightenment in Buddhism

Reality as it is understood in our daily life, the reality we believe we know well, is by no means reality as it is, but the world conceived by the discriminating intellect. It is a highly artificial, secondary reality pressed into the frame of the discriminating intellect and therefore conditioned socially and historically. The "fact" means here the objective fact common to all and the essence of the matter is seen in its self-identity. Reality is believed to be analyzed into substantial entities as its fundamental constituents. The diversity is explained from the combination of the entities, the change from causal law. Human beings objectify themselves and regard the objectified self as true self which is something substantial and which is what it is only by and through itself.

This understanding of reality and the self is easily united with egoism, and this combination constantly produces illusions in a person's understanding of reality.

But this understanding of reality is not ultimate. It can therefore occur that the "primary" reality becomes manifest to us, that we overcome the frame of the discriminating intellect. Our grasp of the reality is then liberated from objectification, conceptualization and substantialization, so that the reality shows itself to us in its aspect before it is set into the frame of the discriminating intellect. At this moment it is revealed that subject and object are neither different nor identical. It is true that subject is subject and not object, that object is object and not subject. But in reality there is no object apart from subject and vice versa. Subject and object are neither one nor two. Reality shows itself namely in its immediacy before it is set into the frame of the discriminating intellect, therefore before it is mediated by conception. It is the primary reality for us, but we need not seek behind it for something like "Ding an sich," because it makes no sense to ask for something apart from subject.

In this state the immediacy of life is found and experienced. Evidently Nietsche knew the immediacy of life, and from this fact we understand the significance of his criticism of modern civilization and culture. But I do not think that he has overcome the way of thinking of the discriminating intellect in a sufficiently radical way. Because of this insufficiency, his understanding of life was united with egoism, with the result that he came to believe, e.g., that the mighty can rightly sacrifice the weak. On the contrary, Buddhism knows the state in which the discriminating intellect is radically overcome. It knows the pure immediacy of life which becomes manifest and is experienced in this state, the immediacy prior to the objectification, conceptualization and substantialization. Not as a matter of objective observation, but as a matter of intuitive experience it has clearly grasped that I and Non-I is neither one nor two. (A Christian knows this fact in his personal relation of love. But a Buddhist knows this in the I and Non-I relation in general). In other words, in the case of the subject-object relation, subject and object are known to make two "poles." Again this becomes clear not as a matter of objective observation, but as a matter of intuitive self-awareness, and the self becomes aware of itself in the immediacy which he has come to know. In this knowledge of him "beings" in general are no longer "beings" as entities, but "poles" which lie in their mutual dependence, mutual implication and mutual reflection. Thus reality becomes obvious as the world of *engi (pratityasamutpada)*. But the essence of Buddhist teaching does not lie in the theoretical cognition of reality as *pratityasamutpada*. It aims at the grasp of the immediacy of life, the immediacy of the work of "the life of Buddha" (Dogen) in the light of which it is known that the self is one pole in the whole of polar relations, that reality as a whole is the world of *pratityasamutpada* as the work of the "life of Buddha". A Buddhist is aware of himself in this immediacy as a link of *pratityasamutpada*. In this state the thinking which objectifies the reality as "being" is overcome. Therefore, in order to express this state, one does not use the language of the discriminating intellect. One no longer speaks here about the transcendent as if it were objective, individual being. "The life of Buddha" is rather at work entirely *as* each self. One cannot ask for the transcendent apart from the human self which acts in immediacy. No doubt one makes discrimination between human self and the transcendent ("the life of Buddha") when he reflects upon the structure of the self, because certainly the self as the work, or the expression, of the "life of Buddha" is at the same time the subject of the discriminating intellect. But in the primary fact of the immediacy of life before discrimination, the "life of Buddha" is at work only *as* each self. Here we see the reason why Buddhists do not want to speak about the transcendent as objective, as something over-against, when they testify to the primary immediacy.

Buddhism and Christianity

Both Christianity and Buddhism understand reality in the frame of integration. We regard the category of integration as the fundamental category of Christian thinking, and we think we can express the world of *pratityasamutpada* also in terms of integration. If this be so, in this category lies one of the main contact points between the two religions. Integration of a person and personal relation is realized when the union of egoism and the discriminating intellect is broken in each person, or rather, we can say that the work of the transcendent towards integration breaks the union. Now in Buddhism the structure of reality as that of *pratityasamutpada* becomes manifest in the self-awareness of the man who has overcome the discriminating intellect and "beings" are perceived not as entities, but "poles" just as in the case in a integrated system.

In primitive Buddhism the view of the substantiality of human self was denied, that is to say, substantialized thinking was overcome. This does not mean solely that beings were found not to be objective entities. This view of primitive Buddhism is at the same time the expression of the self-awareness in which the polar structure of reality has become manifest, and this view leads one also to the breaking down of his egoism. When primitive Buddhism saw in birth, illness, aging and death the main problems of human existence, it did not do so because it wanted to overcome these evils as such, but it saw the basic problem in the fact that man did not accept these as the inevitable destiny of man but clung to happy life in despair. It saw here the vain hybris of man which issues from his non-enlightenedness. Therefore, we understand that Buddhism from the beginning intended to break down the union of egoism and the discriminating intellect.

In primitive Buddhism, though it denied the substantiality of self, the self as the subject of ethical conduct was deemed to be ''being.'' In other words, the self-determining subject in the relation of mutual dependence was regarded as the ''pole'' which is both being and non-being. But in the latter Buddhistic tradition *(Abhidharma)* there appeared again a substantial view of beings *(dharma)*. It was Nagarjuna who criticized this view, deepening and developing the intrinsically Buddhist insight: generally speaking, there can be no relationship between substances, because this is by definition something which is only by and through itself apart from other being. Therefore, is so far as *pratityasamutpada* has validity, ''beings'' cannot be substance, thus ''beings'' in general must be in the relationship of mutual dependence.

Now Buddhism was later accepted in China and many sutras of Mahayana-Buddhism were translated into Chinese. Furthermore, the thought contained in them found a systematic expression there. The Tendai School taught that in spite of the diversity of reality there is a structure that reality is as a whole oneness by virtue of the relationship of *engi (pratityasamutpada)*, in which one thing contains and reflects the others. The Kegon School developed another side of *engi*, namely, its work. Individual ''beings'' which work towards each other contain and reflect each other infinitely just as two mirrors which reflect each other. And in this infinite-fold mutual relationship the individual obtains the limitation of what it is in the whole reality of polar relation. It goes without saying that the above mentioned sides of *engi* are precisely those of integration.

Zen did not intend to lighten the structure of the world of *engi* theoretically, but aimed at man's coming to live in the ''life of Buddha'' which makes up the world of *engi*. We could say that the immediacy of religious life found the purest expression in the way of existence of the Zen masters. The essence of Zen does not consist thus in the teaching, but in the way of living in the immediacy of the ''life of Buddha'' and in the self-awareness given in this way of existence. And the essence of Christian faith does not lie in its origin in the acceptance of creed or dogmas but, from the point of view of integrating work of the transcendent, in the life which lives in the immediacy of the work of love, namely, the life in which love becomes the event of our historical reality.

Buddhism and Christianity

Seen in the category of integration Christianity and Buddhism overlap each other fundamentally. But both religions are not the same; they stand in a polar relation. In the first place, Christian love in something *emeth*. The Christian sees the realization of the *emeth* in the future. This is a vision, not an illusion. And he participates in its realization. The work of love is always the selection of his conduct here and now in the concrete situation towards the realization of authentic human existence in the sense of the entire personality. Therefore, the subject of love is the subject which realizes in historical reality the *emeth* grounded by the work of God. But at the same time it is the subject of the discriminating intellect as the subject of the concrete decision here and now. When such subject looks towards the future and pictures the ultimate realization of the community of love, this realization is understood to be the realization of the will of God which transcends the individual. Therefore, the Christian existence is social, hopes for the realization of the will of God in the future, and understands the faith as the believing participation in the work of God. This participation becomes possible on the ground of the work of God which finds expression in the historical reality through the free decision of the believing man. Thus faith, hope and love have central meaning in Christian existence. In this way it speaks about the will of God which transcends the human self, and the will of God is something over-against the human subject because as the *emeth* that calls for the self-realization of the will of God, it speaks to the human subject and demands response from it. This of course is related to the fact that the Christian pictures a vision towards the future.

On the other hand, the transcendent in Buddhism expresses itself in the immediacy of religious life. Therefore it cannot be present otherwise than as the life of each religious self. Certainly the self reacts to the concrete situation immediately, but the subject of the immediate reaction is at the same time the subject of the discriminating intellect. But in Buddhism, especially in Zen Buddhism, the weight is laid upon the immediacy of the creative reaction without discriminating thinking. Therefore the transcendent "life of Buddha" and the life of each individual are one in the paradoxical relation of "the identity of the contradictory," if we use the term of K. Nishida. In this sense the transcendent is the ground of being-oneself, and the transcendent is to be found nowhere but as each human self. The relation between the transcendent and the self is the "identity of the contradictory" which becomes event in the dynamic work of the transcendent. It is not an ontological relationship between beings and the being itself. If one would speak, nevertheless, of the ground of being, Buddhist transcendence is rather the ground of being *and* non-being, for it is at work both in the life and death of the person. A similar relation is to be found also in Christianity if we pay attention to the "ontological" implication of the grace of God which is opposed to the imperative of God to man. For "I am what I am by the grace of God" (I Cor. 15:10), grace being the ground of "I am". From this point of view even the free decision and the response of the person are

73

seen in the light of the grace of God (John 6:37). If we do not see this matter from the point of view of the personalistic relation between God and humanity, if we do not understand the relation between God and humanity from from the point of view of call and response, imperative and obedience, if we consider the matter purely from the viewpoint of the grace of God as the "ontological" ground of human being, if namely we express, e.g., the nature of Christian love which springs forth from the depth as something immediate or as gift, we can say that God and humanity are, in the relation of mutual indwelling, "one" because God is present in the love of humanity (I John 4:7, 13 ff). Thus, through Christ God and the believer are united to oneness (John 14:20; 17:21). What matters in this aspect is not the subjectivity of humanity but the grace of the transcendent by virtue of which I am I without any subjectivity of mine, the fact that the grace of God makes me live, the fact that I am I not by and through myself, but by the work of God. If we regard the transcendent, as was said above, as the "field" which integrates the "beings" in it, making them into "poles", then the work of the field is on the one hand the imperative which demands obedience from the human subject, but its work is on the other hand the grace by which the egoistic self is changed into "poles", therefore into its original nature. And this change is given to humanity as the gift of God, the fruits of which are love and freedom (Gal. 5:1, 22f), the grace which accepts the sinners and recreates them. If so, the structure of the transcendent is given as follows: God as the transcendent subject (God as personal, God who calls humanity and requires response and obedience from him), and God as the ground of being (God who makes humanity to be what he should be, God who gives to humanity the gift of being, this gift expressing itself as the immediacy of religious life). These two contradictory aspects of God are after all two sides of one and the same God. Both sides form together, if I may use the term in my own way, "the identity of the contradictory." The God of the law is at the same time the God of grace. If this is the structure of the transcendent field as the integrating power, we can say that Christianity tends to understand God as the transcendent subject, therefore as personal, whereas Buddhism deepens into the depth of "the ground of being," or rather, more radically, into the depth of the ground of being and non-being, which is in its nature the "nothing" that works, the "nothing" that expresses itself as the immediacy of the individual religious self, the "nothing" that cannot be present otherwise than in religious immediacy. But Buddhism does not lose sight of the transcendent as the transcendent subject. This is shown in the case of Shinran, the founder of True Pure Land Buddhism in Japan. In the case of Shinran the human self is the self which comes to faith by virtue of the grace of Amida-Buddha, but the human self is at the same time the subject which responds to His call, obeys Him. Though Shinran knows the immediacy of religious life *(Jinen-Honi,* to be so *of itself* because the *Dharma* makes it to be so), he discriminates clearly between humanity and the transcendent, and if we see here the work of the discriminating intellect, we can say further that the subject of the religious life in the case of Shinran is at the same time the subject of the discriminating intellect which works also in the concrete situation here and now, so that the religious subject knows its own egoistic care for itself and believes all the more in the saving grace of Amida.

We can see here the closeness of Shinran to Christianity, namely in the understanding of the structure of the self. But as a whole the emphasis of Buddhism is the immediacy of life which appears when the discriminating intellect has been overcome, so that it tends to the realization of the state of *nirvana*, whereas the emphasis of Christianity is faith in God as the transcendent subject, faith which expresses itself as love which is the response to the call of God in the historical situation here and now, though love is on the other hand the gift of God to humanity. Now as was shown above, egoism and discriminating intellect make a union. Therefore Buddhism which overcomes the discriminating intellect and Christianity which overcomes egoism complement each other, and each religion is grounded on one "contradictory" side of the transcendent.

CHAPTER EIGHT

Some Problems and Possibilities
for Burmese Christian Theology Today

BY KHIN MAUNG DIN

Introduction

This paper is an attempt to bring out some problems and to explore some possibilities for Burmese Christian Theology today. Before proceeding any further, I must clarify some of the terms used here, as well as my purpose for writing this paper.

I have deliberately used the word "Burmese Christian Theology", instead of "Burmese Theology" in order to leave open the possibility of having other theologies besides a Christian theology as such. There can be a Buddhist Theology or even a Marxist Theology, etc. In other words, for me. the scope of Burmese Theology is definitely broader than that of Burmese Christian Theology. In this paper I shall confine myself only to the latter domain.

My aim for making this attempt also needs to be stated clearly. The purpose here is *not primarily* to communicate the Gospel to the Burmese Buddhists. But rather, the main object of this paper is to discover more about the Gospel itself with the aid of some Buddhist and Oriental categories. Genuine theology, in my opinion, should not only try to broaden the present

U Khim Maung Dhin is a lecturer in Philosophy, Arts and Sciences at the University Rangoon, Burma. He is also an honorary part time lecturer in Christian Ethics at the Burma Divinity School, Insein, Burma. This essay is from the South East Asian Journal of Theology Vol. 16, 1975. Reprinted here by permission of the publisher.

boundaries of Christian Theology alone. It should also try and discover new dimensions for theology with the help of the spiritual experience and concepts of men of other faiths.

The aim of this paper is also to seek a theology for today. I want to emphasize this word "today!" Religions as well as political ideologies are themselves undergoing change. Therefore even though we are required to use the concepts and categories of these faiths, we must use them with a sense of relativity. No political or religious concept including any Christian concept, can be regarded as absolutely fixed and final. Any theologizing for today therefore, can only be done relatively, in the context of the ever changing 'today' of history.

I also wish to make it clear from the very beginning that this is not a paper on Biblical Theology. I am not denying the witness of the Scriptures. But my purpose here is to question the validity of translating the most poetical, mystical and religious language of the Bible into only one class of philosophical concepts. If the Church in Burma desires to speak about God in more than poetical or mystical terms, it must also use a theological language derived from the Oriental theological experience.

There had been attempts in the past to construct an indigenous Burmese Christian Theology under the general name: "The Indigenization of Christianity of Christianity in Burma." But most of these attempts were concerned more with the form, rather than with the content of the Gospel. Presentation of Biblical stories in the cultural style of Burmese drama, dressing up of the Nativity Scene in Burmese costumes, use of indigenous musical instruments and melodies for religious hymns and songs,etc., were merely attempts to put the Gospel Wine into Burmese Cultural Bottles. I accept the necessity of employing such cultural forms for effective communication. But to me, the basic theological problem for Burmese Christian Theology, is not that which is concerned with "the Bottle," but that which concerns the "Wine" itself. The Gospel must not only be understood in a Burmese way, but the Burmese and Buddhist understanding of Man, Nature and Ultimate Reality must also become inclusive as a vital component in the overall content of the Gospel.

Hence, any construction of a Burmese Christian Theology for today must take into account, the following three factors: (1) the Christian understanding and experience of the Gospel, (2) the religious experience and concepts of Buddhism and other Oriental Religions, and (3) the socio-political human realities of our times.

It is with this working hypothesis in mind that I shall be taking up some of the problems as well as possibilities for constructing a theology for today. In this paper I will be dealing with only three problems, viz, (a) the problem of God, (b) the problem of Christ, and (c) the problem of Man. It is quite evident that I can only touch them in a very general and limited way.

Burmese Christian Theology Today

The Problem of God

This is a basic problem for Christian theology in its encounter with Theravāda Buddhism in Burma. Some of us would say that is it possible and meaningful to speak of Hindu Theology or Islamic Theology, because in these religions we do find a definite affirmation and acceptance of "the Theos." But many of us question the possibility of a Buddhist Theology or a Marxist Theology, because in these systems there is no "Theos" to "logos" about. But it is my contention that there can be and there *is* in fact a Buddhist Theology, *provided* the theos is understood in Buddhist terms and not in terms of traditional Judaistic, Greek or Western categories.

Theravāda Buddhism has often been labelled as "an atheistic religion" or at best a "non-theistic faith" by many theologians. But before attaching such labels to it, it is important for us to understand properly, what it is that is affirmed, and what it is that is denied by Buddhism with regard to the Theos.

It is true that Buddhism categorically denies the existence of the Theos as a "Personal Being" or "a Creator."/1/ Such a doctrine of God is rejected by the Buddha together with the doctrine of fatalism/2/ according to which all things good or evil are purely determined by past karma alone. In the view of Theravāda, both these doctrines of Theism and Fatalism fail to explain the vexing problem of evil. The theists try to explain evil by appealing to the will of God, whereas the fatalists substitute an unverifiable karma principle in place of an invisible God./3/ It is this sort of Theos that is denied by the Buddha.

But this does not mean that Buddha denies the existence of what can be philosophically described as "the Transcendence" or "the Ultimate Reality." In the Udāna, Buddha is reported to have said: ".....there is, O monks, an Unborn, Unbecome, and Unmade, an Unconditioned; for if there were not this Unborn, Unbecome, Unmade, Unconditioned, no escape from this born, become, made and conditioned would be apparent."/4/

If, by theism, is meant the affirmation of the existence of such a Transcendental Reality, then Buddhism is profoundly theistic!

This raises a serious problem for Christian Theology, especially the view which insists on understanding God as a "Personal Being." Such a manner of describing the Theos has now been challenged by some schools of contemporary theology: Many hold the view that the concept of "Being" is more Hellenistic than Hebraic. A recent attempt by some "Process Theologians" is to use the category of "Becoming" rather than "Being" to describe the nature of God. According to these thinkers the Becoming God does not exclude but includes the nature of God as a Being. "Being" is a relative category within the absolute category of "the Becoming." In the hands of such theologians the traditional conception of God as an already complete, perfect and static Being has given way to a more living dynamic and changing conception of the theos. God is to be seen and understood as a process.

The so called "God is dead" theologians have also challenged the traditional conception of God as a Personal Being. Some of them agree with Dr. Tillich in describing God as "the Ground of our Being." This is also a useful attempt to help Christian Theology deepen its metaphysical category.

But in the view of Theraváda Buddhism both these ways of understanding the Theos or the Ultimate Reality, either as "the Ground of our Being" or as "the Process of Becoming," are still relative ways of understanding the Transcendence. For the true Theravadin, the best way to describe the Ultimate Reality is not to describe it all. The predication of Reality in human terms will distort and relativize its true nature. In other words, for the Theravadins, the Absolute can never be described by relative human terms.

Such a theology is not peculair to Buddhism alone. The Taoists of ancient China also held a smiliar view of Reality. They say that "the Tao is the name of the Nameless One."

My point is whether Christian Theology in Burma should continue to speak of God as a "Person," or "a Personal Being," or even as "a Personality" *in an absolute sense.* Is it not closer to the Truth, to say that God is a Person as well as not-a-Person; that God is a Being as well as a Becoming; that God exists and also does not exist?

Such a way of understanding the theos has been referred to by Professor Jung Young Lee as "the Yin-Yang way of Thinking." (cf. Chapter Two) In that article Professor Lee pointed out the weaknesses of the Either/Or Method used by classical Christian theology in formulating its doctrine of God. He said: "The Either/Or way of thinking in the West not only promoted but shaped the absolute dogma of God. The God of dogma is less than the God of Christianity." Professor Lee advocates the use of the Yin-Yang Way or the Both/And Method for a more progressive construction of Christian Theology.

It seems to me that this Yin-Yang Way is not peculiar to the ancient Chinese philosophers alone. A similar method was also used by the Jains School of India centuries before the birth of Christ. The Jains called their doctrine "Syadváda," which implies the relativity of all human judgements. They qualify their assertions with the word "Somehow" as a prefix to each proposition. Instead of stating categorically that "S is P," they would rather say the "Somehow S is P." But that is not sufficient. One must go on to say that "Somehow S is *also* not P," and even further and say that "Somehow S is *both* P as well as not P." But then, even this last is not final. One must go on to negate that and say: "Somehow *it is not true* that S is both P as well as not P." This last statement is not a return to the earlier statements that S must be *either* P *or* not—P. To use the language of dialectics, it is the negation of the negation. What is meant here is that not only the category of Either/Or, but even the category of Both/And is a relative category which must also be transcended.

Chinese philosophy also speaks of the same method in another form, presenting it as stages of knowledge. To say that all things are Yu (being), or that all things Wu (non-being), is an expression of a lower level of knowledge. The mind arrives at a higher level when it can perceive that all things are neither Yu nor Wu. But there is still an even more advanced plane of knowledge where the understanding discerns that all things are neither not-Yu nor not-Wu. In other words, when the understanding passes through all these levels of knowledge it comes to comprehend the Tao (Reality) as transcending all relative categories.

This peculiar way of understanding Reality is also pointed out by the Vedánta of India. For the Vedantins, Brahman or the Absolute Reality can only be negatively described as "Neti," "Neti" (Not this, Not this).

From such a perspective, "the silence" of the Buddha becomes pregnant with meaning. To the Buddha, the *relatively best way of describing* the true nature of the Transcendence is not to describe it at all. We can discern an almost common methodology in all these major oriental philosophies. The oriental refusal to predicate the Transcendence with western philosophical categories should not be interpreted as the denial of the Transcendence itself. This applies to Buddhism also. Therefore the Buddhist denial of the "existence" of "God" as a "Personal Being" or "a Creator" is not a total rejection of the indescribable, transcendental Theos.

What can we learn from this Oriental Methodology? Should Christian theology continue to keep on referring to God as "a Person," "a Father," "a Him," "a Creator," etc., in an absolute sense? Should we not rather say that somehow God is a Person, as well as not-a-Person, that God is a Father as well as not a Father (a Mother?), that God is a Creator as well as not a Creator, that God is a Thou as well as not a Thou?

How must we interpret God's answer to Moses: "I am that I am?" Is the word 'I' to be understood as referring to a self, a Soul, an Ego, an Atman, a Spirit or even a 'GEIST' as used by Hegel? If that Scripture text means: "I will be to you what I will be to you," as it is now interpreted today/6/, then is it not the case that the answer is to be understood *functionally* and not ontologically? If that is the case, then, metaphysically speaking, such an oriental way of understanding the Theos can be more comprehensive and sometimes even more faithful to the Gospel than most dogmas attached to the traditional Christian doctrine of God.

One criticism made by Traditional Theology with its concept of a Personal God against other theologies which interpret God in non-personal categories, is the problem of entering into an intimate communion with that sort of theos? How, it is asked, can we pray to an impersonal God who is not a Thou but a That? In my opinion, this criticism is valid for those theologies which go to the other extreme of understanding God only and absolutely in terms of an impersonal "That." This should not be a problem for the oriental mind which can conceive God *both* as a Thou as well as a That.

However, it seems to me that the essence of that criticism is more concerned with prayer and communion itself and not with the *onta* of the

Transcendence. Can we pray to an indescribable Transcendence? Can we meaningfully enter into a personal communion with such a Theos? Here again, in my opinion, the Oriental Method of Meditation can open up more profound ways of entering into communion with God. When prayer becomes more than asking, or talking, or *even thinking* then it is arriving at the level of true meditation. And one who prays, or communes, or meditates the Transcendence in such a transcendental way can also find that "peace which passes all understanding." Burmese Christian theology must include the possibility of praying to God in traditional and personal ways, as well as the possibility of entering into a deep and profound relationship with the Transcendence in non-traditional ways.

I can understand the difficulty of Christians in Burma to conceive God in non-personal terms. We are being so metaphysically conditioned by traditional theology that the very idea of a non-personal God becomes totally incomprehensible to us. But this means that we must also be sympathetic to the Buddhists for whom the very idea of God as a Personal Being is incomprehensible. If Christian theology in Burma still persists in speaking of God only and absolutely as a Person, then the Christian God will be reduced to the level of a *Nat* or a *Brahmana*.

It has been suggested to me whether I should not try and broaden the concept of the *Nat* to enable the Buddhists to conceive of God as a Personal Being. I do not deny this possibility as long as the "Broadened Nat Concept" includes the non-personal and non-existential categories also. Even then, there is still the danger of that concept falling into the same error of absolutizing only one aspect of the Transcendence at the expense of the other.

If, instead of trying to broaden the Nat, Burmese Christian Theology tries to understand theism as the acceptance and acknowledgement of an indescribably Transcendental Reality, and if that theology can also accept the validity of non-classical methods of prayer, then the theological differences between Christianity and Buddhism will not be as sharp and as opposed as it opposed as it seems to be today. And the Church in Burma will come to discover a remarkable revelation that God has made in the religious thought, life and culture of our Burmese people.

Before I conclude this section I would like to quote a few passages from Professor David Jenkins' "Commitment and Openness":

".....what I am arguing is that the Ajaltoun experiences make it imperative for us to press the dialogue between men of LIVING FAITHS as a faithful undertaking required by reasons arising from within these faiths and the practice of them. There must be no suggestion either of an attempt to extract 'common religious factors' to reinforce one another against an increasingly 'irreligious world', nor of a desire for cheaply comforting syncretism. The challenge is to pursue that quest and that response which our faith already demands, through and with the help of dialogue.

"Of course, this is a very exacting (as well as a very hopeful) challenge as it implies a readiness to see the bearing (and therefore the theology and practice) of our faith changed. It will be necessary to show, in detail, from the Christian point of view, how loyalty to Jesus Christ and to His God and Father is not only compatible with this but requires this. Theologically I do not see any great difficulty. Psychologically the matter will be very disturbing for the majority of Christians. Theologically it seems to me clear that the "Christian concepts of God and of Christ are not, and cannot be adequate to the living God and His Christ 'Christian' concepts are those which the bodies have hitherto evolved as 'Christian' at the present hold or propagate on the basis of experience hitherto. The absolutizing of these concepts as Christian (without inverted commas), i.e. as wholly commensurate with the reality with which we have to do, seems to me to be clearly theologically wrong in the most literal sense (i.e. *NOT* commensurate with the 'Theos' who is in Christ)."/7/

If Christian Theology in Burma keeps on broadening its scope and deepening its understanding of God, it will come to discover that this one and only God can be worshipped and adored not only in the "Jerusalem Temples" of the Christian churches, but also in other religious as well as the non-religious secular temples of humanity today.

The Problem of Jesus Christ

The second basic problem facing Burmese Christian Theology is the task of formulating a more comprehensive relevant and meaningful Christology for today. This task, I confess, is even more difficult than that of formulating a more comprehensive doctrine of God. I confess with the authors of the WCC Fifth Assembly Bible Studies that "who Jesus Christ is, is beyond us, but...." My attempt in this section is just one relative way of filling in that dotted blank.

Under the theme "Indian Understandings of Jesus Christ" in a bulletin published by the Christian Institute for the study of Religion and Society/8/, the editor pointed out that "There is the need for a pluralism in Christology to meet the diverse needs of the situation. We must think in terms of Christologies rather than a Christology." And in the same Bulletin, Mr. D. A. Thangasamy quoted P. Chenchiah who said: "...more portraits than one are required to catch the transcendental beauty of Jesus of Nazareth." Chenchiah also said: "...we have to wait the larger development of world thought, the reaching of world concepts in politics and history, the processes of Science, before we could see Jesus in the right perspective in the cosmic process." Such affirmations made by these Indian Theologians and their attempt to formulate Christologies from an Indian context have inspired me to take a risk in painting a portrait of "the Theos who was in Christ."

Traditional Christian Theology in Burma has always protected its Christology with the popular Biblical phrase: ".....a stumbling block to the Jews and foolishness to the Gentiles." My question is whether it should always continue to be so. In what sense does "the Christ crucified" *ought* to be a stumbling block and in what sense does it *ought not* to be a stumbling block for men of other faiths?

Some of the traditional biblical terms like "atonement," "sacrifice," "blood offering" may have had supreme religious significance for the Old Testament Jews within their particular culture and history, but these same terms have no religious meaning, and at times, even take on an irreligious or anti-religious meaning for men of Oriental Faiths. For instance, the blood sacrifices of human beings made in the history of our Burmese people belong to the ancient primitive, animistic and pre-Buddhistic period. Such primitive practices were gradually but surely abandoned after the arrival of Buddhism in Burma. In such a religious context, if conventional Christology insists on using those relative Jewish concepts in an absolute way, then it will be imposing an *unnecessary stumbling block* to the "Gentiles" of the East, and the fault will be more with the preacher than with the hearers of the Word.

In other words, if the Gospel is meant to be universal, we must interpret it in terms of truly universal categories. The historical relativity of the Jesus of Nazareth should not be confused with the universality of Jesus, the Christ. I am not denying "the raw fact of Jesus!" Neither do I deny the special revelation made through him. But I question the authenticity of universalizing him from a purely Jewish context and in mostly Jewish terms. To forumlate a more relevant Christology for today we must be able to distinguish the particularity and temporality of the Jesus event from the universality and eternality of the Christ event in the ongoing process of universal history.

In other words the Christ event ought to be interpreted *Kairologically* rather than chronologically. The "Chronos" of the Jesus of history is to be understood as a means to reveal the "Kairos" of Christ. Instead of emphasizing only one relative aspect of the incarnation as an historical and chronological happening of the distant past, Christian theology would do well to discern more about the continuing Incarnation, the ongoing Immanence, ministry, crucifixion, and the resurrection of the Transcendent Christ in the Kairological 'now' of every moment of history.

Perhaps Jesus Christ can be better understood through the Yin-Yang and Jaina way. Somehow Jesus Christ is a man (or fully human); but somehow he is not a man. And yet, somehow he is *both* fully man *and* fully God. But even this statement is still relative and conditional. To the eastern mind, including Buddhism, if Christ is divine, then he transcends all human categories. So we are led to the humble confession that "who Jesus Christ is, is *beyond* us...." Even some Hindu way of conceiving Christ as an avatara or describing him with the Buddhist concept of "Bodhisattva," can never be adequate for the Christ who is truly ONE with God.

Formulating a Christology from this perspective may enable the church to experience and recognize the living Christ in the changing process of history. Christ will be seen not only *from* the context and in the contest of Jewish history alone, but also *from* the context and *in* the context of the universal history of humanity. The historical advent of Jesus reveals the coming of God to man not only in that particular moment of history, but even *before* that time, as well as the periods following that historical moment and the ages to come. It is in this sense also that we can better understand the Cross as the "Centre" of history. The preparation for the coming of Christ can also be discerned in the particular histories of other people. One task of Christian theology in Burma therefore, is to try and discover *how, when* and *in what manner,* the living Christ has already come to our people even before the arrival of Christianity in Burma. The church in Burma needs to see Jesus Christ as an ongoing, living dynamaic reality in the life of our people, as well as other peoples, yesterday, today and forever.

From this it follows that in our attempt to seek the living Christ we shall not only refer to and reflect on what the historical Jesus had said in the Gospels but *also listen* to what He has spoken, and keeps on speaking in and through the living faiths and ideologies of other men. We shall seek the Word that has already come and dwelt among them. Such an understanding of Jesus Christ may perhaps remove some unnecessary stumbling blocks that stand in the way of men of other faiths to come to Him.

But the question still remains. In what sense will "the Christ crucified" still be a stumbling block, or ought to be a stumbling block, in spite of the above attempt to universalize Him, i.e. to make the truth of Christ become inclusive and not exclusive? To answer this question I propose to set up the following criteria:

Jesus Christ will be, and ought to be, and is in fact a stumbling block for the following:

I. Any faith or ideology that absolutely denies the reality of the Transcendence.

II. Any faith or ideology that can never accept the possibility of that Transcendent becoming Immanent in any way whatsoever.

III. Any faith or ideology that accepts the possibility of the Immanence of the Transcendence, but fails to discern the happening or the happenedness of that possibility in human history *including their own.*

IV. Any faith or ideology that totally rejects the witness of the scriptures regarding the revelation in Jesus Christ, even though that revelation was made in a relative and limited context.

V. Any faith or ideology that rejects the *'Kenosis'* of Christ.

A very important question can be raised here. Am I not using the same traditional Either/Or Method in setting up the above criteria? *Either* faiths or ideologies do not belong to categories I to V *or* they will always regard Christ as a stumbling block. Is not this proposition implied by the above criteria?

My reply to this very relevant question is that if we consistently follow the

Yin-Yang Way, then even that criteria must be understood in a relative and not in an absolute sense. The very meaning of words used here as for example 'the Transcendence" 'Immanence', 'Revelation', 'Kenosis', etc. are relative and are still in the process of change. We cannot deny the possibility of a faith or an ideology rejecting "Transcendence" in one sense and accepting it in another sense. The contemporary quest for a *secular meaning* of the Gospel suggests the relativity of all theological concepts. Therefore the above criteria when used in the Jaina Way, can still allow us to affirm that somehow Jesus Christ is *still* a stumbling block and yet somehow He *is not* a stumbling block to men of other faiths and ideologies.

One lesson then, for Burmese Christian Theology is this: No Christology, traditional or contemporary, has said the final word about God in Christ. We can formulate our own Christology, even from a Buddhist context, or from a socialist context, without becoming trapped forever by traditional dogmas, or being misled by false interpretations.

Here again, as a conclusion to this section, may I again quote Professor David Jenkins: "....the truth, the uniqueness and the absoluteness of Christ are not *EXCLUSIVE* but *INCLUSIVE,* that the fulness of Christ lies only in the *END* when *All Things* are summed up in Him."

The Problem of Man

The theological question "Who is God?" should also begin with the question "What is Man?" In fact, I think this is the more crucial question facing all humanity today.

Traditional Christian theology has more often depended on the Bible alone to provide the answer to this question. To construct a progressive theology of Man we must go beyond the biblical concepts which are primarily "religious" in character and take into account also the empirical study of Man made by the sciences and the humanities of today. Christian theology should also listen and learn from the other religious accounts of man explored by other religions. Other truths about man must become inclusive in the One Truth of the Gospel. Here again, we must be careful to distinguish our "Theology of Man" from the all-inclusive Gospel. Any Theology of Man is and will still remain "a theology." Its primary aim is to relate the Theos to Man and Man to the Theos. But this does not mean that we must confine our study only to theological and religious issues. In our attempt to relate God and man, we must also make use of the other normative and empirical studies of man.

It is not my purpose here to give an answer to this problem: "What is Man?" Neither is it my aim to point out what similarities and differences exist between the Christian understanding of man and others. My object here is only to point out some problems and possible solutions to this important question from one perspective.

One of the problems faced by Christian Theology regarding man, is the problem of his SIN. What do we mean by SIN? How do we understand the classical doctrine of *original* sin? If we prepared to interpret "the Fall" as a symbolical rather an historical fact, then "the doctrine of the original sin" must be reformulated in the light of the historical, anthropological, psychological, sociological, political and cultural discoveries also. (Sin as an evil arising from purely egoistic motives and actions is not exclusive to Christianity alone. Other religions as well as most ideologies more or less hold similar theories of evil also).

Christian theology with its emphasis on obedience and disobedience to God's will, seems to emphasize sin as being more volitional than intellectual in nature. Eastern thought, including Buddhism, tends to emphasize the intellectual aspect more than the volitional. Ignorance or avidya is regarded as the primary source of evil. It is ignorance that leads to attachment which in turn leads to all sorts of evil. Christian Theology in Burma can better understand and explain the nature of sin and evil by taking into account the intellectual aspect also. Jesus prayed on the Cross to "forgive them, for *they know not* what they do." If "they" had really "known," then perhaps they might not have crucified him.

The classical Christian doctrine of sin also tends to be rather individualistic in its interpretation of evil. It seems to regard sin or evil as arising from independent decisions of isolated individuals. It therefore fails to understand sin in a relational contest, with the result that the socio-political nature of evil became almost neglected. These are just some pointers for a construction of Burmese Christian Theology which is also called upon to explain the nature of man.

Related to the problem of sin, is the problem of "conversion." What do we mean by conversion? Does conversion to Christ mean the acceptance of the concepts and methods as propagated by the established Church? Does some one become a convert only when he or she has confessed Christ in a "Christian" way? Are there not also possibilities of confessing Christ in "non-Christian" ways? Do we not sometimes impose our own "*modern laws of circumcision*" as a pre-condition for the conversion of modern "Gentiles?"

If our motive for mission is not just proselytism, then our understanding of conversion to Christ must be broadened. With such a broadened concept, perhaps we may come to discover today that many from both the East and the West have come, or are already on their way "to sit down with the sons of Abraham, Isaac and Jacob." They will be astonished to find themselves honoured and invited to share His glory, they who had never known or confessed Him as their lord and saviour; for unknowingly they had simply been carrying out His Will.

In other words, does conversion really matter? Is not commitment to the living Christ more important than becoming converted in the traditional way? And is not this commitment to Christ universal enough to embrace even those, who, without acknowledging him, are already committed to His cause? Here again, the Yin-Yang method can help us understand more about the relation between conversion and commitment. Somehow conversion implies a definite confession of Jesus Christ as Lord, and yet somehow it may not require that explicit confession.

Another important problem faced by Christian Theology in Burma is the doctrine of salvation. The present controversy between ''the other-worldly salvationists'' and ''this-worldly humanists'' is also spreading throughout the churches in our country. But, theologically speaking, this need not be a crucial problem for the Church in Burma. If the Church in Burma is faithful to its oriental heritage, then it will not commit the error of absolutizing only one relative aspect of salvation. To the oriental mind, salvation itselt is *a mystery* which transcends all human ways of understanding it. No theology of salvation can therefore make absolute claims for itself.

The more important problem for Burmese Christian Theology is that which concerns *the desire* for salvation. For the true Buddhist, he who takes the path to Nirvana, must not do so out of attachment, or craving, or the desire for Nirvana. A truly liberated person is not even conscious of the fact that he has attained salvation. In other words, the very desire for liberation itself must be transcended before one can acquire final liberation.

What then can we learn from this Buddhist Theory of Non-Attachment? One popular belief held by many Christians in Burma, is the continuity of the Self, or the Soul, after death. This reflects a craving of the Self for existence in the hereafter. It may be due to this belief that our present doctrine of Resurrection is clouded by our present misunderstanding of immortality. Such a theology seems to be trapped by ''reward-punishment'' concepts. Christian soteriology should also be formulated from the perspective of Non-Attachment. This will have a very sobering effect for both the ''salvationists'' and the ''humanists.'' Humanistic Theology can learn to overcome its obsession with over-activism in the seculum. We must learn to become detached from our own revolutionary actions. We must do our best, but at the time we must really learn to say with our Lord: ''It is finished.'' The salvationists on the other hand can learn to rid themselves of craving for heaven. We must dare to die without forcing God to resurrect us. We must really learn to say with our Lord: ''Father, into Thy hands, I commend my spirit.''

I mentioned in my introduction that any attempt at Burmese Christian Theology must also take into account, the socio-political human realities of our times. This is not the only source from which we can construct our theology. Nevertheless, relatively speaking, with the context of today, this has become the most basic foundation. The economical, political, social and personal crises of our times are undeniable, existential realities. The common problems, struggles, suffering, hopes and frustrations among us, have already broken down the barriers between Christians and Buddhists in our land. I admit the necessity of metaphysics for theology. But no amount of armchair philosophy or abstract theology can save the concrete, struggling humanity of today.

We do require more comprehensive categories for theology. But we must never forget that God, in Christ, has spoken a *human language*, a *concrete language*, for *concrete humanity*. It is in this concrete field of human relations that both Christianity and Buddhism, both the East and the West, both the Marxists and the Non-Marxists, meet their common neighbour in need. And it is in this common meeting, loving, caring and struggling for and with their common neighbour that all religions and ideologies develop together toward their common destiny. The final test for both Christianity and Buddhism therefore, is not the test of their knowledge of God, but the test of their concrete love for man. So the most important problem facing Burmese Christian Theology today is the problem of *How to Feed His Lambs?*

/1/   *sisara nimmána vá*
/2/   *pubbekata hetu váda*
/3/   *By U Aye Maung, "Buddha and Buddhism", Vol. II, page 19.*
/4/   *Udána; Viii, 3: nissaranam pannayetha.*
/5/   International Review of Missions-*July 1971*
/6/   *See the* WWC Fifth Assembly Bible Studies
/7/   International Review of Missions-*Oct. 1970 (Faithful Dialogue)*
/8/   *Religion and Society Vol XI. No. 3, September, 1969*

CHAPTER NINE

Horizons On Christianity's
New Dialogue With Buddhism

PAUL F. KNITTER

There is something different, something new in Christianity's dialogue with Buddhism over the past decade. Most of the works surveyed in this paper (see Bibliography) indicate a notable shift from the earlier "let's see the differences so we can establish the superiority" attitude to an approach which wants to take differences seriously, understand them correctly, in order to learn from them. The following pages will try to describe what this new attitude is discovering. After some preliminary considerations of the new attitude's methodology, I will highlight—much more is not possible—"converging insights" in four major areas of the Christian conversation with Buddhists. In each area I will also add my own reflections on how these new insights might be pursued in order to "correct" certain ambiguities in present-day Christian doctrine and practice.

Paul F. Knitter received the Th.D. from Marburg University, West Germany and is presently Professor of Theology at Xavier University (Cincinnatti, OH 45207). His publications, most of which focus on the dialogue between Christianity and World Religions, include: Toward a Protestant Theology of the Religions *(1974), and articles in* Concilium *(1980),* The Journal of Ecumenical Studies *(1975, 1979),* Horizons *(1978), and* Neue Zeitschrift für systematische Theologie und Religionsphilosophie *(1971, 1973). His essay* "World Religions and the Finality of Christ: A Critique of Hans Kung's 'On Being a Christian.' " *appeared in the first volume of this series* "Interreligious Dialogue: Facing the Next Frontier," *Ridge Row Press. 1981. He is an Associate Editor of* Horizons. *Taken from* Horizons: Journal of the College Theology Society. *6/1 (1981) pp. 40-61. Reprinted by permission of the publisher and author.*

Christianity and the Religions of the East

I. A Different Method for Dialogue
Much to Learn and a Need to Learn It

While all of the works surveyed in this study evince a genuine respect for Buddhism and are a clear move byond the "poor pagan" mentality, a few of the authors still stand on the same platform that sustained earlier, apologetic studies of Buddhism: they argue that Christianity and Buddhism represent two totally opposed, absolutely unbridgeable religious views, or that the basic claims of Buddha, when compared to those of Christ, are radically inadequate (Callaway, Hossfeld, Aldwinckle). But these are the exceptions. The majority of the authors approach the conversation with Buddhists with a firm conviction that there is much for Christians to learn and, given the crisis of Western Christianity, an urgent need to learn it. A frequent image is that of "the covenant with the East": as the Fathers recognized a "covenant with the Greeks" from which Christianity could (and certainly did!) learn, today the same transformative encounter can take place with the East (Johnston, 1970, xiv; Gilkey, 2; Merton, 1975, 313).

For the conversation, however, to be fruitful, it must have as its starting point a deep commitment to Christ and to the truth discovered in him. Yet the depth of this commitment must be matched by the breadth of one's openness to the truth that may be contained in Buddha's message. Such openness is called for not only as an evident prerequisite for authentic dialogue but also as a demand of the Christian claim that God's love and revelatory presence are universal (Drummond, 207; Swearer, 49; Waldenfels, 206-07).

But in this dialogue, all the authors insist, the evident differences between Buddha and Christ must not be slighted; only if they are taken seriously can anything be learned. There are recurrent warnings against a facile syncretism which reduces all religions to a common denominator or against a simplistic arationalism which wants to cut away all doctrines in order to inhale a "common essence" (Merton, 1968, 43; Johnston, 1978, 43; Rupp, 3-26). Yet though it is admitted that these differences can sometimes make for "unbridgeable gaps," the common expectation of the authors is that it is especially at the points where Buddhism most differs that Christianity has most to learn. Drummond speaks of "converging foci" (206-07). This reflects a growing insight in the Christian conversation with Buddhism (and with other religions) that truth, especially religious truth, is not a matter of either-or but of both-and (Kreeft, 514-15; Spae, 1977, 3, 25; deSilva, xii-xiii). Every religious assertion must, somehow, be balanced by its opposite. One of the most recent and eloquent cases for this "both-and" quality of religious experience and doctrine is John A. T. Robinson's *Truth is Two-Eyed.*

The Experiential-Praxis Basis for Dialogue

Another new insight into the method for dialoguing with Buddhism is the growing recognition that the partners must somehow "pass over," i.e., personally enter into the experience of the other religion. Dialogue must, to some extent at least, be based on a praxis of the other religion (J. Dunne, ix-xiii). This is particularly called for in the dialogue with Buddhism. To a great extent, Christians have misunderstood and therefore misused Buddhist language. Language, as found in Theravāda and Mahayana texts and in Zen literature, is not meant primarily to provide "explanation" but "experience" (Merton, 1968, 36-38; Johnston, 1970, 173). "Buddhist terminology...is largely phenomenological and descriptive and it aims to portray an experience rather than a reality. It is not metaphysical but soteriological, and if we interpret it ontologically, Buddhism appears atheistic, monistic, or pantheistic" (Gardini, 34-35).

Merton articulates a growing consensus when he suggests that therefore the conversation with Buddhists must first be a *communion* before it is a *communication*. It is a communion which originates in one's own religion and which is based on "the science of an ultimate experience." It enables Christians "to penetrate the ultimate ground of their beliefs" and allows them to touch the ultimate ground of Buddhist beliefs. Such communion, while it still recognizes "the very important essential differences" between Christianity and Buddhism, unveils the possibility that both "in their inner reality...end up with the simplest and most baffling thing of all: direct confrontation with Absolute Being, Absolute Love, Absolute Mercy or Absolute Void..." (Merton, 1968, 61-62; id., 1975, 310-12; Johnston, 1978, 77-78, 85-86; Swearer, 113-15; Dubarle, 71).

While this communion is "beyond the level of words," it can enable Christians to "find a common ground of verbal understanding" (Merton, 1975, 315). Here we have a handle on the immense problem of language in the Christian-Buddhist conversation. Both traditions have developed in isolation from each other and therefore have "no common language." Yet with the experiential starting point of "communion" we can attempt a new method of dialogue: "...dialogue is that form of communication in which the means of communication has to be created in the course of the process of communication itself" (Sangharakshita, 58, also 59-63). We can perhaps discover that our "words," with all their baffling differences, are more complementary than contradictory. Merton therefore suggests, "the real area for investigation...might after all be theology rather than psychology or asceticism." But he adds: "..it must be theology as experienced in Christian contemplation, not the speculative theology of textbooks and disputations" (1968, 58).

A further guideline in the new dialogue bears mention, even though it is not found as an explicit point of consensus among the authors. Swearer reminds us that the conversation can be bogged down with an overconcern for correct interpretation, for historical accuracy, for knowing whether the historical Buddha or the historical Jesus really said or meant this or that. Such questions, no doubt, are important. But they should not distract us from the fact that the dialogue is to be carried out between believers not between beliefs. It concerns not the *ipsissima verba* or the *verissima facta* of Buddha or Jesus but the way these two archetypal figures have been understood and followed throughout history and especially in our present day (Swearer, 16).

II. God and God-Talk
Converging Insights

1. *Buddha was not an atheist:* There is a clear consensus among most of the authors that to label Buddha an atheist or to declare that Nirvana or *Sunyata* are utterly godless is, as stated above, to abuse Buddha's language—or lack of language (deSilva, 67-74). Buddha is recognized as a religious practitioner who, as the parable of the poison arrow attests, wanted to resolve a practical problem not propose a new religious theory (Drummond, 73,115); as Marx might put it, his primary concern was to transform the subject not to understand it. And because he realized that all words and theories are both inadequate and distractive, he refused to speak of God or Brahman/Atman. We should respect his silence, not fill it with our hasty interpretations (Johnston, 1970, 173; id., 1978, 107-12; Merton, 1968, 81; Spae, 1977, 19).

Yet many of the authors cautiously—sometimes not so cautiously— suggest that if we enter into the words that *are* used in the Buddhist scriptures and especially if we regard the practice of contemporary Buddhists, we will recognize that the Buddhist experience of Nirvana, *Sunyata, Satori* is not unrelated to the Christian experience of God (deSilva, 138-45). Drummond states that after considering "...the range of Buddha's teaching on Nirvana, I feel compelled to affirm that in some authentic way he was in contact with aspects or dimensions of the Reality that Jesus terms the kingdom of God" (127). Dumoulin sees in Nirvana a genuine recognition of "Transcendence" (1974, 97-98). Johnston, witnessing the sense of participation, affirmation, and "pure dependence" experienced in *Satori,* holds that we are dealing with an experience "...upon which (for the Christian) it is impossible to put any name except that of God" (1970, 125). Buddhist Emptiness, therefore, is a "rich emptiness" (Johnston, 1970, 33), which may be a more accurate way of describing the Christian experience of the *pleroma* or fullness of God (Merton, 1968, 85; Panikkar, 1978). *Sunyata,* Vos suggests, can be translated "relativity," an attempt to describe the essential interrelatedness of all reality in a larger Whole (33)./1/ Whatever the propriety of such Christian interpretations, they express the willingness to affirm, and learn from, Buddhist experience and language of the Ultimate.

2. *The immanence, non-duality, and suprapersonality of the Ultimate:* While some authors express concern that Buddhist language often seems to dissolve any possible distinction between the Ultimate and the finite (Johnston, 1970, 41, 83-84; Fox, 10), the clear consensus is that to brand

Buddhism as inescapably monistic is a rash judgment./2/ The Buddhist challenges the Christian to embrace the logically more frustrating but personally more rewarding experience of the unity and diversity of the Ultimate and the finite, of Nirvana and *Samsara*. While *Sunyata* truly *is* every finite reality, while each particular entity truly is (and is not just "a piece of") *Sunyata*, still "particularity really exists"; *Sunyata* is what it is, the Absolute, in every particular, so that we have "an interpenetration of Absolutes" and still only one Absolute (Fox, 48-50; Dumoulin, 1979b, 102-14).

This is mind-boggling indeed and therefore an invitation to Christians to stretch their minds towards a fuller appreciation of the immanence of God. As modern theologians recently and mystics through the centuries have reminded us, Christians have missed this immanent God because of their unbalanced insistence on His Otherness and Transcendence (Johnston, 1970, 179). In Buddhism we can detect the immanent God of the Johannine writings which, in defining God as love, portray him not as a *doer* but as the *doing* (in us) of something, a God whose "reality...is not to be sought beyond the phenomenal" (Bruns, 30-33, 46, 89). Here is the God who cannot be localized, put in *a place*, either above the clouds or in our hearts (Johnston, 1971, 24). Here is a God truly encompassing, neither in us nor outside of us; but we and the world in Him (Kreeft, 521-22).

To experience, with the Buddhist, the immanence of the Absolute is to discover—or rediscover—that the relation between God and world-humanity is not monistic (simple identity) or dualistic (clear distinction) but *non-dualistic*. A number of the authors suggest that any experience of God which has not yet felt this non-duality is incomplete or immature. The Cartesian "cogito," with its radical subject-object distinction, may be a profitable starting point for the natural sciences, but it constitutes a "false start" for our understanding of the Ultimate. Instead of beginning with distinctions, we can and should start with the original unity between the Ultimate and the finite—a unity which is available, Buddhists tell us, in a non-reflexive awareness which can best be described as "consciousness itself" or "pure consciousness" (Kreeft, 525; Merton, 1968, 23-24). In this consciousness, which is given with our very being, God is known neither as an objective reality nor simply as a subjective experience. God is known to be radically beyond our distinctions between subject and object. Therefore, when Christians speak of God as an objective other, they must remind themselves that they are speaking only *quoad nos* and not *quoad* the reality of God; and when Buddhists maintain that the Absolute is our subjective consciousness, they too must be reminded that they are speaking adverbially not adjectivally, i.e., they are describing how they experience the Absolute, not what the Absolute is (Kreeft, 525). A true religious experience is the experience of God being subjective in us; it is to touch the "Single Center of all beings," the "still point of the turning world," the *ipsum esse* subsisting in us and we in it; it is an experience in which it is impossible neatly to locate ourselves or the Self of God. The Ultimate and the finite, then, are not "one"; yet neither are they "two"; they make up a non-dual Reality in which both are and have their being in each other (Kreeft, 526-27; Merton, 1968, 9-13, 23-24, 71-73).

But does such a conversation with Buddhism still allow for a *personal* God? Reservations are voiced that the Buddhist perception of the non-duality between the Ultimate and the finite, while establishing a splendid vision of unity, easily renders meaningless any talk of personal community among humans or with God (Fox, 180-83). Yet there are converging insights among the authors that the experience of Nirvana is not utterly devoid of personal qualities. Drummond finds a basis for this in the frequent references in Buddhist texts to Nirvana or the *Dharma* as "the Loverly" (124, 193). C. Dunner and Merton go further. They claim that the Buddhist experience of Enlightenment is not contradictory to but can include the experience of "Being (which) has fallen in love with beings" so that "secret name" of Being might well be "Father" (C. Dunne, 51-56, 39-41). Buddhist praxis indicates that to realize Nirvana as Absolute Reality is to experience it as "Absolute Love": "Pure Being is Infinite Compassion...Absolute Emptiness is Absolute Compassion" (Merton, 1968, 84-87; Johnston, 1978, 67-68).

The majority of the authors, however, want to qualify such personal language. They accept the Buddhist admonition that much of Christianity's personal theism has limited and "offended" the Ultimate. God understood as Thou, for all its merits, has led to an anthropomorphized Deity, a totally-Other, who controls our lives or who can be used by humans to control their fellows. Buddhists therefore underscore the reminder of Ratzinger that "the personal dimension of God infinitely transcends human personhood, so that the concept of person, as much as it is illuminating, still proves to be an inadequate similitude" (in Dumoulin, 1974, 168). Our authors clumsily search for a more adequate language: God is personal but not a personality (Bruns, 45); God is "pre-personal" (Dumoulin, 1974, 164), an "unpersonal personal" (Waldenfels, 181-82), "supra-personal." Better to admit that personal language of God is essentially inadequate, that God is both personal and impersonal (Robinson, 13-40). Only when one has felt and recognized this non-dual, more than personal quality of the Ultimate, can one fittingly address it as Thou (Lassalle, 68).

3. *The Non-Being of God:* Gilkey describes his reaction when, for the first time, a Buddhist (Masao Abe) asked him why Christian theology begins with being rather than nonbeing. It "blew my mind," he admits; and it led him to suggest that this focus on divine nonbeing might more deeply and coherently reveal the Christian God than has traditional "being-centered" Western theology (Gilkey, 2-3; Spae, 1979, 30-40; Johnston, 1978, 115-25). God's reality and activity transcend and therefore include

96

both being *and* nonbeing. Christian theologians have missed this. "God is being qualified dialectically and yet essentially by nonbeing, and so his mystery transcends the categories of both being and nonbeing. It is in this dialectical pattern...that he manifests himself in all his works; and it is on this pattern alone that the self can find itself—by losing itself" (Gilkey, 10). Creation is possible *only* if God's being is "emptied," i.e., limited by nonbeing (Dumoulin, 1974, 180-82; id., 1979b, 144-53; Gilkey, 10-11; Waldenfels, 191-93). This transcending dialectic is contained even more clearly in the deepest implications of the Christian understanding of incarnation and the cross in which Deity realizes itself in "letting-go," in embracing Nothingness (Swearer, 109-11). Reality, God's and ours, unfolds only in this constant movement into and embrace of what is not Itself (Waldenfels, 178, 197-207; Gilkey, 11).

A Corrective for Christian-Doctrinalism and Dualism

1. One of the aspects in Christian consciousness, both past and present, which stands in urgent need of a "Buddhist balance" is what might be termed "doctrinalism." Simply stated: Christianity seems to have taken its words and concepts, whether biblical or papal, much too seriously. This obsessive insistence on right words or doctrines (orthodoxy) blurs the fact that all religion originates from a deep personal experience and not from an affirmation of propositions (Merton, 1968, 39-41, 56). Orthodoxy provides a clear and distinct concept of God which too easily becomes Freud's transcendent crutch for our insecurity and anxiety (Fernando, 1979, 93). And the security of right knowing debilitates so readily the primacy of right acting.

Our Buddhist brothers and sisters remind us of what our mystics all along and our theologians in their better moments have admitted: that to experience and to know God is to encounter *das Geheimnis schlechthin*–absolute mystery! This is mystery which, as much as we are grasped by it and dare to speak of it, will always remain beyond our words and dogmas. Theology, therefore, if it is to be true to its task, must ultimately and always be a *reductio in mysterium* (Waldenfels, 186-89). And Christians, while they must "cling to God," need not and ought not to "cling to views and ideas about God" (Johnston, 1970, 190; Lassalle, 79-93).

Yet Christians will remind their Buddhist partners that words/doctrines are important, even necessary. In stressing the emptiness of words and the limitations of the intellect, Buddhists run the risk of not being able to "say anything about anything" (Johnston, 1970, 92;id., 1978, 43; Waldenfels, 159-76). If Christianity is the Body of Christ and the People of God, it needs some kind of a "common language" (Merton, 1968, 47). And because it claims the incarnational immanence of God in the world, it will not look on the forms or symbols of God in the world as meaningless illusions; while the faceless mystery of God cannot be contained in any *one* human face, it can be reflected in *many* faces (C. Dunne, 75-82). But in making such affirmations, Christian remain in need of the balance of Buddhist negation: as much as Christians affirm their words and doctrines, they must be ready to negate them; they can proclaim the value and even necessity of doctrine *only* if with equal insistence they recognize its inadequacy. Buddha might use a paradox here: words about God can be valid and useful only if they flow from a profound experience of silence. Behind and within all Christian doctrine there must be "...a silence which prepares the way for the word and the silence which is the word's highest utterance" (C. Dunne, 23; Panikkar, 1971, 84-89; Steindl-Rast, 175-79).

2. The Christian encounter with Buddha's understanding of the Ultimate can also be, I suggest, an invaluable aid in addressing another area of incoherence in Christian proclamation: *dualism*. Christianity, to be sure, proclaims itself as a "this-worldly" religion. More than any other of the world religions, it claims that it is best able to affirm and guide the "basic faith" of secularity in the ultimate value of this world and human involvement in it. And indeed, the central symbols of Christianity—kingdom, incarnation, resurrection—are this-wordly and non-dualistic in that they affirm a God intimately involved in history and working with human action. Yet despite the non-dualistic content of these symbols, despite the rallying calls of theologians to affirm this world, many Christians—and this includes theologians—remain "anonymous dualists." The reason for this is that they continue to interpret their non-dualistic symbols in a basically dualistic philosophical framework—usually traced back to Neo-Platonism.

Dualism, sometimes anonymously and sometimes quite consciously, infects and debilitates Christian affirmation of the *humanum* and *mundanum* (Rupp, 38, 69). How can the dualistic "God of theism" be truly immanent in history when He is perfect unto himself, in need of no other, immutable and related to the world *rationis tantum?* How can life in this world truly prepare for and be part of the future Kingdom when, as even many theologians of hope insist, that Kingdom will arrive as an other-worldly "coming," not as a this-worldly "becoming," a "mighty act of God" carried out not because of but despite the actions of humans. The eternal significance of human action is thus jeopardized by the sovereignty of God's grace; at the most, human activity is meaningful only as an "admission ticket" to or a "proleptic sign" of another divine order./3/ How can we take the "supernatural existential," the non-dual relation of nature and grace seriously when, in the final analysis ("double gratuity!") nothing in us or in God *requires* the bestowal of grace?

Many Christian thinkers, liberation and especially process theologians, are attempting to root out this prevailing Christian dualism. Some of the converging insights in the new dialogue with Buddhists can be of vital help in enabling them to coherently explain what the symbols of incarnation and resurrection really imply. The Buddhist experience of the supra-personal immanence of the Absolute in the finite can confirm and perhaps refine the process notion of panentheism: God will not be seen so much as a Super-Being relating to finite beings but as the unitive Mystery which lives and moves and has its being within finite beings, as they have their being in It. And the paradoxical non-duality which Mahayana Buddhism claims to be the relation between Nirvana and *Samsara* will enable the Rahnerians to carry through with their notion of the supernatural existential and admit that "nature" cannot be without "grace," nor "grace" without "nature." A non-dualistic notion of God-world will also lend coherence to the claims of the liberation theologians, for if God is subjective in us, he cannot carry out his liberating action without us (nor we without him) so that our actions *are* his and the Kingdom we build here on earth *is* His Reality. The new conversation with Buddhism, then, would seem to enable Christians to become more fully and actively aware of the Non-Duality which is inherent, but often blurred, in the Christian vision.

III. The Selfless Self
Converging Insights

1. *A Misunderstanding:* The consensus of authors examined for this study are in basic agreement with Merton's assessment that most Christian discussions about the Buddhist view of *Anatta/No-self* have been, like the discussions about Nirvana, "completely equivocal" (Merton, 1968, 118; Swearer, 75; Drummond, 138-40). Again, the blame can be pinned on an abuse of Buddhist language. In his talk about being a No-self, Buddha was not proposing a metaphysical doctrine but an ethical invitation; he was not arguing an "eternalist" or an "annihilationist" concept of the soul but urging a radically different way of experiencing ourselves and the selves of others (Swearer, 179-80; deSilva, 30-32). The problem is that Christians have understood that language much too literally; or they have taken their own language about the "new self" or about the "self in Christ" so literally and simplistically that they are blind to the possible complementarity between the No-Self and the New Self (Merton, 1968, 118). In fact, some would argue that *Anatta* is a *via negationis* and the New-self a *via affirmationis*, both trying to draw us, along quite different paths, to the same amazing discovery: that the human self can be so transformed, in consciousness and in way of acting, that it no longer resembles the self it thought it was. It is so *new* as *not* to be the original self (C. Dunne, 65-67; Swearer, 80; Drummond, 142, 147; Merton, 1968, 76-77; Kreeft, 520).

2. *The Meaning of Anatta:* Recognizing past misunderstandings of *Anatta,* our authors move on, in surprising agreement, to try to grasp what the Buddhist No-self really implies. They recognize that Buddhism provides Christians with an opportunity to know and experience that the true reality of the person does not consist in being an *individuum*, a given entity; rather, the

true self is radically, essentially, constantly in relation to other selves and to all reality; its "being" is constantly one of ongoing "dependent co-origination"; its being is relating. Therefore, the true self is a selfless self, constantly losing-finding its self in its relations with others (deSilva, 90-103; C. Dunne, 16-17). Many of the authors use the psychology of Jung to explain and confirm this. It is possible to break through our ego-consciousness and experience a consciousness in which there is no ego, in which we are aware of ourselves-at-one with reality around us, vitally related (Johnston, 1970, 54; Drummond, 146-48, 195; Merton, 1968, 64; Franck, 77). In T. S. Eliot's terms, "you are the music" (Johnston, 1970, 23). According to Aquinas, *intellectus est quodamodo omnia*—our selves, in a sense, are all things (Johnston, 1968, 55).

3. *The Self-in-God:* Converging insights among our authors point out that the Buddhist *Anatta* doctrine can aid Christians in more fully appropriating the content of such expressions as to be "in Christ," "united with God," "a temple of the Spirit," or of the text (cited by almost all the authors), "I live, not yet I, but Christ lives in me" (Gal. 2:20). Having "passed over" to Buddha's experience of *Anatta,* Christians can realize that such language means more than an ethical imitation of Christ, more than being filled with God as glass might be filled with water. Rather, Buddhists suggest that these Christian claims are inviting us to a non-dual experience of Christ/God (Swearer, 82-83; Merton, 1968, 118-20; Johnston, 1970, 75-76; Drummond, 151-52). It is an experience in which we become aware of the claim of the mystics that "the soul *is* God" (Johnston, 1970, 75); or, phrased more cautiously, "...that God is (among other things) my true identity" (Kreeft, 521). In arriving at the depths of our consciousness we discover that there is no *self*-consciousness; rather, we are conscious of ourselves with the consciousness of God; we truly participate "in the mind of Christ" (Phil. 2, 5). This experience is not only one of immense peace in that it affirms the value of our divine being; but also, in it we find ourselves operating out of a new *principium,* a new center which is no longer the self-concerned, ratiocinating ego. We no longer find ourselves "obeying" God's law, but simply being and carrying out our true identity: a No-self at one with God and others (Swearer, 82-83; Franck, 134).

4. *The Fall:* A number of the authors find that the Buddhist understanding of *Anatta* provides needed clarification for the Christian notion of Sin and the Fall. In the light of our true nature as No-selves, our sinfulness is not seen as a corruption of human nature due to some past event; "original sin" is not an ontological separation from God. Rather, the root cause and essence of our sinfulness is ignorance—the pseudo-knowledge acquired from eating of the Tree of Knowledge which leads us to think that we are individuals and that the purpose of existence is to maintain and augment that individuality (Franck, 97). Sin stems from a false self-consciousness which

makes the self aware of what is good or evil for itself (Merton, 1968, 127). The Fall, therefore, is the prevailing disposition of humans—fostered through generations of collective bad karma—''to treat the ego as objects of desire or of repulsion'' (Merton, 1968, 82-83; Fox, 60; Drummond, 101-02; Dumoulin, 1979a, 22-26).

A Corrective for Christian Individualism

Perhaps the most valuable lesson which Christianity can learn from these converging insights concerning the *Anatta*-doctrine is to recognize the *individualism* which has infected the church's all too Western interpretation of the Gospel. In our present state of world affairs, this lesson appears more urgent than ever. The undialectical affirmation of the self and of being which animates so much of Western politics, economics, philosophy, and theology, ''may be,'' in Gilkey's words, ''the principle of world destruction'' (8). The inability to see the value of non-being and of the No-self, the insistence that the welfare and growth of the individual self or the national self cannot be jeopardized has led to the domination and exploitation of other selves and of nature, making earth an endangered planet. How much has the church bought into and even fostered this insidious sacrality of the self? The new conversation with Buddhism is suggesting to Christians thay they will not be able to make a meaningful contribution to ''a new world order'' unless they and their theologians (even process theologians!) rid themselves of the vestiges of Western Substantialist and existentialist philosophy and its overemphasis on the ultimate value and inviolability of the individual.

It must be stressed that to learn from the Buddhist No-self is not simply a matter of Christians affirming more clearly what they already know. It will lead to a radical revision of Christian attitudes. It will help bring about what John Cobb feels is a much needed ''postpersonal form of Christian existence, in which Western Christianity is finally able to free itself from its attachment to individualized personal existence as a final good'' and in which ''interpersonal (and international) relations can be understood in a different way.''/4/

It is only this post-personal form of Christian existence, which understands the True Self as the Selfless Self, that will enable Christianity, together with Buddhism, to further the ''quantum leap'' which humanity today must make if its evolution is to continue: the evolutionary leap from individuality to communality, from a world of divided, warring tribes to a ''global village'' (Franck, 86-87). Only if human beings cease understanding themselves as individuals, only if they profoundly realize that to be themselves they *must* be part of others—only then will they be able to form authentic community, whether in the church or among nations; only then will they be able to get beyond the patriotism and nationalism that continue to hamstring efforts for global community (deSilva, 146-59; Fox, 71).

IV. Value of This World and of Action in It
Converging Insights

1. *Buddhism not world-denying:* While many of the authors recognize the potential for Buddhism, especially when understood monistorically, to be a "cop-out" on history (Rupp, 51, 54; Dhavamony, 53), they voice a practically unanimous opinion that Buddhism is not essentially a world-denying religion. To judge it so is to fall prey to Western scholars' all too simplistic dichotomy between the mystical, passive religions of the East and the prophetic, active religions of the West (Johnston, 1978, 10). Many authors call for recognition of the fact that today Buddhism is just as intent and just as successful as is Christianity in adjusting to the world-affirming faith of contemporary men and women (Dumoulin, 1974, 150-58; id., 1979a, 29; Spae, 1977, 22). In doing this, Buddhism is returning (like Christianity) to its early sources and proving its "original universal character" which is "essentially humanistic" (Dumoulin, 1974, 61; id., 1979b, 84-87).

The authors agree that from what we can know of the original message of Gautama, the First Noble Truth does not imply a condemnation of the finite world and life in it. Rather, the First Truth reveals that, since all finite reality is in constant "dependent co-origination," everything is a "no-thing" and must not be made absolute. To make anything in the world ultimate and to hold on to it with all one's being is to grasp at an ultimately disappointing idol (Drummond, 186-88; Swearer, 62-68; Kreeft, 527). Realizing this, one can "sit loose in the saddle" as one moves on to an active involvement in the world (Drummond, 107-09). Therefore Buddha, like Jesus proposed a revolutionarily new view of society without being a social reformer. While he could accept the favors of kings and rajas, Gautama demonstrated a dangerous "freedom from any concept of the sacral king" (Drummond, 198). And even though he did not call for the abolition of the caste system (as Paul did not reject Slavery), his *Anatta* doctrine and his acceptance of all men (and later women) into the *Sangha* constituted "a radical rejection of both principle and practice of caste" (Drummond, 198, 63-67; Rupp, 64-68). Drummond argues that many, if not all, of the world-denying attitudes found in Theravada literature do not stem from the Buddha but are most likely "the result of later developments in Buddhist monastic communities"; he compares such attitudes with similar world-denying developments in early Christianity, even in St. Paul (Drummond, 150, 100).

2. *Are history and evil real?* It is not easy to focus a clear consensus among the authors concerning their interpretations of Buddhism's response to this question. As we have seen, Gautama's original message and especially its Mahayanist interpretation contain a recognition of the need to act in the world. But many of our authors point out that it is difficult for Buddhists to coherently ground this need to act in a recognition that time and process are real, that there is the genuine possibility of things going wrong and that

therefore it is necessary to counteract evil and work for a better world (Rupp, 50-52; Merton, 1968, 132; Robinson, 94). There is, then, a general recognition among the authors that in these areas of the dialogue, Buddhists perhaps have much to learn from Christians (Spae, 1977, 23).

But the warning is voiced that it is too simplistic to brand the Buddhist experience of time as cyclic. Given the central Buddhist affirmation that bad *karma* can be overcome and that here is a process of rebirths, one might better speak of an *upward spiral* movement or time within *Samsara* (Spae, 1977, 4; Dumoulin, 1979b, 119-24). But more importantly, it is recognized that the Buddhist insistence that the fullness of Reality is to be experienced in the *Now* is not totally opposed to the Christian insistence on history. In fact, the Buddhist Now is a needed balance for Christianity's exaggerated concern with the historical which tends to place "salvation" primarily in a fact of the past and leads to a fundamentalistic "absolutizing [of] the relativities of history" (Robinson, 54-55). Also, Christianity's preoccupation with the *future* tends to blur the fact that while Jesus proclaimed the Kingdom to come, he also, paradoxically, announced that it *is* now (Merton, 1968, 138).

Concerning the reality of evil, many of the authors remind us that it is again an abuse of Buddhist language simply to conclude that if evil is described as an "illusion" it is therefore not real. For Buddhism, there is no dualistic distinction between the subjective and the objective orders, between the *ordo cognoscendi* and the *ordo essendi*. Therefore, "...a change (or a lack) in consciousness is also a change (or lack) in the real" (Rupp, 38). This is corroborated if we take seriously Socrates' and Newman's equation between true knowledge and true virtue; what we truly know (Newman's "real assent") or do not know really affects and *is* what we are or are not (Kreeft, 528). If all this is then understood within the framework of the Buddhist experience of Reality-as-Now, we can happily recognize that while we must strain all efforts to overcome the present real evil of ignorance, ultimately all evil and all ignorance is *not* real; every instance of evil is a *"felix culpa"* (Kreeft, 535). In Buddhist terms, all ignorance is contained and overcome in the fullness and the dynamic interrelatedness of Nirvana; in complementary Christian terms, all evil can and *will* be an occasion for good and for greater unity, i.e., an occasion by which the Kingdom-to-be is realized as the Kingdom-now. Ultimately, evil *is* an illusion. "Death, where is thy sting?" (1 Cor. 15:55).

3. *The natural need to act in the world:* These converging insights as to the "illusion" of history and evil are confirmed by further insights among our authors concerning the Buddhist (especially Mahayanist) non-dual distinction between *prajna/bodhi* (wisdom) and *Karuna* (compassion). To be swept away by wisdom into the quiet sea of *Sunyata* is also to be swept up into the dynamic stream of compassion for all beings. It is impossible truly to be wise without actively being compassionate. Some of the authors mention

the frequent Christian claim that *karuna* is not the same as *agape* since it does not really admit of any "other" to love; but they go on to point out that while this may be true in theory, there is no difference between the Buddhist practice of compassion and the Christian practice of charity. Evidently, such theory is missing something (Dumoulin, 1974, 119-20; Kreeft, 534). As to the further Christian claim that *karuna* aims at bringing others to enlightenment, while *agape* is intent on changing both the person and society, Fox responds that compassion "will do whatever it must to awaken men to wisdom"; and that includes the relief of poverty, the abolition of oppression, the establishment of a just social-political order (62-66). For the Buddhist, the fundamental motivation for such efforts towards social change is not the intrinsic superiority of one social-economic order over another but the desire that all men and women experience enlightenment and know the relativity of all individuals and theories. Fox, however, adds that in regard to the relative adequacy of any one social system, Buddhism shows a greater affinity for socialism than for capitalism (74-79).

A Corrective for Christian Activism

Thanks to liberation/political theologians, Christians today are becoming more aware the Christian life in the recent past been excessively a matter of "individual piety," that today they are called to act in the world, that liberating praxis is of the essence of the Gospel. In order to carry out this urgent program of liberation and to avoid certain excesses of their own, liberation theologians can learn much from the new dialogue with Buddhism. Their Buddhist brothers and sisters offer them two crucially important insights into why praxis so easily becomes activism, or, why there can be no effective liberation without spirituality.

First, the new conversation with Buddhism, as described in this section, tells the liberation theologian that it is not sufficient that liberation praxis be based on careful social analysis and on a concrete political program; it must also be *grounded in the individual's contemplative or mystical experience* of his/her and the world's nondual relation with God. Praxis must be fruitfully wedded not only to *theoria* but also to *sophia*. Base Communities must foster not only a social "raising of consciousness"*(concienciamento)* but also a mystical "deepening of consciousness." Buddhists would offer a number of reasons for this.

—Only if our praxis is rooted in and sustained by the profound nirvanic realization that our actions *are* God's, that they are not just our feeble efforts but part of a larger, indefatigable divine process—only then will we truly know what we are doing; only then will we continue doing it in face of the crucifying opposition that all social liberation confronts. Without such mystical grounding, our acts become activism: isolated, scattered, frantic, mindless (Merton, 1975, 349).

—Also, while Buddhists will learn from the liberation theologian that sin is systemic, part of social structures, they will also remind the liberationist that the root problem is not social structures but human consciousness. Yes, sin does infect the body politic, and the body may be so infected that immediate, even revolutionary surgery is needed. Yet the Buddhist warns that the infecting bacteria is human ignorance, a false consciousness which, because it believes in individual egos, creates a false picture of society. Only if this bacteria, this false consciousness is destroyed can social structures truly be changed.

—Buddhism therefore clarifies both the means and the ultimate goal of liberation praxis. The final end of all social involvement is *not* to fashion a new social order or to dethrone multinational tyrants or to remove poverty and hunger (although these certainly are immediate and urgent ends); rather, the principal goal of liberation is to bring all men and women to personal enlightenment, to a mystical experience of their No-selves and essential interrelatedness in the Kingdom. Such enlightenment must also be considered part of the necessary *means* to the ultimate end. If it is not, the immediate achievements of social change and dethronement of tyrants will be short-lived.

Second, the new conversation with Buddhism tells liberation theologians that if their praxis is not to become activism, it must not only be grounded in contemplation; it must also be *detached from its own action*. The Buddhist insistence on detachment and the Christian insistence on involvement must paradoxically and creatively include each other. "...[T]he mystical centre needs the prophetic centre if it is not to become airborne...But equally the prophetic centre needs the mystical centre if it is not to become arrogant, narrow and unlovely..." (Robinson, 64-65). If we are truly detached from our praxis we all too easily consider our action the only way to effect change; we are inclined to crush anyone in its way; or we ourselves are crushed when our actions do not yield their intended fruits. To be truly free *for* action and involvement we must be free *from* it. And this freedom is the fruit of the mystical experience by which we know that our feeble actions are part of a larger liberation-process, and that while in the moment they are necessary, in an ultimate sense, they are not. We can act without seeking the fruits of our actions. The mystical experience of our nonduality with God/Kingdom embues us with "the double capacity to be fully and effectively invested in what one takes to be morally required activity; and yet also to be also to stand back and laugh at oneself" (Rupp, 83). It equips a person with "the freedom from concern that goes with being simply what he is and accepting things as they are in order to work with them as he can" (Merton, 1968, 31). The Buddhist insistence on detachment, then, enables liberation theologians to appropriate, in their praxis, the full implications of the traditional Christian doctrine that we are liberated "by grace" and not by our works in themselves; it enables them to grasp the freedom-from-and-for acting contained in the Gospel images of being like the birds of the air and the lilies of the field, of not being overconcerned with what we shall eat or wear in order to seek *first* the Kingdom of God in the assurance that then all will be added and liberation will take place.

V. Jesus and Buddha: Mutually Unique Converging Insights

1. *Similar missions:* The authors who explicitly take up a comparison of the "persons and works" of the "persons and works" of Jesus and Buddha do so, for the most part, with caution (Drummond, Armore, C. Dunne, Williams, Hossfeld, Dhavamony, Aldwinckle)./5/ They avoid facile generalizations about Jesus and Buddha being two faces of the same God or about one identical message in two different languages. Yet these authors to recognize certain basic similarities in the missions of the Christ and the Buddha.

The missions of both consisted basically in *revealing* something and in *modeling* what was revealed. Buddha, like Jesus, was recognized as an authoritative teacher. Both were seen to be preaching an urgently important message (the *Dharma*, the Gospel); and both were acclaimed as "speaking with authority"—the authority that comes from having an extraordinary experience of what they were talking about (Nirvana, the Father) (Drummond, 182-84; Dhavamony, 83-87). Also, both were claimed to embody, to model the full reality of their revelation. Thus, Buddha was called "he who has arrived" (Tathagata) and Jesus, "he who is to come." Or more simply, both were experienced as "Master" or "Lord" who carried out their exalted roles not by domineering but by showing the way (Dhavamony, 50-52; Nhat Hanh in Berrigan, 107). And from what we can cautiously know of the self-awareness of both Masters, it seems that Buddha, like Jesus, was animated with a sense of universal mission; all peoples must hear the message. Such an awareness of personal mission, according to Drummond, "has no parallel in the previous history of India" (44, also 80).

As to the content of what was revealed and modeled, the previous three sections of this study indicate the common consensus among our authors that the messages of Buddha and Jesus concerning the Ultimate, the Self, and the World are clearly different but that the differences are ultimately much more complementary than contradictory. Amore crystallizes this complementarity, which he calls "One Message," in Jesus' doctrine of "the Pure Mind" found especially in the Gospels of Luke and Matthew; the One Message is that of orthopraxis, i.e., the same ethical vision (58-95). Williams agrees and throughout his book argues that the hub of Jesus' message is the same radical call to destroy the ego and to live in interrelating love as is found in Buddha's message (see esp. 27-35; 48-74). C. Dunne, for all her concern to face squarely the differences between Jesus and Buddha, summarizes the attitude of many of our authors: "...from a Christian perspective, I see

Gotama as a precursor, preparing the way of the Lord. From a Buddhist perspective, I see Jesus as a true successor of the Buddha''(10)./6/

2. *Similar glorification myths:* Few of the authors explicitly consider the processes by which Jesus and Gautama were further understood and ''glorified'' after their deaths. Dhavamony rules out the validity of any such comparison (52-53). J. Dunne and especially Amore would disagree. Dunne makes the theological claim that we can recognize a genuine incarnation of God in all humans (x, 94-95). Amore, arguing phenomenologically, shows that especially in the Mahayanist school there developed ''the nearly complete deification of the Buddha''; this process ''had a considerable impact on the earlier, more conservative Buddhist sects as well'' (51). Intrinsic to this interpretation is what Amore terms ''an ancient, legendary pattern'' of descent—the Ultimate descends to humanity to become part of it. Both Christianity and Buddhism are, according to Amore, incarnational religions. He points out that while there were forms of Docetism in Buddhism as in early Christianity, their overriding affirmation is, expressed in Christian terms, that God is ''embodied'' (16, 57). Elsewhere I have argued more extensively that both Jesus and Buddha were experienced and interpreted according to similar glorification-incarnation myths./7/

A Corrective for Christological Exclusivism

What has been suggested so far in this section, as well as in this entire study, compels Christians to take a new and more critical look at the exclusivism that has marked their understanding of the uniqueness of Jesus. The new context of religious pluralism, exemplified sharply in the new dialogue with Buddhism, forces new questions which urge new answers concerning Jesus as ''One Mediator'' (Robinson, 121). If the incarnation and divinity of Jesus can be understood in terms of Enlightenment, i.e., the personal realization and living of divine-human nonduality, if Gautama seems to have experienced just such an Enlightenment, if the Buddhists are on to something when they claim that we should expect ''other Buddhas''— then Christians must ask whether their traditional claims that Jesus is exclusively unique or even inclusively unique (e.g., in the ''anonymous Christianity'' model) are accurate. This is not to deny the uniqueness of Jesus, but it inquires whether we have misunderstood it and the New Testament language about it./8/ Robinson uses a distinction which poses the question incisively: ''From being *totus Christus* and *totus Deus*, the one who is utterly expressive of Godhead, through and through, so that in him there in no unChristlikeness at all, he becomes *totum Christi, totum Dei*, the exhaustive revelation and all sufficient act, so that apart from him there is nothing of God and no Christlikeness at all'' (104). To be *totus Deus*, must Jesus be *totum Dei?*

In the dialogue with Buddhism, Christians can recognize the possibility that both Jesus and Buddha are mutually unique. Both preserve their distinctive difference and importance. And in a sense, both can be said to remain absolute in that they present their followers with a salvific revelation or *Dharma* which calls for total commitment and which is claimed to be meaningful for all people of all times. But this will be an absoluteness which is not defined by its ability to exclude or include other revelations; rather, Jesus and Buddha will be *proven* absolute insofar as they are able to relate to other's truths, include and be included by each other. Christians, then, can continue to be totally committed to Jesus the Christ and to claim that for them God has decisively been revealed in him; but they will also feel not only the possibility but the need to "clarify, complete and correct" (Robinson, 125) their understanding of Jesus and of God through dialogue with Buddhism as well as with other religions./9/

* * * * * *

This study has tried to show that the new Christian conversation with Buddhists is just such a "clarifying, completing and correcting" dialogue. In understanding better their Buddhist brothers and sisters, Christians have the opportunity to understand better their God is beyond all words and truly immanent in the world, that they themselves are radically social beings able to transform society only if they mystically realize this, and that their Savior is a Christ who defines God but does not confine Him.

Bibliography

Aldwinckle, Russel F.
> 1976 *"Jesus or Gotama?"* in More Than Man: A Study in Christology *(Grand Rapids: Eerdmans), pp. 211-46.*

Amore, Roy C.
> 1978 Two Masters, One Message: The Lives and Teachings of Gautama and Jesus *(Nashville: Abingdon).*

Berrigan, Daniel and Hanh, Thich Nhat
> 1975 The Raft Is Not the Shore: Conversations Towards a Buddhist Christian Awareness *(Boston: Beacon).*

Bruns, J. Edgar
> 1971 The Christian Buddhism of St. John *(New York: Paulist).*

Callaway, Tucker
> 1976 Zen Way, Jesus Way *(Rutland, VT: C. E. Tuttle).*

Cobb, John B., Jr.
> 1977 *"Buddhist Emptiness and the Christian God,"* Journal of the American Academy of Religion, *Vol. 45, pp. 11-25.*

Dhavamony, Mariasusai
> 1979 *"The Buddha as Saviour,"* in Christianity and Buddhism, *M. Dhavamony and C. Geffre, eds.,* Concilium, *Vol. 116 (New York: Seabury), pp. 43-54.*

Drummond, Richard H.
> 1974 Gautama the Buddha: An Essay in Religious Understanding *(Grand Rapids, Eerdmans).*

Dubarle, Dominique
> 1979 *"Buddhist Spirituality and the Christian Understanding of God,"* in Christianity and Buddhism, *pp. 64-73.*

Dumoulin, Heinrich
1974   Christianity Meets Buddhism (LaSalle, IL: Open Court).
1979a   "Buddhism–A Religion of Liberation," in Christianity and Buddhism, pp. 22-30.
1979b   Zen Enlightenment: Origins and Meaning (New York: Weatherhill).
Dunne, Carrin
1975   Buddha and Jesus: Conversations (Springfield: Templegate).
Dunne, John
1972   The Way of All the Earth (New York: Macmillan).
Fernando, Mervyn
1972   "Self, Reality and Salvation in Christianity and Buddhism," International
        Philosophical Quarterly, Vol. 12, pp. 415-25.
1979   "The Buddhist Challenge to Christianity," in Christianity and Buddhism, pp. 88-96.
Fox, D. A.
1975   Buddhism, Christianity and the Future of Man (Philadelphia: Westminster).
Franck, Frederick
1974   Pilgrimage to Now/here (Maryknoll: Orbis).
Gardini, Walter
1976   "Critical Points of the Buddhist-Christian Dialogue," Japanese Religions, Vol. 9,
        July, pp. 33-47
Gilkey, Langdon
1978   "The Mystery of Being and Nonbeing: An Experimental Project," Journal of Relig-
        ion, Vol. 58, pp. 1-12.
Griffiths, Bede
1977   Return to the Center (Springfield, IL: Templegate).
Hossfeld, Paul
1974   "Jesus (der Christus) und Siddhartha Gautama (der Buddha)," Theologie und
        Glaube, Vol. 64, pp. 366-89.
Johnston, William
1970   The Still Point: Reflections on Zen and Christian Mysticism (New York: Harper &
        Row).
1971   Christian Zen (New York: Harper & Row).
1978   The Inner Eye of Love: Mysticism and Religion (New York: Harper & Row).
Kreeft, Peter
1971   "Zen Buddhism and Christianity: An Experiment in Comparative Religion," Jour-
        nal of Ecumenical Studies, Vol. 8, pp. 513-38.
Lassalle, H. M. Enomiya
1974   Zen Meditation for Christians (LaSalle, IL: Open Court).
MacCormick, Chalmers
1972   "The Zen Catholicism of Thomas Merton," Journal of Ecumenical Studies, Vol. 9,
        pp. 802-17.
Merton, Thomas
1968   Zen and the Birds of Appetite (New York: New Directions).
1975   The Asian Journal of Thomas Merton (New York: New Directions).
Panikkar, Raimundo
1971   "Nirvana and the Awareness of the Absolute," in The God Experience, J. P.
        Whelen, ed. (New York: Newman, pp. 81-99.
1978   "Sunyata and Pleroma: The Buddhist and Christian Response to the Human Predi-
        cament," in The Intra-Religious Dialogue (New York: Paulist), pp. 77-100.
Robinson, John A. T.
1979   Truth Is Two-Eyed (London: SCM Press).
Rupp, George
1979   Beyond Existentialism and Zen: Religion in a Pluralistic World (New York: Oxford
        University Press).
Sangharakshita, Maha Sthavira
1979   "Dialogue between Buddhism and Christianity," in Christianity and Buddhism, pp.
        55-63.
deSilva, Lynn A.
1978   The Problem of the Self in Buddhism and Christianity (New York: Barnes &
        Noble/Harper).

Christianity and the Religions of the East

Spae, Joseph
1977   The Buddhist-Christian Encounter, *Pro Mundi Vita Bulletin, July-August, Vol. 67.*
1979   East Challenges West: Towards a Convergence of Spiritualities *(Chicago: Chicago Institute of Theology and Culture).*
Steindl-Rast, David
1972   "Christian Confrontation with Buddhism and Hinduism," Monastic Studies, Vol. 8, pp. 171-87.
Swearer, Donald K.
1977   Dialogue: The Key to Understanding Other Religions *(Philadelphia: Westminster).*
Vos, Frits
1979   "The Discovery of the Special Nature of Buddha: Sudden Enlightenment in Zen," in Christianity and Buddhism, *pp. 31-39.*
Waldenfels, Hans
1976   Absolutes nichts: Zur Grundlegung des Dialogs zwischen Buddhism und Christentum *(Basel-Freiburg: Herder).*
Williams, Jay G.
1978   Yeshua Buddha: An Interpretation of New Testament Theology as a Meaninfgul Myth *(Wheaton, IL: Theosophical Publishing House).*

Footnotes

/1/   *John Cobb, from his process perspective, diverges somewhat from the general direction of Christian interpretations of* Sunyata. *Comparing it with God, he speaks about "two absolutes" which complement each other.* Sunyata *expresses our essential interrelatedness, our unity in dependent co-origination (analogous to Whitehead's understanding of "creativity"), while God is the guiding "principle of rightness" which "participates in every instance of dependent co-origination" (11-12).*

/2/   *Again, Callaway strongly disagrees with this consensus; he is certain that Zen is nothing but "idealistic Monism" (see 162-65; 232-33). In all the other areas of "converging insights" which are still to be considered in this study, Callaway stands in stark disagreement.*

/3/   *For a further unveiling of the dualism that hides behind the eschatology of theologians of hope like Moltmann and Pannenberg, see:* Langdon Gilkey, Reaping the Whirlwind *(New York: Seabury, 1976), pp. 226-38; Jose Miguez Bonino,* Doing Theology in a Revolutionary Situation *(Philadelphia: Fortress, 1975), pp. 138-50.*

/4/   *Christ in a Pluralistic Age (Philadelphia: Westminster, 1975), pp. 220, 212.*

/5/   *Jay Williams in his Yeshua Buddha stands as somewhat of an exception to this statement. His book presents a thoroughgoing retelling of Jesus' message from the perspective of Mahayana Buddhism.*

/6/   *While Aldwinckle admits clear similarities in the missions of Jesus and Buddha as well as in the manner in which they were interpreted and "divinized" after their deaths (see 211-26), he holds to a definite opposition between their messages. Following the more traditional Christian interpretation of Buddhism, he argues that Buddha's Gospel contradicts that of Jesus in three key areas: Buddha could admit of no personal Transcendent, he denied the reality of the self, he preached an essentially other-worldly doctrine (227-35).*

/7/   "Jesus-Buddha-Krishna: Still Present?" Journal of Ecumenical Studies 16 (1979), 665-68.

/8/   *For further indications that New Testament language about Christ does not require an exclusivistic understanding of his uniqueness, see* P. Knitter, "World Religions and the Finality of Christ: A Critique of Hans Kung's On Being a Christian," Horizons 5 (1978), 153-56 *and* Interreligious Dialogue: Facing the Next Frontier *(Scranton: Ridge Row Press, 1981) pp. 202-221.*

/9/   *I have tried to show how such an understanding of Jesus' uniqueness can ground a unitive pluralism of religious experience in "Christianity as Religion: A Roman Catholic Perspective," in* What is Religion? An Enquiry for Christian Theology *(Concilium, vol. 136), ed. David Tracy and Mircea Eliade (New York: Seabury, 1980, pp. 16-19.*

CHAPTER TEN

Wisdom and Love as the Basis for Preaching in Buddhism and Christianity
An Essay in Comparative Homiletics

BY PAUL MARTINSON

P erhaps no pair of concepts is more central to Mahayana Buddhism than *prajna* (wisdom) and *karuna* (compassion). They constitute the twin experiences of the bhodisattva — that enlightened being who in compassion disdains the final realization of *nirvana* so as to return to the sentient world, bringing it relief and salvation. Whether in Tibetan tantra or in Chinese and Japanese Pure Land and Zen, this inner religious structure, of attainment of wisdom and compassionate return, is central. Preaching is one mode through which compassionate return is given expression.

One might not be inclined to think of *sophia* (wisdom) and *agape* (love) as a similarly central pair for Christianity. *Agape* to be sure deserves central status, but *sophia*? If, however, one turns to a principal New Testament text on preaching, I Corinthians 1 and 2, we may not be so quick to make the disclaimer. In this text the wisdom of God which was expressed in the

Dr. Paul Varo Martinson is Associate Professor of Theology of Religion at Luther Theological Seminary in St. Paul Minnesota. Born in China Dr. Martinson has long specialized in Chinese Studies with many scholarships and fellowships in the field. He also has many publications on China and Christianity. Most recently he spent a sabbatical in the Far East. Two of his most recent essays are "Humanism Revisionism; Translation and Comment on People's Daily Essay," in Ching Feng for Nov. 2, 1980 and "Confucius Lives; A Theological Critique of the Current Chinese Reappraisal of the Confucian Tradition," also in Ching Feng, 1982. This present essay is taken from Dialog, Vol. 19, 1978, pp. 174, 180 and is reprinted by permission of the publisher.

outpouring of love in the cross, links wisdom, love and preaching into an indissoluble unity. Furthermore, Christian thinking, which turned to *agape* as a central category for understanding the *work* of Christ; turned to the *sophia* or wisdom texts of the Hebrew writings as a central resource for understanding the *person* of Christ. Thus, though the paired-use of *wisdom-love* is not a common Christian formula as is the *prajna-karuna* formula in Buddhism, yet the basic conceptuality that requires both is present. And it is the *agape* cross-event wrought by God's wisdom that constitutes the core of Christian, or at least Pauline and Johannine, preaching.

Wisdom

It is not by chance that both *prajna* and *sophia* are opposed to conventional notions of wisdom. For Paul, conventional wisdom was epitomized by Greek philosophy. For our purposes we might say that it was wisdom that at the simplest level argued from appearance to reality (the sun goes around the earth, good people ought to be rewarded); at a higher level argued from rational categories to reality (causality-implies first cause), or dealt with reality speculatively (matter is the distant end product of an emanation from God and inherently evil); and at the instrumental level confidently indulged in rhetoric and its tricks. In contrast to all this is the wisdom of God articulated in the cross. Appearance proves misleading: the good don't get rewarded, the remote first cause is somewhat mixed up in contingency by being bound up with suffering inflicted by men and women, the cross strangely invests matter with value rather than being a demonstration of its inferior value, and rhetorical tricks only serve to confuse the lean and clear lines of a story that packs its own power. In short, divine wisdom confounds the accepted arrangements of world and reality inherent in conventional wisdom.

For the Buddhist, conventional wisdom is that wisdom whereby we conduct our normal lives. We eat because we are hungry, we build houses to protect our bodies, we work to earn a livelihood, we laugh because we are happy, we fight because we are greedy — and so on. Conventional wisdom takes life, so to say, for real. But again appearances are misleading. The more we live by the rule that what I want is a real want, the more we enter into a world of delusion. Is the ''I'' that wants really worth providing for? Is it (the subject) in fact real? Is that which is wanted worth striving for? Is it (the object) in fact an available entity? Conventional wisdom simply assumes that wants are genuine wants, and that the sought after satisfactions are real satisfactions. It lives with a discriminating conceptuality that yields an impossible and undesirable subject-object world — I am the subject, everything else is the object. And so, with everybody thinking the same, we have striving, contention and strife.

Prajna is wisdom of an utterly different kind. It is, first of all, an analytic wisdom. Under its powerful rays the very world that appears before our eyes dissolves. We take life from cradle to grave as a single continuum. What is born at the beginning dies at the end. But what makes us so sure? Aren't all the cells of my body changed many times over throughout life? Isn't everything we know of in constant process? Where then lies the unchanging? In fact, existence, according to *prajna*, is simply an endless sequence of momentary instants or configurations — it is, so to say, cinematic in character. What looks like a continuous movement is merely a projection, illusory and with no substance.

One may also analyze spatially. You look out the window and see a tree — or at least you think such is the case. But then a high school student takes a twig, cuts off a section, and peers at it through a microscope. The reality changes as one beholds it at the cellular level. Then some scientist analyzes the same bit at the molecular level, and what appears solid turns mostly into space. At the atomic level things become even less substantial, and more distressingly so at the sub-atomic level — and so on ad infinitum. Where then exists that tree? It is an appearance, no more, no less.

Such analytic procedures that preface *prajna* — true insight — are somewhat disconcerting to conventional wisdom. But *prajna* is insistent. It is the false notion of a self-that-subsists-in-itself together with an equally false notion of objects-that-have-their-own-subsistence that lies at the root of the human problem. Much better to realize the false assumptions of such thinking. Then one sees the obverse, synthetic side, that the self is contingent to everything else. In consequence, everything, including the insubstantial, contingent self, is co-incidental. Totality and individuality are not to be distinguished. Individuality is known only in the totality, yet this totality itself is devoid of independent subsistence, being empty. The moment one discriminates, notions of subject-object come into play and we are back again in the old game of wanting, seeking and thinking we find.

Thus both Pauline *sophia* and Buddhist *prajna* are impressive negations of the final validity of conventional wisdom. But they are so in different ways. Under the laser beam of Buddhist *prajna*, even the divine *sophia* of Paul dissolves. There is no sub-sisting God, much less a cross and one crucified. These too are mere appearances, arisings and passings away. To the Buddhist Paul is still woefully conventional. Inversely, Buddhist *prajna* becomes for a Pauline view merely one more mode of speculative wisdom. It is nothing more than a particularly sophisticated epistemological maneuver to avoid guilty accountability and to claim the identity of my own reality — or unreality as the case may be — with absolute reality. For the Buddhist the *mode of consciousness* (a right *knowing*) is the supreme concern; for Paul it is the *mode of conscience* (or *knowing of right*). The wisdoms are of two kinds.

113

Christianity and the Religions of the East

Love

We must now look at love in each case. Buddhist love *(karuna)* is related to wisdom *(prajna)* in a provisional or instrumental way. The secondary character of *karuna* is clear from this striking and characteristic passage taken from the *Diamond Sutra* (a highly condensed version of the vast *prajna* scriptures):

> "The Lord (i.e., Buddha) said....a bodhisattva should produce a thought in this manner: 'as many beings as there are in the universe — all these I must lead to Nirvana —. And yet, although innumerable beings have thus been led to Nirvana, no being at all has been led to Nirvana.' ..."

The text then goes on to explain that the notion of "being" itself is false and that the one who holds it has not yet been enlightened. This obviously puts the bodhisattva, who has vowed to save all beings, in a terrible predicament. Compassion indeed motivates the bodhisattva. Yet this *karuna* that motivates requires the belief that there are beings that need saving, while *prajna* which is its basis says that the very notion of beings-to-be-saved and a being-that-saves is false. Love and wisdom seem to be at absolute loggerheads.

The only thing that saves the situation is the real subordination of love to wisdom. Actually, compassion and wisdom are the same reality. The only difference is in perception. Wisdom as passive knowing has awakened to the true nature of reality. Since in this knowing no distinction is made between subject and object, in its activity it also acts without regard to such distinctions. To the unenlightened this appears as altruistic action, compassion, concern for the other, whereas in fact there is no concern since there is no other that concerns one. What in its interiority is really *prajna*, to unenlightened beings appears in its externality as compassion. There is thus no real conflict, the problem is merely perspectival.

Another way to say essentially the same thing is to say that the enlightened bodhisattva turns in compassion to the world as *if* it were real and needed salvation. Having saved this world it is then revealed that there was really nothing to save. The *as if* finally dissolves into the absolute *as is (tathagata)*. *Karuna,* having served as means to salvation, ceases to be.

Wisdom and love in the Christian setting have a quite different relation. While in Buddhism wisdom is constitutive of ultimate reality, for the Christian it is love. Love constitutes what wisdom is. There are numerous Pauline passages, for instance, that express this. In Romans 11 Paul, after concluding on the note of divine mercy, bursts into a doxology in vs. 33 on the depths of divine wisdom. In Eph. 3:19 we read of "knowing the love [ἀγάπην] of Christ, which is beyond all knowledge [τῆϛ γνώσεωϛ]." More striking, we read in I Cor. 13 that whereas knowledge of the conventional and limited kind will pass away, a true and full knowing (ἐπιγνώσομαι) which finds its perfection in love (ἀγάπη) will constitute the experience of the eschaton.

It becomes apparent then that the internal structures of *prajna* and *agape* are strikingly different. Buddhist *prajna* entails a peculiar asymmetry. In itself, *prajna* is enlightened *as-is-ness;* but faced towards the conventional world *prajna* transforms into the *as-if-ness* of *karuna.* Clearly one is to leave the latter in the finding of the former, though the latter was instrumental in making that finding possible. *Agape* does not possess such an asymmetry. Love constitutes God's wisdom. He is wise because he is love; not vice-versa, for "God is love." But not only does love constitute absolute reality, it also constitutes the divine will for conventional human reality in this world. As scripture avers, love sums up the whole of the commandments. *Agape* is thus proper for both absolute and relative experience.

It is probably this interior asymmetry of *prajna* that accounts for the importance of the *prajna-karuna* formula in Buddhism. Were *prajna* alone affirmed, Buddhism would lose all contact with conventional reality in an unmitigated transcendence. *Karuna,* provisional and subordinate though it be, saves Buddhism from this. In this *as-if-ness* absolute and relative are conjoined, even identified *(nirvana* is *samsara, samsara* is *nirvana),* but in such a way that *prajna* is the finally norming category. On the other hand, within Christianity love is proper to both God and world. Therefore there is no need for a wisdom-love formula to hold absolute and relative together. The linkage is achieved in the relative by the absolute via incarnation: the *as-if* (supposition) syntax of the *prajna-karuna* formula is replaced by a *so that* (result) syntax of the incarnational formula of Christian confession.

The two wisdom-love formulae inwardly impell Buddhist and Christian to missionary, that is, preaching activity. We will want to see in what sense this is so, and to what preaching it leads.

Preaching

Preaching occupies a central place in the religious activity of both Buddhism and Christianity. The Buddha's first public act after Enlightenment was to preach. Pious iconography depicts this preaching event as the 3rd Great Miracle, the first being Birth, the second Enlightenment and the fourth Decease. The Enlightened One, the Buddha, sets in motion the wheel of *Dharma* (teaching, law, truth, gospel) with his first sermon, displaying thereby his spiritual sovereignty. He chose as his first audience five former disciples who had deserted him at the critical juncture before his enlightenment. They were converted. Henceforth the Buddha spent some 40 odd years in itinerant preaching, dying (according to tradition) at 80 on his final preaching mission.

In the centuries following his death a vast corpus of literature developed, much of it drawn into the extended Buddhist canon that dwarfs our Christian scriptures many times over. A principal class of texts is the *sutras* (cf. English sutra, thread), the others, in the Pali canon, being *vinaya* or regulations for the religious life, and *abhidharma* or scholastic elaborations of the basic teachings. The countless extant *sutras* purport to be the sermons, preachments or discourses of the Buddhas. Their characteristic form is to locate the Buddha at some important preaching site of his earthly career, surround him with a numberless audience of monks, nuns, male and female lay devotees, and indeed all beings in the cosmos, place him in the pose of meditative insight, present him with a request from the audience that he proclaim the truth of liberation, and elaborate his response in a discourse, which may or may not allow for further interchange with the audience.

The formalized body of canonical literature was thus a vast corpus of stylized sermonic discourses. No doubt the literature had some close relations to the early Buddhist practice of preaching. Preaching monks were important instruments in the dispersion of Buddhism throughout the Asian world. According to tradition, which has some basis in fact, there was an explosion of missionary activity reaching out in the four directions during the pious reign of Asoka (ca 274-232 BC, the Buddhist Constantine), and as a product of the third Great Council which he summoned. Be that as it may, the religion was in fact widely preached.

Over time the form of this preaching has continually changed, with a progressive loss in its missionary function — a function that seems to be coming back with the propagation of Buddhist faith and practice to the West. Pure Land, Zen and Tantra all retain important preaching forms. Not long ago I sat with my class of 13 seminarians in lotus, or semi-lotus position (some of us couldn't even manage that for long) in the meditation hall of the recently established Minnesota Zen Meditation Center, overlooking Lake Calhoun. For an hour and a half Katagiri-roshii, in full-lotus position, discoursed to us in a style that I could only call sermonic, quietly articulating the basic faith claims of Buddhism, and applying these assertions to our daily lives. Significantly, his sermon was in form and essentials a precise contemporary rendition of that original sermon whereby the Buddha first turned the wheel of Dharma long ago.

We hardly need expatiate on the importance of preaching in the course of Christianity's historical development. From the itinerant preaching of Christ, through that of Paul and the early missionaries, up to our own day, there have been many transformations in function and form of this religious activity. Suffice it to say that historical-critical and related studies have shown to what degree the shaping of our own canon was an outgrowth of the preaching activity of the early church.

So as to understand the place of preaching in Buddhism and Christianity and to relate this to its basis in wisdom and love, let us take a sermonic story from each of the canons — for the Christians the parable of the so-called "Prodigal Son" — we could say the "Compassionate Father" — and for the Buddhists the so-called parable of the "Burning House" — also a form of the "Compassionate Father" motif. The first comes, of course, from Luke, the latter from the Lotus-sutra, the *Saddharma-pundarika*, probably the single most influential *sutra* of East Asia (Mahayana) Buddhism. We shall begin with the latter first.

Wisdom and Love in Buddhism and Christianity

Story I — The "Burning House"

An elderly gentleman of some wealth possessed a house which, though spacious, was in an extreme state of disrepair. It had only one entrance. One day he returned home to find it engulfed in flames. Distraught, for his house was full of children, he cast about for a way of deliverance. The boys, it seems, had no inkling of the fire, much less fear of it, playing their happy games within. To rush in and rescue by brute force might lead to more chaos than help. The old man's attempts to reason with the boys fail. In desperation he attempts a deception. He announces that he has ready for them a rich assortment of carts and toys of all kinds for them to claim. No sooner is he finished then all rush out to lay claim to their choicest items. Contrary to what they expect, they eventually receive only one kind of gift — but it is the best of all — each an expensive bullock-cart. The parable then ends with this question: "Now, Sariputra, what is thy opinion? Has that man made himself guilty of falsehood by first holding out to his children the prospect of three [or a variety of] vehicles and afterwards giving to each of them the greatest vehicles only, the most magnificent vehicles?" The point of the story then becomes clear in Sariputra's response: "By no means, ... since it was a skillful device to persuade his children to go out of the burning house .... If that man, O Lord, had given no single cart, even then he would not have been a speaker of falsehood."

The story is rich with symbolism, most of which passes by our dull ears unnoticed. The burning house symbolizes *samsara* or worldly existence, insensitivity to pain symbolizes ignorance *(avidya),* the father of course represents the Buddha, the 3 vehicles the various paths, the one vehicle being the supreme pathway of the bodhisattva, and so on. For our purposes, however, only two things need be said. First, this parable is spoken from the viewpoint of enlightenment. Only after the Buddha has passed through the many stages of meditative consciousness does he address the audience. Second, the concept of *upaya,* accommodation or skillful means, of which deception is one case, is absolutely central to the Buddhist activity of preaching.

The point of the story is hardly the trivial notion that the end justifies the means — that falsehood is just fine so long as you do it for good ends. A much stronger claim is made, that "deception" is integral to the task of preaching and compassionate liberation. Inherent in the human situation is false consciousness. An appeal to human-kind can only be made in terms comprehensible to it. The *upaya* doctrine is a potentially radical doctrine of accommodation. In this case the father ostensibly appeals to greed so as to lead to a greater deliverance.

But this is only a special example of the entire meaning of the Buddha's existence. In this same *sutra* it is made clear that the Buddha's life and death were only a subterfuge, a pretense. In fact, the Buddha had attained deliverance aeons ago, he was nothing less than the eternal unconditional liberated

117

consciousness in its absolute character. The historical Buddha merely appeared on earth to accommodate to our state of ignorance, preaching and teaching to lure us on from ignorance to knowledge.

This doctrine of *upaya,* skillful means, is obviously predicated upon the *prajna-karuna* formula. This gives to Buddhist preaching and teaching its peculiar form of the mystical hermeneutic of the double truth. There is conventional wisdom and true insight. Though the former is indeed false and illusory, the Buddha acts *as if* it is true, appealing to unenlightened beings by using every device of rhetoric and persuasion possible. Though there is no independently existing subject or object in reality, yet the Buddha makes his appeal as if this were so. To those on the conventional level he first teaches conventional moral values, attracting by the preaching of gods and heavens, and terrifying by the preaching of hell and suffering. To others who are ready he preaches the doctrine of the non-existence of a self-subsisting self so as to lead to higher realization. Finally, to the well-prepared, he gives the full-teaching not only of the non-existence of the self and the other, but the final identify of absolute (truth) and relative (illusion). What at one level is proclaimed as true, at a higher level is negated, and so the process of "subrating" continues till right consciousness replaces false.

It is probably not necessary to show how consistent this view of the function of preaching is with the twin doctrines of *prajna-karuna* discussed above. Preaching consists in words spoken from enlightenment *(prajna)* as a compassionate and accommodating means to lead from ignorance to insight *(karuna)*. In the context of the double truth hermeneutic (or the principle of subration) it is not an overstatement to say that compassion requires a holy falsehood to be effective towards deliverance of humanity from ignorance.

Story II — The "Prodigal Son"

Since we are on more familiar ground when we turn to Christian preaching — though the complexities are certainly just as great — we can spend less time. The story that concerns us is the prodigal son. This son takes his inheritance prematurely, runs off and has a gay and frivolous time with it, winding up in a pig pen. Here he "comes to himself," resolves to return home and seek servitude, but upon return is embraced by a father mad with delight, and reinstated with honor amidst great celebration. The incongruity of treating a worthless son as though he were a returning hero doesn't even cross the father's mind. It does, however, that of his elder son. That son's resentment is met by the charmingly naive excuse of the father that "this my son was dead, but now he is alive."

Here we once again have a compassionate father. And, once again, we have a story of inexhaustible symbolic meaning. But as before only a point or two need be made for our present purposes. First, the historical context for this parable is crucial to its understanding. There is, we might say, a battle of conscience between Jesus and his opponents. His opponents pass unfavorable judgment upon certain classes of society — sinners they are called. It is not the unfavorable judgment as such that is at issue but the self-exoneration that it implies — they who make the judgment imagine themselves to be the righteous. It is to such a situation that the parable is addressed. Second, the parable is double-edged. It both justifies and condemns. While the prodigal pronounces self-judgment, the father forgives. While the dutiful son protests indiscretion, the father reminds. In the end the act of the father discloses both the liberating truth discovered by the prodigal and the constricting pretence and saves. The hermeneutic at work here is perhaps best stated as that of Law and Gospel.

If these two parables are at all indicative, and we will assume that they are, Buddhist and Christian preaching enter into the human reality at rather different points: Buddhist preaching cleaves consciousness, Christian preaching cleaves conscience; one arouses primarily a new psychic awareness of absolute reality the other moral awareness of absolute import. The respective hermeneutic dualities — double truth, law-gospel — are appropriate to the carrying out of these tasks.

Cleaving Consciousness

Are these two preachments antithetical? Let us consider further the Buddhist entree into consciousness. Sitting at the feet of lotus-seated Katagiri-roshii we were quietly invited to consider the matter of cancer. Supposing one should be afflicted with this disease. It is indeed suffering! Yet in this cancerous suffering one experiences the truth profoundly, directly! How so? All existence is conditioned — what more profound and intense realization of this than through cancer? In accepting suffering and the truth of conditionedness that it teaches, one has the opportunity to awaken to unconditioned consciousness which perceives suffering from a different perspective — not as an ''I'' that suffers this disease'' (false consciousness which discriminates subject and object) but as an individualized moment that poignantly concentrates the truth of the conditionedness and suffering of all moments, and therefore precludes an attitude of grasping for or of seeking to possess, and resists attachment to any moment (enlightened consciousness which does not discriminate). Wisdom which knows the true nature of all existence thus compassionates without attachment amidst all existence. To arise and to pass away is the course of reality. The one who clings to the arising clings to a false reality. The Buddhist proclamation would cleave one from such a consciousness.

At certain points this Buddhist entree hits home with the Christian as well. Where, however, the Buddhist will speak of wisdom, the Christian will speak of faith. Faith too implies a stance towards consciousness. Faith, as wisdom, is a non-ego consciousness. Faith, as wisdom, is a radical acceptance of finitude, of conditioned existence. In this courageous acceptance of finitude, without egotistic resentment, faith and wisdom coincide. The nihilism Christians often object to in Buddhism turns out to be a conviction that faith too ought to share.

But the conviction is shared differently. Buddhism has a doctrine of finitude, but it lacks a doctrine of creation. Faith has both. In Buddhism existence is analyzed into its constituents and dissolved in this acid. The more composite an existent, the more illusory its claim to reality. The Christian will gladly accept the analysis into constituents, even should this analysis have to be *ad – infinitum* – after all creation is *ex nihilo,* having no sub-sistence save in God! But the Christian will not recognize the Buddhist interpretation as possessing any prior hold on truth. Greater compositness does not necessarily mean greater irreality.

A linguistic analogy might help. Speech enables communication and the sharing of meaning. But speech means sentences, sentences phrases, phrases words, words syllables, syllables phonemes, phonemes phonetics and so on down the line. What is striking here is that, in certain ways at least, greater reality attaches to the more composite level, not the less composite. At the level of meaning, a sentence that communicates a message has a higher claim to value than a mere noise from the throat or a detached phonetic symbol. To be sure there is a limit to this value — it is relative. But to limit is to qualify, and to qualify is to value. Finitude is not irreality but limited value, that is, creation.

The absolute and relative need not be seen with the Buddhist as either contraries or identities, or both, or neither — all of which ontologically amounts to the same thing. It might just as well be that they are co-relative in a distinguishable way — the one (relative) conditioned, the other (absolute) self-conditioned. And it may well be that just at that locus where this dual-conditioning (of uncreated and created) meets is to be found true realization and final meaning.

Cleaving Conscience

Christian preaching cleaves conscience. What Buddhism, side-stepping a doctrine of creation, calls false ego-consciousness, Christian faith radicalizes by re-defining as false ego-conscience. False ego-conscience is the pretense of conditioned individual will, willing to be against or in place of, rather than responsive to, self-conditioned absolute will. It is a guilty *as if* presuming to be the *as is.* And it is here we are returned to the Biblical parable. The prodigal son chose independence, demanding his portion of the inheritance. He would squander it as he chose without reference to its source. His coming to his senses was a sudden awakening to a new consciousness of the relative and interdependent character of existence — "my father's paid servants have food. . ." — being an observation on the cohesiveness of the mundane, work-a-day world we properly belong to — and coincidentally an awakening to a new conscience about the meaning of

these relations — ''I will ... go to my father and say ... I have sinned ...''
Creational consciousness and moral awakening are here simultaneous.

The ''dutiful son'' while superficially accepting the creational relations of
interdependence — he has remained at home, worked in the fields, and dined
regularly with father and friends — by his attitude of moral superiority
excepts himself from relationship to his brother and denies the very claims
that relationship places upon him. False conscience and false consciousness
about creational relations are also co-incident.

If the father in the parable is in any sense symbolic of divine reality, then
he must be a symbol in the first instance of the self-conditioned, and indeed
he is. His love drives him to anguished longing for his lost son. He could
have chosen to dismiss him as a good-for-nothing. But the idea of disinheri-
tance doesn't occur. Instead, he has given the son the inheritance prematurely, together with his freedom, and thereby makes himself vulnerable to
loss. By sharing and giving, even prematurely, the father clearly makes a
statement which says that relationship is only fully possible where there is
freedom without coercion. Playing loose with social precedents (he has been
called an unduly indulgent father) is not to deny creational relationships but
to affirm the radical personal depths which alone make such relationships
genuine. Giving the inheritance thus restates the meaning of creation. And
this creational consciousness is coupled with the self-risking ''conscience''
of love.

This father symbolizes the self-conditioned giving of the Creator. It is
only a small step further from the pain of the Father who gives, to the pain of
the Son — the truly dutiful one — who is given. And here, at incarnation and
cross, the dual conditionings meet in absolutely good conscience.

Our comments must draw to a close, though this study in a comparative
homiletics has hardly begun. Preaching as a mode of religious activity has
been of decisive importance for the self-understanding and world effectiveness of both Buddhism and Christianity. The preachings have now circled
the globe, and not only *do* we, we *must,* speak to one another. Can we hear
our separate preachings? Do we understand one another's speech? Should
we? Will our preachings convince? Does yours? On what basis? Buddhism
has a bias towards transcending wisdom; Christian faith towards incarnating
love. Which better defines which? Which defining is more true to that reality
being defined, and perhaps at the same time confessed? Will our preachings
tell? Ought they? How?

CHAPTER ELEVEN

Christian Theology in an Asian Setting: The Gospel and Chinese Intellectual Culture

BY DOUGLAS J. ELWOOD

I n spite of past failures to effectively communicate the Christian faith in diverse cultural situations, Christian theology is properly "contextual" in character. All Christians everywhere are responsible to reflect upon their faith in awareness of the creative tension between the "content" of the Gospel and the "context" in which the Christian community exists. This is what the church has always meant by *theologia in loco*. The Christian Conference of Asia (EACC) calls it "living theology," defined as "the manner in which a Church confesses its faith and establishes its historical existence in dialogue with its own environment."/1/ Dr. Shoki Coe of Taiwan, Executive Director of the Theological Education Fund, has expressed the contextual nature of theology and theological education in the meaningful slogan, "Faithful to the text, relevant to the context." The "text" here refers to the Christ-Event and to the content of the biblical message as received. The "context" refers not only to the Christian community in which the individual Christian stands, but also to the local folk

---

Douglas J. Elwood, an American educated in Scotland, has taught Christianity in the Philippines and Taiwan, Parts of this essay were read at a student seminar, other parts at a faculty forum, Tainan Theological College, Taiwan, where the author was a Professor of Theology (1972-75). For further background on this topic, the author refers to the Louvain and Bastad studies: "Theological Implications of the New China," *and* "Christian Faith and the Chinese Experience." *(Geneva and Brussels: LWF/PMV, 1974.) This essay is from the* South East Asian Journal of Theology: *Vol. 16, n. 1975, and is reprinted by permission of the publisher.*

traditions, the classical culture, the impact of modern secular culture, and the socio-political environment with which the Christian community must be in constant dialogue. Since there are many contexts to which one must relate, an ''inter-contextual'' method is required./2/

Re-Contextualizing the Text

''Context'' is one of the important words that seems to reflect the spirit of our time, according to James Burtness. Specialists in the field of education, for instance, now speak of ''contextual education.'' An emphasis on context insists that there is no such thing as a naked text; it is always clothed with something (from the Latin *contextus* meaning ''that which is woven together''). Thus we may speak of our own sociocultural, religious, political, and economic environment seen as a whole./3/ What my Homiletics professor at Princeton Seminary used to say is as true in Systematics as it is in Homiletics: ''A text without a context is a pretext.'' The point is that no text can be taken hold of — whether it be a sentence or a number, a person or an event — until it is ''related'' to something. And since the meaning of the text will always be relative to the context in which we choose to set it, the choice of context will always be an extremely important one./4/ Since the Gospel was first received in a cultural and historical context, adds Burtness, our task becomes one of ''re-contextualizing'' the biblical text. In the past, unfortunately, the Christian faith has too often been handled non-contextually, ''dogmatically.''

It is now fairly well known that the Third Mandate of the Theological Education Fund encourages a program of ''contextualization,'' which has special relevance for the Christian faith in Asia. The concept is defined by the TEF Committee as ''the capacity to respond meaningfully to the Gospel within the framework of one's own situation,'' and this capacity is regarded as ''a chief characteristic of authentic theological reflection.'' Not just a catchword, it is ''a theological necessity demanded by the incarnational nature of the Word.'' The concept implies all that is implied in the more traditional term ''indigenization,'' but seeks at the same time to press beyond it. Here is the basic difference:

> Indigenization tends to be used in the sense of responding to the Gospel in terms of a traditional culture. Contextualization, while not ignoring this, takes into account the processes of secularity, technology, and struggle for human justice, which characterize the historical moment of nations in the Third World./5/

The TEF Statement is careful to distinguish ''authentic'' and ''false'' forms of contextuality. The false kind leads to uncritical accommodation and yields only another form of ''culture-faith.'' ''Authentic contextualization is always prophetic, arising out of genuine encounter between God's Word and His world, and moves toward the purpose of *challenging and changing* the situation through rootedness in and commitment to a given historical moment." Though it stresses local and situational concerns, it "draws its basic power from the Gospel which is for all people."/6/

To take Taiwan today as a case in point, one would have to consider both the narrower and the wider context — the narrower one of Formosa with its independent history and culture; the wider context of Taiwan in relation to the larger Chinese population of Asia, and as belonging to the still larger Third World of developing nations. Similarly, the Christians of Taiwan must see themselves not only as a local community but also as a part of the Chinese Christian community in Asia, and in the widest sense as a part of the ecumenical Christian movement./7/ Theological reflection of Christians in Taiwan, therefore, should be done in the context of all these concentric relationships. As already implied, above, there are at least four layers of culture that must be considered in any encounter of the Gospel with Asian cultures today: (1) The classical culture; (2) the local, folk tradition; (3) the growing technological culture; and (4) the culture that is emerging as a result of the tension between the old and the new.

In addition, there are two processes of contextualization. One is the spontaneous expression of Christian experience through the life-style and folk-ways of the people who are committed to the Christian faith. Actually, this process goes on unconsciously in any situation where a host-culture welcomes an alien religion. The results may be favorable or unfavorable. Presumably this is the way in which Mahayana Buddhism was assimilated so completely by the Chinese. The other process of contextualization is a more intellectual one — the task of conscious reinterpretation on the basis of certain guiding principles. Ideally there should be dynamic interaction between the uncritical expression of Christianity by the worshiping, witnessing community, and the critical process of reinterpretation by its Christian scholars. Since it is difficult to deal with the whole context at once, this paper is limited to a discussion of aspects of the more neglected task of intellectual contextuality.

Ethical Principles

There are three interrelated principles which can be helpful in guiding the encounter of the Gospel with people in Asian cultures. These were neatly formulated by the directors of Christian Study Centers in Asia at their meeting in Kyoto, in 1971. One is the principle of "dynamic accommodation," which involves an understanding and appreciation of values and structures which enable the Christian to live as an accepted member of society. The second principle is "critical confrontation," which implies that the Gospel brings certain aspects of the culture under judgment as alien or opposed in spirit to the demands of the Gospel. The third is "positive transformation," which implies that negative aspects of the culture are to be creatively transformed, if possible, in a manner which will express Christian faith and support the Christian life in new patterns./8/

More recently, the Southeast Asia Graduate School of Theology has proposed what is called the "Critical Asian Principle" which, according to Dean Emerito Nacpil, is designed to operate at various methodological levels: (1) "It is a way of saying where our area of responsibility and concern is, namely the varieties and dynamics of Asian realities. We are committed to understand this context both sympathetically and critically." (2) "It is a way of saying that we will approach and interpret the Gospel in relation to the needs and issues peculiar to the Asian situation. It functions therefore partly as a hermeneutical principle." (3) Thirdly, "it is a way of saying that a theology worth its salt at this time in Asia must be capable not only of illuminating Asian realities with the light of the Gospel, but also of helping to manage and direct the changes now taking place along lines more consonant with the Gospel and its vision for human life."/9/

Theological Freedom

Any statement of the faith, to be intelligible to the people, has to make use of the thought-forms and concepts of the culture and society within which it is being undertaken. This almost goes without saying. Christianity began in a Hebrew cultural environment, with a Hebrew or Aramaic vocabulary, and the Gospel's first great encounter was with Judaism. When the first Christians began to proclaim the Gospel to peoples of Greek cultural background, they had to use a different vocabulary. Gradually the language of Christian theology changed, incorporating many Greek terms and ideas such as *logos* and "substance," alongside the Jewish ones already in use. It is quite natural to expect, therefore, that a similar pattern will follow as the Gospel confront more directly the thought-forms and life-ways of particular Asian cultures.

There is such a thing as "theological freedom," says theologian John Macquarrie, which is "the right, within limits, to stress viewpoints and use methods which, in the situation, seem to need stressing."/10/ This would apply both to the cultural and the historical situation. This freedom must be used responsibly, of course, to avoid undue exaggeration, omission, or distortion of the Gospel. But this theological freedom allows Christians of Taiwan, for instance, to interpret the historic doctrines of the Christian faith in terms of their own cultural experience and historical situation. Indeed, it is an obligation of every Christian to give serious consideration to the viewpoints and methods which need stressing in his own context. Certainly this does not mean that we have to begin all over again to lay a new spiritual foundation, such as searching for a native Messiah or another Trinity of national heroes. We have to start, of course, with what is "given" and "received", including the Christian heritage of faith as it has come to us. A safe rule might be not to reject so much as to select from that heritage as we have received it in alien cultural forms.

Neither could we afford to be uncritical in the use of local "building materials" from the depository of traditional culture, but we should be deliberately selective there as well. The end result would be that we would not "sweep anything away," but instead "purify" it in the light of Christ — something like the familiar Asian rice-cleaning practice. Our task is not to destroy and replace but to renew and transform what is already given. Nor is it enough merely to construct a theology that is "acceptable" and popular with the general public. Ours would then be like the message of the "false prophets" of Old Testament times who were popular because they told people only what they wanted to hear!/11/ Doubtless a combination of accommodating processes is required, ranging from adaptation and assimilation to reinterpretation and reconception. This paper is only exploratory and does not attempt to suggest exactly what in the Christian faith could be adapted to Chinese thought, or how much of Chinese thought might be assimilated by the Christian understanding. These are tasks which must be done by Chinese Christians.

The Changeless and the Changing

M. M. Thomas, India's outstanding lay theologian, draws an important distinction between the "changeless" and the "changing" elements in Christian thought, based on the findings of the first Indian Theological Conference held in Poona, in 1942, where they spoke of the "Word of God" as "the absolute element — the central core" which must determine the shape of any expression which is to be recognizably Christian — and "the relative element" which is "the expression, interpretation, and application" necessary for presenting the Gospel to others./12/ The justification for changing what can be changed is stated forcefully by Shoki Coe when he says, "The Word of God did not come to us men as 'pure' Word in itself; it came as Incarnate Word in the humanity of Jesus of Nazareth at a particular time and in a particular place." We must therefore emphasize the Word that seeks to become incarnate through Christ's Spirit in our contemporary setting./13/

The late D. T. Niles, of Sri Lanka, once referred to Christianity in Asia today as a "potted plant" which has been transported to Asia without having been transplanted in Asian soil. Here is the full statement:

> The Gospel is a seed sown in the soil of culture. The plant bears the mark both of the seed and of the soil. There is one Gospel; there are many "Christianities." In Asian countries, Christianity is a potted plant which needs to be rooted in the cultural soil of the East./14/

This reminds us that the structures and forms in which the Christian message has come to us are not in themselves sacred; as St. Paul would say, they are only the "containers" in which the "treasure" is carried: "We have this treasure in clay pots, to show that the transcendent power belongs to God and not to us." (II Cor. 4:7) Part of our theological task is to replace the "clay pots" with more appropriate ones, so that the treasured message will speak to Asian Christians in terms of Asian cultural experiences. But we should be warned that it is not enough merely to adapt a Western theology to the Taiwan context, for instance. In the past this has been the Japanese pattern, adapting European theology to Japan and producing "Japanized Barthians" and "Japanized Bultmannians." Some of the younger Japanese are now rebelling against the "Germanic captivity" of Japanese theology./15/ What is called for is a more direct contact between the biblical faith and particular Asian cultures.

It is just as important, however, that a Chinese or Taiwanese Christian theology not be an exclusive or esoteric theology — "made in Taiwan for Taiwanese." It must be an ecumenically-oriented theology: the distinctive contribution of the Taiwan church to the theology of world Christianity. Some critics of the Bangkok Conference on "Salvation Today" felt that the report of Section I went too far. It was right in saying that "proper theology includes reflection on the experience of the Christian community in a particular place at a particular time. Thus it will necessarily be a contextual theology...." But the Report went on to say that a relevant and living theology is one that "refuses to be easily universalized because it speaks to and out of a particular situation." It appeared to some that the Report became one-sided at this point because, although it uses the qualifying adverb "easily," it tends to overlook the important truth that "there is a core of hard historic fact... which remains normative and which forbids us to make the 'context' *alone* decisive for our thinking and teaching."/16/ Here is caution against over-enthusiastic contextualizers.

Christianity — An Asian Faith

Sometimes we hear it said that in Asia Christianity is a foreign religion. But we should never forget that it came to birth on Asian soil, its Founder was an Asian, and the Bible is fundamentally an Asian book. One of the speakers at the Singapore Congress on Evangelism, in 1968, reminded the delegates that "the First Adam was an Asian and so was the Second." Furthermore, it was in Athens and Philippi — "Western" cities — where the Apostle Paul had to suffer for proclaiming a "foreign divinity" and for teaching an "Eastern" religion! Shoki Coe, speaking at a meeting of the Division of World Mission and Evangelism, WCC, in Mexico, in 1963, had this to say about the Bible: "Our depths are known to us in the Bible. This is an Asian book. Preserved and mediated to us by Europe and America, it must be reclaimed by Asians in their task of re-building. This Bible must speak to a new Asia through commentaries in Asian terms. Its riches must be mined by Asians for a word in season to neo-Confucianism and resurgent Buddhism." Christianity was originally an Eastern phenomenon, but the theological thought-forms in which it reached the East are not the thought-forms of Eastern peoples. This offers a challenge to the Asian Christian to rediscover Christ-as-an-Asian, the Bible as an Asian book, and Christianity as an Asian faith.

Toward an "Asian Theology"

It would be more accurate to speak of "Asian theologies" or of "Asian theological thinking," for Asia is not singular but plural! However, although there is a very wide cultural diversity in Asia, there is also now among many Asians a growing "Asian consciousness." Dr. Russell Chandran, Principal of United Theological College, Bangalore, speaks of a new sense of "Asian solidarity" based on the common experience of most Asians — those, at least, outside the Communist orbit. He mentions five factors that contribute to it: (1) Rival faiths claim the loyalty of great masses of people; (2) among Asian intellectuals there is a growing apathy toward traditional religions and a new confidence in science and technology for the improvement of man's lot; (3) most Asian countries share the common experience of having only recently emerged out of colonial domination; (4) great masses of people in most Asian societies are in the grip of poverty, hunger, disease, illiteracy, and allied social evils; and (5) in most Asian countries reactionary forces are still at work retarding the progress of human development./17/

Emerging at the same time is a "Third World-consciousness" among Asians who identify with other developing countries in Latin America and Africa. Some now, in fact, speak of a "Third World theology" by which they mean especially a Theology of Liberation or Human Development./18/ Such a theological approach is concerned with laying the foundations for a more just, free, and human society in the context of the liberating power of Christ. In one of his many editorials M. M. Thomas speaks of "Asian theology" as "a response to the challenge to make faith relevant to life in the midst of the Asian social revolution." "It is a small matter," he adds, "whether it gets systematized or remains unsystematic. The important thing is that it should emerge."/19/

The history of the Church in Asia, understandably, has been marked by theological dependency and hesitation. This was especially noticeable at the Bangkok Assembly of the Christian Conference of Asia (EACC), in 1950, where most of the Asian churchmen were suspicious of any attempts to express the Christian gospel in the thought-forms of the older Asian cultures. This came as a surprise to observers who remembered the ecumenical conference in Tambaram, India, twelve years earlier where it was frankly acknowledged that indigenization was an absolute necessity if the Christian gospel was to survive in Asia, in view of the resurgence of older Asian faiths. Very different from the Bangkok meeting, however, was the CCA Consultation at Kandy, Sri Lanka, in 1965 — fifteen years later — which marked the beginning of a new era of Asian leadership in the development of what they called "an authentic living theology." One of the Statements issued by that important meeting is titled "The Confessing Church in Asia and Its Theological Task." The document acknowledges that "the Asian Churches so far, and in large measure, have not taken their theological task seriously enough, for they have been largely content to accept the ready-made answers of Western theology or confessions.'' Part of the reason is a fundamental misunderstanding of what theology, in reality is:

> A living theology is born out of the meeting of a living Church and its world....Theology is a living thing, having to do with our existance as Christians and as Churches. A living theology must speak to the actual questions men in Asia are asking in the midst of their dilemmas; their hopes, aspirations and achievements; their doubts, despair and suffering... Christian theology will fulfill its task in Asia only as the Asian Churches, as servants of God's Word and revelation in Jesus Christ, speak to the Asian situation and from involvement in it./20/

The Apologetic Task of Theology in a Chinese Context

One of the problems with theology in a Chinese context is the historic lack of communication between Christian scholars and Chinese intellectuals. Philosopher Wing-tsit Chan cites this as a major reason ''few mature Chinese intellectuals have been converted to Christianity.'' So long as Christianity fails to come in contact with the Chinese intelligentsia, says Chan, ''it will have failed to reach the nerve center of the Chinese people.''/21/Confucian scholar Tsung-san Mou regards Chinese Christians as having ''abandoned their nationality,'' although he does not make the same judgment about Chinese Buddhists or Muslims! This means, in theological terms, that attention must be given to the neglected ''apologetic'' task of Christian theology, which seeks to relate faith to culture and to make the Faith intelligible to the non-Christian. In the spirit of the Kandy Consultation, the Christian message must be shown to give the answer to the actual questions Chinese are asking.

Thus far in the Chinese setting, where theology has been stressed at all, it has been an emphasis on the ''confessional'' task of theology, which addresses itself primarily to the believer and the Christian community. For this reason Karl Barth has been more attractive to Chinese Christians than, say, Bultmann, Tillich, or Moltmann. The confessional task of theology is an important one, to be sure, but with the onslaught of secularism a widening conversation is called for between Christian intellectuals and the representatives of the rich cultural heritage of China. This is precisely what the Church in China has failed to do in the past, according to Sverre Holth, and ''this is the reason Christian thinking has not captured the imagination of Chinese intellectuals or made much of an impact on the cultural life of the Chinese.''/22/ Christian philosopher C. M. Wei, in his book *The Spirit of Chinese Culture,* says that if Christianity is to attract the Chinese people, it must not only capture the hearts and wills of the people, but also their minds, esthetic sense, and imagination./23/

The Possibility of a "Confucian Christianity"

Most Chinese intellectuals repeatedly deny that Confucianism is a religion, insisting that it is an ethical value-system and, indeed, the cultural ethos of all Chinese. It may be appropriate, therefore, to speak of the possibility of a "Confucian Christianity," by which is meant the Christian message understood and expressed in terms of Confucian thought. This is not to assume that Confucianism is the only important philosophical influence in China, for Taoism and Buddhism have had even greater influence on Chinese art and literature. But Confucian thought is a more suitable point of contact for Christian theology because, like Aristotelian and Platonic thought when adopted by the Western Church, it is not committed to any particular organized religion. Although some contemporary Japanese Christian theologians are using Buddhist philosophy as a point of contact — notably Seiichi Yagi (c.f. Chapter 7) and Katsumi Takizawa—the problem is that Buddhist philosophy is committed already to the Buddhist religion. Taoist philosophy is also somewhat less suitable, because a popular Taoist cult developed in China alongside classical Taoist philosophy.

There is fairly wide agreement that Confucian thought has had the most enduring influence on the thought-patterns and life-ways of Chinese people everywhere. It is now recognized that this influence, too, is waning. Nevertheless, concludes Julia Ching writing in *International Philosophical Quarterly* on the subject, "Will Confucianism Survive?" it "will always be relevant" if by Confucianism we mean "a dynamic discovery of the worth of the human person, of the openness of the self to the transcendent, of man's fundamental relationship to others in a human society based on ethical values."/24/

C. M. Wei, in his book previously cited, seriously advocates the idea that Chinese can be regarded as somehow a *preparatio evangelica* in a way similar to the role of Hebrew culture in relation to the coming of Christianity. Fu-ya Hsieh, likewise, in his recent book, *Chi Tu Chiao yu Chung Kuo Shi Hsian* (Christianity and Chinese Thought), refers symbolically to classical Confucianism as "the Law and the Prophets" which Jesus said he had come "not to abolish but to fulfil." He sees no reason why Chinese thought cannot also be the "forerunner" of Christ. This does not mean that the Chinese classics can become literally the "Old Testament" for Chinese Christians, but it does mean that they might perform a similar function in supplying a background and framework for the Christian message in the Chinese cultural context. Hsieh regrets that Chinese theologians and preachers have not had the same courage of faith as the Bible translators in using Chinese concepts to convey Christian meanings, an example being the term *Tao* as a dynamic equivalent of *Logos,* recalling that the author of the Fourth Gospel also borrowed his term from Greek culture./25/ This is part of what is meant by "Confessing the Faith in Asia Today," as the CCA document states it: "The responsibility of interpretation includes discover-

131

ing the thought-forms in our cultural heritage and investing them with new meaning and new depth in the light of the Gospel as the Christian community confesses its faith in its setting.''/26/

The Chinese Roman Catholic convert of an earlier generation, known as Dom Lou, is reported to have said it is a totally mistaken idea to think that a follower of Confucius has to give up his loyalty to Confucius in order to be loyal to Jesus Christ. Dom Lou professed to be a Confucian and a Christian. What the Japanese Christian, Kanzo Uchimura, once said concerning the Japanese might be paraphrased here: A Chinese by becoming a Christian does not cease to be a Chinese. On the contrary, he beomes more Chinese by becoming a Christian! There are also precedents in Indian Christianity for the same emphasis. Brahmabhanduev Upadhyaya, a famous Bengali convert, and Manilal Parekh, a convert from Jainism, both called themselves Hindus even while being baptized Christians. ''I am a Hindu by birth,'' Upadhyaya once said, ''a Christian by rebirth; I am a Christian Hindu.'' These men continued to accept Hindu culture and thought insofar as it did not conflict with commitment to Christ. Another well-known example is Sadhu Sundar Singh./27/ This becomes possible in Asian cultures because, to be an Indian, for example, is — for most Indians — to be a Hindu, just as to be Chinese is to be in some sense a Confucian. Here it is not so much a religious as a cultural self-identity. It should be possible for a Chinese intellectual also to say, ''I am a Confucian by birth, a Christian by rebirth; I am a Christian Confucian.'' It should be possible to speak of ''Confucian Christians'' in somewhat the same way in which in the West we are accustomed to speaking of ''Aristotelian Christians,'' ''Christian Platonists,'' ''Christian Existentialists,'' and even ''Process Theologians.''/28/ It remains for Chinese Christians to work out a careful interpretation of Christianity along Confucian lines of thought. What is most obvious is that a Chinese Christian theology must grow out of dialogue with Confucian thought, utilizing the principles of dynamic accommodation, critical confrontation, and positive transformation, as outlined above.

Most Western theologians have used Aristotle or Plato, Kant or Hegel, Whitehead or Heidegger, selectively. Their philosophies have seldom been adopted as total systems. More often than not they have served as useful points of contact or frames of reference for theological construction. A clear example is the way in which Karl Rahner and John Macquarrie make use of Martin Heidegger, or Jürgen Moltmann and Johannes Metz make use of Karl Marx. It is in this way that Confucian thought can serve a useful purpose in the contextualizing of Christianity in a Chinese setting, particularly since — in spite of the modern criticisms of Confucius — no other important indigenous philosophy in China has arisen to take its place. Pandipeddy Chenchiah, lay theologian and leader of the ''Re-Thinking Christianity Group'' among Indian Christians, has put it pointedly: ''We do not see any reason why Aristotle and Plato, Kant and Hegel, should be regarded as safer guides for Christian theology than the Indian philosophers Sankara and Ramanuja."/29/ And, we might add, than Chinese philosophers like Mencius and Chuang-tzu, Mo-tzu and Yang-ming Wang. Any ancient system of thought, of course, needs to be reinterpreted in the light of new knowledge. In the process of reinterpreting Confucianism, insights from contemporary philosophy can be useful, especially from Process Philosophy and Existentialism, both of which have been immensely helpful in the task of reinterpreting Christian thought in the twentieth century. The most exciting encounter will be that between a reinterpreted Christianity and a reinterpreted Confucianism.

The purpose of this encounter is not to restate Confucian thought in Christian terms, which thus far most Chinese Christian writers who have written on the subject of indigenization seem to be content to do. What the late Paul Devanandan of India once said of Indian Christian thought might be paraphrased for Chinese Christian thought: We seek neither to Confucianize Christianity nor to Christianize Confucianism; our goal is not a Christian expression of Confucianism but a Chinese expression of Christianity./30/ Uncritical accommodation makes Christ a mere "Christ-of-culture" rather than a "Christ-transforming-culture."

Christian Humanism As a Possible Chinese Theology

To say that Confucianism is a philosophy or ethic uncommitted to any particular organized religion does not mean that it has no religious content. On the contrary, it is unmistakably a religious philosophy, however much some Confucians have tended to minimize this element in Confucian thought./31/ Professor Yi-pao Mei, Luce Visiting Professor in Humanities, and my colleague for two years, at Tunghai University, Taiwan, draws an important distinction between "positive" and "negative" types of humanism. The negative type is a revolt against theism, associated in the past with Western naturalistic humanism scientific and Marxist — and now also with Maoist thought. Confucian humanism, however, is of the positive type, stressing the unity of man and Heaven, and the elevation of man above bestiality. Man is encouraged to cultivate his inner essence *(ren)* to the fullest extent. With his manhood actualized he is worthy of forming a triad with Heaven and Earth. Confucian humanism, then, is not anti-theistic. The human and the divine are not opposed but juxtaposed. This makes Confucian philosophy an appropriate point of contact or frame of reference for Christian theology. What is more, this kind of humanism has been revived in recent years in Hong Kong and Taiwan, under the general label of "New Confucianism."/32/ Supportive of this approach is the emphasis in recent ecumenical theology on "Christian humanism," particularly in the thought of the leading Roman Catholic theologian Karl Rahner. Christian humanism and Confucian humanism are not the same thing, to be sure, but there are significant points of contact, as thinkers like Fu-ya Hsieh and Tian-min Lin have labored to show.

Existentialist theologian John Macquarrie argues for the need in a secular age to begin theological reflection with man. Calvin rightly began with the doctrine of God, for this was an intelligible way to begin in an age when most people were conversant with theological language. But in a secular age we have to consider the alternative. If we can begin from the humanity which we all share, says Macquarrie, and "if we find that this humanity points beyond itself for its completion, then we have indicated the place of the word 'God' on the map of meaningful discourse." In any case, Christian theology is as much a doctrine of man as it is a doctrine of God./33/ A Chinese approach to theology, then, might begin with an analysis of human nature. When we seriously face the question, "What is man?" or, more personally, "Who am I?" this question already implies the question of God. Essentially it is the other side of the same question, as Bultmann has tried to show.

Paul Tillich has pointed out that all modern Protestant theology is an attempt to unite two trends in Christian thinking — the "classical" and the "humanistic." The great liberal theologies of the 19th and 20th centuries wrought a synthesis of the two./34/ In the mid-twentieth century we have seen the rise and fall of a theology of protest against all comfortable syntheses; namely, the theology known as Neo-orthodoxy. In the second half of this century we are rediscovering once again the humanistic trend in Christian thinking. We may trace the beginning of this rediscovery to the influence of an important book by the Roman Catholic philosopher Jacques Maritain, called *True Humanism* (1936), and somewhat later to the influence of Protestant theologians like Friedrich Gogarten, Dietrich Bonhoeffer, and Reinhold Niebuhr.

The most notable expressions of this new "Christian humanism were evident at the Second Vatican Council (1962-65) and at the Geneva Conference on Church and Society, WCC (1966). Pope Paul reaffirmed the Roman Catholic emphasis in his encyclical *On the Development of Peoples* (1967), stressing the point that Christian humanism is a "transcendent humanism." On the Protestant side, the New Testament concept of "the new humanity" in Christ, and its implications for "humanization," has come to be recognized as a primary goal of the Christian mission, having moved into the center of discussion since the Upsalla Assembly, WCC (1968).

Roger Shinn, in his recent book *The New Humanism,* reaffirms the ecumenical emphasis on Christian humanism since Vatican II and the Geneva Conference, but he is careful to distinguish what he calls "self-confident humanism" and "grace-ful humanism." The first lives by a confidence in man's capacity to realize and enjoy his potentialities, similar to the optimism about human virtue in most Confucian thought. The second type is Christian humanism which lives by a trust in a grace given to man. "I call it a grace-ful humanism, because it is response to a gracious gift, including the gift of human existence itself. It means a grateful life, which combines appreciation of and discontent with the world, with society, with the self.'' What distinguishes Christian humanism from other humanistic philosophies is that ''it is not so much a matter of looking within oneself for the norms of humanity as it is a perpetual awakening to new possibilities and new graces that are given.''/35/ The two kinds of humanism are not entirely opposed or even separable, concludes Shinn, ''but there is a difference worth thinking about,'' and this difference is especially important to consider in the Christian dialogue with Confucian humanists.

''Christianity and Chinese Humanism'' is the theme of a recent issue of *Ching Feng: Quarterly Notes on Christianity and Chinese Religion and Culture* (March, 1974). Editor Peter K. H. Lee, who is also Director of Tao Fong Shan, Hong Kong, is not at all satisfied with previous efforts to relate the Gospel and Chinese thought. Chinese Christian thinkers, he says, are often content merely to point out structural similarities, ''rarely look at Chinese thought critically, and seldom deal with it in a ''historical context.'' The net effect of this approach is the impression that the Confucian tradition already contains everything that is of value in Christianity. Thus, the radical character of Christian teaching is not allowed to challenge Confucian thought. Dr. Lee appeals to his fellow-Chinese theologians to be more willing ''to be critical of their cultural heritage and to take the forces of living history seriously; otherwise their thought is not sound Christian theology and is not truly indigenous to the contemporary Chinese situation.''/36/ He himself finds the humanism of Yang-ming Wang, the sixteenth-century idealist philosopher, a useful point of contact for the construction of a Chinese Christian theology.

The genuinely humanistic approach, with man as the starting-point of theological reflection, and basic Confucian principles as a frame of reference, suggests a methodology for contextualizing Christian thought in a Chinese setting. Other proposed methods may complement this one. For instance, a Korean theologian, Dr. Jung Young Lee, has suggested using the Chinese *Yin-Yang* (''both/and'') principle to balance the dominant ''either/ or'' way of thinking characteristic of much Western thought./37/ The problem with most attempts thus far is that they tend to build on too narrow a foundation. When the critics finish tearing it apart, there is little or no platform left to stand upon. For this reason, the broader platform of common ground between Christian humanism and Confucian humanism allows for varieties of interpretation without destroying the foundation on which the structure rests.

A Chinese Christian humanism will be concerned, among other things, with the quest for the truly human in a rapidly changing society. It will seek to clarify the similarities and differences between the Christian view of man and the Maoist view of man. It will stress the biblical basis of ''true humanism'' in terms of the conviction that God is ever-active in the world, ''making and keeping human life human.'' Therefore, nothing that is truly human can be alien to Christ. It would take several papers to work out the implications of a Chinese Christian humanism. The intent of this paper is merely to suggest some of the possible lines of thought. Moreover, this is a task for Chinese Christians. Nor can the Chinese theologian afford to ignore the insights in Taoist and Buddhist philosophies. One would expect, however, that a humanistic approach to Christian theology in a Chinese setting would be based primarily on the spirit of Confucianism.

Christian theologians of Taiwan and Hong Kong, together perhaps, can make a unique contribution to the theology of the church ecumenical. Beyond this, Christian thought can also be enriched by its contact with the Chinese intellectual heritage. C. M. Wei says that Christian theology needs the enrichment which Chinese culture can bring to it./38/ No single Church, nation, or generation can exhaust the full depth and meaning of the Christian faith, and none can properly claim that its interpretation or confession holds the whole truth. As Dr. Frederick C. Grant has put it, ''The actual realization of all that Christianity is, ought to be, and may in time become, is still only partial and far from complete.''/39/ We may well conclude that some of the dimensions of meaning in Christian thought will remain undiscovered until its truths are received, understood, and expressed in the framework of Chinese thought-forms. The CCA document on ''The Confessing Church in Asia and Its Theological Task,'' referred to earlier in this paper, expresses the conviction that ''Christ has more of his truth to reveal to us, as we seek to understand his work among men in their several Asian cultures, their different religions, and their involvement in the contemporary Asian revolution. In the past we have been too inhibited by our fear of syncretism and too tied to inherited traditional and conceptual forms of confession to make such ventures.'' We have forgotten that ''even as people of other times and cultures made their own confession, we too must do the same in our time and culture. When we make absolute the written confessions of the Churches of another culture or age, we become incapable of discovering the new depths of truth God can reveal to us in Christ amidst Asian life.''/40/

Dr. Visser t'Hooft has pointed out that ''mutual correction'' is one of the great functions of a truly ecumenical theology. ''Every historical form in which Christianity has expressed itself,'' he says, ''needs to be challenged by other forms of expression in order that it may not become frozen, that it may remember its own limitations.'' For instance, ''Western Christianity needs to be questioned from the point of view of an Asian Christianity....''/41/ We need to remember, of course, that the Asian Church is still in the ''Apostolic Age'' of its history, a period in which the central doctrines of the Faith were being forged and shaped under the heat of controversy with a variety of heresies. Historically, the Apologists were the first theologians; only later did the great Church Fathers emerge. How can we expect it to be otherwise in the Asian Church?

Christian Theology in an Asian Setting

/1/   M. M. Thomas, *"Preface" to* Introduction to Indian Christian Theology, *by Robin Boyd (Madras: CLS, 1969). Thomas here paraphrases the Kandy Consultation report, 1965.*

/2/   *It was at the Nairobi Assembly of the WCC that this term was introduced with reference to a new method of doing theology.*

/3/   *See Editorial in* IRM, *LXI, 244 (Oct., 1972).*

/4/   James H. Burtness, *"Innovation as the Search for Probabilities: To Re-Contextualize the Text," in* Learning in Context *(London TEF, 1973), p. 10.*

/5/   *Policy Statement of the TEF Committee, "Theology in Context,"* SEAJT, XIV, 1 *(1972) 64-67.*

/6/   Ibid. *Italics added.*

/7/   *One of the problems facing the Taiwan church is that it has been cut off from any participation in the international community, including the World Council of Churches. See the news report on Taiwan in an (1975) issue of* CCA News.

/8/   *Report of a "Study Center Directors Consultation."* Japanese Religions, VII, 1 *(1971), p. 54f.*

/9/   *Emerito P. Nacpil, "The Question of Excellence in Theological Education,"* SEAJT, XVI, 1 *(1975), p. 58.*

/10/   John Macquarrie, Principles of Christian Theology *(N.Y. Scribners) p. 17.*

/11/   *For example, Ezekiel denounced false prophets who foretold peaceful security when they knew very well that this was impossible (13:1-6).*

/12/   M. M. Thomas, The Acknowledged Christ of the Indian Renaissance, *(London: SCM, 1969), p. 312f. See Marcus Ward, Our Theological Task (Bangalore, 1946) for a full report of the Poona findings.*

/13/   Shoki Coe *"Confessing the Faith in Asia Today,"* SEAJT, VIII, 1 & 2. *(1966) p. 84.*

/14/   D.T. Niles, *as quoted in Chandran Devanesen,* The Cross Is Lifted, *(N.Y.: Friendship Press, 1954), p. 11.*

/15/   *Professor Hideo Ohki, of Tokyo Union Theological Seminary, in a plea to his countrymen, said, "Deliver Japanese theology from Germanic captivity!" Quoted by Seiichi Yagi, another protesting theologian, and translated by Joseph Spae in* Christianity Encounters Japan, *(Tokyo: Oriens Institute, 1968), p. 201.*

/16/   Lesslie Newbigin, *"Salvation, the New Humanity, and Cultural-Communal Solidarity,"* Bangalore Theological Forum, *V, 2(1973), p. 9.*

/17/   J. Russell Chandran, *"Confessing the Faith in Asia Today,"* SEAJT, VIII, 1 & 2 *(1966), 91-94. See also M. M. Thomas, "Preface,"* The Christian Response to the Asian Revolution *(SCM 1966).*

/18/   *See the issue at* Mission Trends No. 3: *"Third World Theology" (Paulist Press, Paramus, N.J. 1976).*

/19/   *M. M. Thomas, Editorial,* Church and Society *(EACC), II, 3 & 4 (Dec., 1965), p. 1f.*

/20/   EACC, *"Statements Issued by a Consultation on Confessional Families and the Churches in Asia," (Kandy, Sri Lanka, 1965), in* International Review of Mission, *LV, 2/8 (April, 1966), 199-204. For examples of this "living theology" in Asia see the following collections: G. H. Anderson (ed.),* Asian Voices in Christian Theology *(Orbis Books, 1976); D. J. Elwood (ed.),* What Asian Christians Are Thinking *(New Day Publishers, Manila, 1976); and G. P. Vicedom (ed.),* Christ and the Younger Churches *(SPCK, 1972).*

/21/   Wing-tsit Chan, Religious Trends in Modern China *(Octagon, 1970), p. 261*

/22/   Sverre Holth, *"Towards an Indigenous Theology,"* Ching Feng, *XI, 4, (1968), 24f.*

/23/   Francis C. M. Wei, The Spirit of Chinese Culture *(Scribners, 1947).*

/24/   Julia Ching, *"Will Confucianism Survive? A Critical Re-Assessment of the Heritage,"* International Philosophical Quarterly *(March, 1975); reprinted in* Ching Feng, *XVIII, 4 (1975), p. 214.*

/25/   *I am indebeted to Mr. Paul Kong, a seminarian of China Evangelical Seminary, Taipei for translating for me portions of Hsieh's book.*

/26/   EACC, Confessing the Faith in Asia Today, *Section II: "Some Responsibilities of Confessing Churches" (1966).*

/27/   *See the article, "Implications of Vatican II for Mission in Asia,"* Teaching All Nations, *(EAPI), IV, 3 (1967), 321.*

/28/   *Cf. A. C. Bouquet, "Revelation and the Divine Logos," p. 182 in G. H. Anderson (ed.)* Theology of Christian Mission *(McGraw-Hill, 1961).*

137

Christianity and the Religions of the East

/29/   Quoted in Christianity in the Indian Crucible, ed. by E. Asirvatham (Calcutta, 1955), p. 95f.

/30/   Quoted in Visser t'Hooft, "Accommodation – True and False," SEAJT, VIII, 3 (1967), 5-18.

/31/   See Wing-tsit Chan concerning the "unmistakably religious" character of Confucianism, in The Great Asian Religions, by W. T. Chan, et al., (Macmillan, 1969), p. 105f.

/32/   Chief spokesmen of this "New Confucianism" are Chun-i T'ang Tsung-san Mou, and Fo-kuan Hsu, three of the five men who signed the "Manifesto to the World on Behalf of Chinese Culture," a translation of which appears in the Democratic Review (Hong Kong), IX, 1 (Jan., 1958). For materials in Chinese produced by these modern Confucians see Re Sheng (The Young Sun), a Hong Kong journal, especially 1958-60. In line with the emphasis on Confucianism as an essentially "theistic" philosophy, Wing-tsit Chan begins his Source Book in Chinese Philosophy (Princeton, 1963) with the statement: "If one word could characterize the entire history of Chinese philosophy, that word would be humanism – not the humanism that denies or slights a Supreme Power, but one that professes the unity of man and Heaven." (p. 3)

/33/   John Macquarrie, "How Is Theology Possible?" New Theology No. 1, edited by Marty and Peerman (Macmillan, 1964), p. 22f.

/34/   Paul Tillich, Perspectives on 19th and 20th Century Protestant Theology, edited by Carl E. Braaten (Harper & Row, 1967), p. 5.

/35/   Roger Shinn, Man: The New Humanism (Westminster, 1968), pp. 174-78.

/36/   Peter K. H. Lee, "An Interpretative Summary: "Christianity and Chinese Humanism,'" Ching Feng, XVII, 1 (1974), p. 49.

/37/   See his article, "The Yin-Yang Way of Thinking: A Possible Method for Ecumenical Theology," IRM, LX, 239 (1971), 363-70. (cf. Also Chapter 2 of this book) See also his book, The I; A Christian Concept of Man (Philosophical Library, 1973), in which he applies the Yin-Yang logic to the Christian understanding of man; also "The Spirit and the Unity of Change," Encounter XXXIX, 2, (Spring, 1973), 147-61, in which he applies the same to the Christian idea of God.

/38/   C. M. Wei, op. cit. p. 27.

/39/   F. C. Grant, Basic Christian Beliefs, (N.Y.: Methodist Church, 1960), "Preface."

/40/   EACC, "Statements Issued by a Consultation on Confessional Families and the Churches in Asia," IRM, LV, 218 (April, 1966), p. 201.

/41/   Visser t'Hooft, "Asian Issues in the Ecumenical Setting," pp. 59-62 in A Decisive Hour for the Christian Mission (FACO 1950).

CHAPTER TWELVE

A Covenant With the Chinese

By LANGDON GILKEY

The Model of Covenant

I have lived relatively long as a young ignoramus in China, and been twice to Japan as a visitor. Thus I can smell oriental smells, whiff oriental meanings, and feel oriental shapes and forms almost as well as anyone. I am a relative "know-nothing" about Chinese religions, cultural and political history, and about present day Maoism. I know too little about the Chinese present, therefore, to try to suggest concrete ways in which Western Christians may relate their faith to this new reality. What I may be able to do is to discuss theological principles according to which such an interrelationship may be assayed.

Our question concerns the relation of Christianity or of Christian faith to the new, powerful, promising, and attractive reality of China. This question is usually posed as the question of "mission," of bringing or of not bringing *our* gospel, *our* religion, *our* church to the Chinese. Such a posing of the question — with, let me admit, immense backing from both Bible and tradition — is, I shall suggest, historically and theologically misleading, or

Dr. Langdon Gilkey is Professor of Theology at the University of Chicago Divinity School and is well known in theological circles for both his scholarship and leadership. Born in China and interned there during the war, Dr. Gilkey often writes on the relationship between China and Western, especially Christian, culture. This essay is taken from Dialog, *Vol. 17, 1978, pp. 181-187 and is reprinted by permission of the publisher.*

139

better, almost fatally tempting. Its implications are that *our* religion, in its present forms is transcultural. As a result the question that is then put is: in what ways do *their* culture and *their* religious life need *our* religion and so *our* church? Already latent here, I suggest, are the seeds of the imperialism, and the ultimate ineffectiveness — for in spiritual matters the two are opposite sides of the same coin — of recent Christian invasions of China.

In the place of this model of ''mission'' I would like to propose the model of ''covenant.'' By covenant in this context I mean the patristic concept of the ''covenant with the Greeks'' through which the Fathers — or some of the more liberal of them — legitimated the synthesis of Hellenistic culture and the gospel, out of which synthesis what we now call Christianity arose. Here, therefore, we are speaking of *our* history and of the formation of *our* religion — so immediately everything is less, much less imperialistic and utterly different! This is, I say, a more helpful and accurate model with which to ponder the subject of our conference, the relation of Christianity to the old and to the new China.

The Catholic religion, and so of course ultimately Protestantism too, resulted from the movement of an apocalyptic branch of Hebraic religion into the new and alien world of late Hellenism. This was a world replete with social, political, and ethical norms and goals strange to those of the earliest Christian communities, and a world reflectively structured by alien philosophical categories and permeated with a religious orientation utterly different from their own. Out of a slow, deep and essential interpenetration of these two realities arose our Christian religion: an interpenetration in the areas of rite, of symbol, of ethical obligation, of forms of church organization, and finally of categories and concepts of reflective thought. Hellenistic culture was tranformed in part — unfortunately only in part! — by the Christian leaven. In turn Christianity was expressed and made real within forms and categories of the Hellenistic world.

Heresy appeared when the religious dimensions of Hellenistic life quite overcame the affirmations of the gospel. No historian, however, can deny that both the orthodoxy that combatted and conquered heresy, and the creeds that sealed the victory, were themselves saturated with the categories of Hellenistic culture and permeated with the characteristics and aims of Hellenistic religion. This synthesis, pace Harnack, was immensely creative and anyway inevitable. It expressed and uncovered elements in the gospel essential to its full witness; and it was surely in part this Hellenistic component that made it possible for the gospel to be a basic formative factor of medieval culture and so of subsequent Western civilization.

One other ''covenant'' may be mentioned; the covenant with the modern West. Modernity's science, its history, its psychology, its political, economic and social norms and goals, its moral and human self-understanding, its sense of time, history and human destiny, have impinged, as both a lure and a threat, on the older synthesis with Hellenism. Liberal and post-liberal Protestantism sought for two hundred years to establish a creative covenant with the modern Renaissance and Enlightenment; Catholicism is finally seeking to do so as well.

Think what the implications of *this* covenant are for "missions"! Much of what we most treasure and defend in modern Christianity has arisen from this synthesis: its acceptance of pluralism, its tolerance, its emphasis on autonomy, its awareness that all dogmas and forms of religion are historically relative, its drive to transform the world in the name of justice and of love. As Hellenism once did, modern life, in its synthesis with Christianity, has uncovered and emphasized invaluable elements of the gospel latent and even denied before.

We cannot repudiate this paradigm of the covenant and be ourselves as contemporary Christians. We know in ourselves and in those we respect that a living Christianity always appears in the form of a "covenant" with the cultural life in which it seeks to live. The absence of such a covenant or synthesis heralds either imperialism, the heteronomous imposition of an alien synthesis on the life of a new culture, or — and this is always the *final* result — ineffectiveness, emptiness and disappearance.

The church has consistently refused to apply the model of covenant in relation to other cultures. Forgetting how its own synthesis arose, the church has sought to send other cultures this synthesis. Or, put another way, it has sought to send *itself:* its traditional language and concepts, its dogmas, doctrines and theologies, its institutional structures and forms, its rites and liturgies, its rules and norms. One cannot, as a modern Western Christian, look at any of these traditional forms of dogma, law or polity and not *feel* their Hellenic origin and so what is to us their anachronistic character. We are all dedicated to bringing this whole religious corpus "up to date": in theology, liturgy, canon law, moral philosophy, church structure. And yet we, who can hardly wait to bring this inherited corpus into the deepest union with the forms of the modern culture we share, are apt to feel an infinite risk when we contemplate, if we do, a synthesis with another cultural substance entirely.

I need not press the irony in all this. Do we think these forms save us, or that God cannot use the forms of others as he has used ours? Can he not establish a covenant with the Chinese as well as with pagan Hellenism and pagan modernity? Would not a Chinese Christian feel the same need of "aggiornamento" in terms of *his* culture as we feel in terms of ours — and one that goes not only into the peripheral realms of social policy but one that penetrates — as does ours — to the very heart: to rites, liturgy, theology and moral understanding?

Preliminary Cautions

Three comments should be made before we turn directly to the issue before us. The first is that at least at the present there is hardly any prospect of the sort of synthesis that historically the covenant principle has represented, namely a deep interpenetration of Christianity and Chinese culture. Christianity has little present prospect of entering massively the Chinese scene. Only Hellenistic Christians could create the synthesis that became orthodoxy; only moderns can write contemporary Catholic theology. Interested Westerners are probably like early Bedouin converts trying to foresee the forms of the 4th and 5th century creeds!

We, to be sure, are deeply influenced by the present Chinese civilization; correspondingly we are asking the question about our relation, as Western Christians, to that culture. *They* are scarcely asking that question! At present it is their theoria and faith, their patterns of being human, that are impinging with power on us. Our questions, let us be clear, may (like theirs) be really more about the shape of future *Western* culture and of *our* Christianity than about theirs!

Secondly, a further word should be said about imperialism. A religion can be imperialistic on two scores, interrelated but separable. 1)Religion is imperial when it accompanies, appeals to and profits from the military, economic and political power of its culture. This we have done enthusiastically: first with Constantine, and then across the globe, the Church accepted security, wealth, prestige, honor and glory from Caesar — and has in our day paid for it both in Caesar's coin and in the honor of our Lord's name. (2) A religion is imperialistic when the cultural forms which it inevitably bears — for no religion but has a cultural expression — are made absolute and so are forced upon that new cultural situation. In the case of Christian mission the Western cultural forms and institutions of Christianity were regarded as identical with the gospel and the grace being mediated, by both Catholics and Protestants. Thus instead of pointing beyond itself to its non-Western Lord and its transcendent God, Christianity pointed to itself as a Western religion — and sealed its own doom.

These two forms of imperialism are avoidable if one is aware of them — and if we understand that God's covenants are wider than we think, as his rain falls on all. The greatest present danger is that we may, in consciously rejecting both military and economic power and Western social, economic and political culture, fail to see how Western our religion and our Church are, and so seek again to move our religion and our church into union with the new China.

As is evident, the question of imperialism is not directly related to the question of the universality of a religious reality. In order to avoid imperialism one does not need to repudiate the claim of a religion to universal relevance. Universal religions — Buddhism, Christianity, liberal democracy and Marxism — can proceed into new cultural situations without imperialism, solely by means of the persuasive power and relevance of their message, and have sometimes done so. On the other hand, each has proceeded into new situations imperialistically. Let us also note that anyone who demotes Christianity from the status of a universal faith to a "culture religion," relevant only in its own cultural and historical situation, has already relinquished Christianity and adopted in its place some *other* universalist faith, possibly liberal democracy or Marxism.

Each universal faith tends quite naturally to reduce the status and pretensions of its victims and its rivals. For each realizes, and rightly, that the essential structure of its own belief is radically compromised if its claims to universal relevance are rejected. The theological trick in all these matters — for cultural systems such as liberalism and Marxism quite as well as for explicit religions such as Buddhism and Christianity — is to preserve the sense of universal relevance, and so of truth, along with that clear sense of our own relativity which alone can dissolve imperialism and generate charity.

Thirdly, we should note that there are two different levels of any cultural whole with which a religion is to make synthesis, and correspondingly two different levels of religion. This was true of Hellenism and of the modern West, and it is surely also true of present China. There is first of all the level of cultural life as such: science or forms of inquiry and of truth; social and political thought; forms of art; social and personal norms, mores and goals; and so on. Second there is the religious dimension, a dimension that appears in each cultural whole however "secular" it may regard itself to be, a dimension that is explicitly expressed in organized religion. In an avowedly secular culture such as the modern West or Maoism, the cultural life as such is all that is recognized. Most discussions of a synthesis of Maoism with Christianity that I have seen, have only this secular level of Chinese reality in mind.

The Cultural Covenant

We shall, then, first seek to deal with the cultural level. How might Christian faith relate to the social, political, economic and moral reality of present China? It is on this level that to me the clearest gains for Christianity and for our common future appear. The synthesis of Christianity with the modern West has had many creative results. But undoubtedly this covenant has brought with it an emphasis on the *individual:* his or her salvation in heaven; his or her conscience, automony and freedom of spirit; his or her property and its rights — all of which, for better or for worse, have reconstructed Christianity from the medieval and feudal phenomenon it was into a democratic and bourgeois one. I do not wish by any means to repudiate this inheritance in its entirety. But it is, especially in its American variants, desperately weak on the communal side.

The embeddedness of the individual in responsibility to the community, the ineradicability and value of relationships and their obligations, the priority, therefore, of community obligations over obligations to the self, the absolute importance of the category of the "common good" — all of these emphases are peculiarly oriental, as the Confucian tradition in both China and Japan witnesses. They reappear in modern, progressive and so creative form in Maoist thought and in the reality of the new life in China: in the principles of the Mass Line, in the polarity of elite and peasant, in the emphasis on the social origin and character of knowing and of theory, and in the identity of the substance of China with the whole *People* of China. The same creative rebalancing of forces appears in the subordination of technology to the people's needs, of the authority of the expert and the power of the pragmatic technician to the political and moral goals of society, and in the insistence that all theory be reinterpreted through praxis.

These phenomena are not just the politicization of life, the absolutization of an ideology, as many American observers maintain. They represent in principle the reintegration of elements of culture sundered in our own cultural experience and so in destructive conflict and dissolution. In the West, there is a continuing struggle between the individual and the community, between rational organization and moral purpose, between technology and human need. We perceive our sundered and self-destructive reality; but our theories remain only theories, separated as protests from the sundered reality. In China the beginning of a reunion of these separated polarities appears as an actual and a powerful social *reality,* (compound of Confucianism and Socialism,) that seems to have effected not only a redirecting of public policy but even more of individual motivation and of obligation. As Western life created a new pluralistic society and a new individual autonomy — as well as new theories about each — so Chinese life seems to be creating a new society and a new individual oriented towards the common good, using Marxist theory and Western technology and rationalization for human purposes. If, as I believe, the central social and political crisis facing us at present requires a new synthesis of the tradition of individual freedom with the communal character of human existence, then it is surely modern China that will provide the inspiration and the guidance for the creation of that synthesis.

The Religious Covenant

Every cultural whole, however, has a religious as well as a cultural dimension, a religious substance which maintains cultural life's unity, power and meaning. Each culture expresses in all its cultural forms a particular vision of what is ultimately real, true and valuable, and lives out in all aspects of its life that stance towards being and meaning. Such a view of culture as having a religious substance has been expressed in varying ways in 19th and 20th century theoretical sociology and anthropology; it has been set in theological form by Tillich, and in a poorman's version by myself. Let us note that it represents an antagonistic position both to the exhaustively secular interpretation of culture of the Enlightenment and of Marxism, and to the natural-supernatural interpretation of culture of traditional theology. For here the natural is permeated with the supernatural, while, as we have argued, the church is also expressive in all its religious forms of its cultural locus.

Needless to say, this religious dimension of culture's life complicates the relation of a religion such as Christianity to any given culture. For therewith the problem arises not only of the relation of Christian faith to the culture as such, but also its relation to the *religious* elements of that culture. It has historically been here especially that the real issues of a covenant of a synthesis have appeared.

Concerning this problem the Church has been clear in theory and ambivalent in practice. Heresy is constituted by a capitulation to the *religious* idolatries of a culture, not by a use of its cultural forms. The gnostic, Arian and Manicheean heresies sought to set into Christian symbolic forms the religious visions of the Hellenistic world. They were countered by peculiarly Christian symbols expressing a non-Hellenistic religious orientation: ex nihilo, Trinity, Incarnation, resurrection of the body, etc. We should note, however, that none of the orthodox fathers eschewed Hellenistic cultural categories in expressing what became orthodoxy. In order to effect their Christian opposition to Hellenistic religion they used the categories of Hellenistic culture.

The Same point could be made about the so-called "neo-orthodox" in the modern synthesis. In order to express their "orthodox" theology meaningfully, they used modern categories of interpretation, and they deliberately sought *not* to combat the secular science, history, psychology and so on of their time. In order to express a *traditional* theological position, they counter what they regard as the false *religious* dimensions of modern culture: its rampant individualism, its scientism, its principle of autonomous self-sufficiency, its belief in progress and so on.

The problem of the relation of Christian faith to the religious dimension of culture — when the liberal consciously accepts culture and even the orthodox must use cultural concepts — dominates the theological controversies of both the ancient and the modern church. It can hardly fail to be the most important issue in our problem: the relation of Christianity to either the old or the new China.

A synthesis is possible and necessary only when each side has something to offer. I have indicated at length what ancient and present Chinese cultural reality may offer to the West and to Christianity: the strong moral and communal emphasis of Confucianism, now refashioned in an egalitarian rather than a hierarchical manner and oriented forward to new possibilities in history rather than backward to a sacred past. Here *both* the Confucian tradition and the Marxist tradition have been transformed in relation to one another, a genuine covenant, a monument to Mao's genius. That the very different Western cultural emphasis on criticism, individual autonomy and the value of the person has in the past and even in the present something to offer China, I do not doubt. But what does *Christianity* have to contribute?

I shall try to suggest an answer in three points. All involve transcendence and our relation to it. Since Christianity is a religion, and thus a mode of being in relation to the divine, what it has to offer is primarily a new form of *that* relation, a form which transforms but does not replace the various aspects of cultural life in the world. Correspondingly, what the faith offers to Maoism is essentially a new shape to the religious dimension of Maoism — as Christianity sought to do with Hellenism and with Western modernity. Christianity does not replace the cultural life with which it is in covenant; it has no science, politics, sociology or economics to offer of its own. Hopefully by transforming the religious substance of the culture into one of its own shape, (here is the relevance of the symbol of the Kingdom) it will transform and deepen *all* of these common aspects of culture into a more perfect realization of what they themselves intend. Our three points, then, seek to clarify how the Christian tradition might reshape the religious dimension of Maoism into a truer and more creative form. Clearly my argument is circular: Maoism is incomplete on these three issues *only* when viewed from a Christian (or some other) perspective. From its *own* perspective it naturally needs no complementary principles, no grace beyond what it may itself provide. But this circularity is characteristic of all intercultural and interreligious discourse, and so, while it is well to recognize it, it should not deter us.

Point One. That there is a religious dimension to Maoism is undoubted. Like its sister, Western Marxism and its distant cousin, the liberal view of Evolutionary Progress, Maoism presents a global viewpoint encompassing a view of reality as a whole and of its meaning, as a whole. This viewpoint is set in a symbolic structure of remarkable depth and consistency, that calls for participatory faith, commitment and obedience. The symbolic structure stabilizes and shapes institutions and the forms and the values of communal existence; it grounds the meanings of daily life; it structures the patterns of education; and it guides political action. Above all, in answering the deepest questions of the meaning of life, it relates human beings to the categories of the absolute and the sacred, and thus provides their fundamental principles of judgment and renewal, the grounds of confidence and hope, and so the possibility of their creative existence. This is not to say the Maoism is a "religion"; it is only to say that like any fundamental cultural reality, it contains and lives from a religious substance and religious dimension.

Now my first question is: what happens when this religious dimension is latent or in fact denied, as is the case in China? The denial does not remove the religious elements: the sense of the relation to *the* ultimate reality of process, to *the* meaning of history, to *the* promise of future fulfillment. Mao's genius is clearly evident in the way he prevented that claim to absoluteness from settling onto and rendering ultimate any *particular* plan or theory: the elite vanguard, the proletariat or peasants, the party, the nation. There is here a sense of transcendence that is able, to a remarkable degree, to be permanently critical of each of the polarities of socialism in process.

A Covenant with the Chinese

The preservation of transcendence is crucial lest absoluteness settle again (as it did in Russia) on theory and on the party elite, or lest the religious dimension itself be entirely lost in a pragmatic expertise ultimately indistinguishable from Western counterparts. Modern history is replete with creative cultural experiments whose religious dimensions were unheeded and suppressed. The meanings of such a culture can then disintegrate into superficial triviality. Its norms and its call to justice can dissolve — and finally, in reaction, the absolute can return in primitive, parochial, and demonic form. A cultural whole — and the more redemptive it is the more the risk — that understands itself to be "religionless" is continually in danger of a profanization that loses its essential religious substance, or of a self-absolutization that leads to the demonic. Both have occurred, often in quick succession, in the West, and both still threaten us. China is by no means invulnerable to this possibility. Where the transcendent is not known and acknowledged, the creativity of a cultural substance is always in danger.

Point Two. The necessity of the transformation of social institutions — of the structures of government, of property, of the relations of production, of the interrelations of social groups and classes — has been one of the major creative themes of modern world culture. It is the central theme of the forces of liberation everywhere. This theme has historically been a creative result of the covenant of Christianity with secular modernity. Its roots are, to be sure, in important part Biblical. But it has been only in modern history that it has, for various reasons, become part of the self-interpretation of the Church and so of her understanding of her obligations. What does Christian faith, if it recognizes this "demand" for the transforming of the institutions of society as its own obligation have to say to a movement and a society centrally devoted to that transformation?

The answer, obviously itself dependent on a Christian view of our historical existence, is grounded in a distinction between our estrangement on the one hand and its consequences in cultural life on the other, between what has traditionally been called "sin" and what we might term "fate." The warped and unjust institutions of our common life of government, property, race, group, family, sexuality — can and do become a "fate" for those who live under their domination. Such institutions, incarnating injustice, can be inescapable for those born into them; they prevent and constrict our freedom to constitute ourselves and to share in the determination of our own destiny; they separate us from one another and from all meaning and worth. The suffering that arises from unjust social institutions is the clearest sign of the fallen character of history, and, as modern theology has pointed out, of the ravages of sin in history.

Since such institutional structures are the result of sin, and since they create suffering and encourage further sin, they defy the will of God for human community and are an offence to the Kingdom. On the basis of scripture and of the implications of every basic Christian symbol, therefore, the eradication, in so far as it is possible, of "fate" in this sense is an ultimate obligation of the gospel. Liberation theology, and the thrust of Maoism — as of the humanitarian movements of the 18th and 19th centuries — are essential aspects of theology. Correspondingly, both faith and theology are required to unite themselves with authentic political, economic and social movements of liberation whenever the latter appear. True theology is inescapably political theology dedicated to social liberation.

On the other hand, warped institutions are not the *cause* but the effects of history's must fundamental problem. Consequently, political and economic liberation, however crucial, is not the sum total of the gospel. For these institutions in this distorted form do not appear from nowhere; their warped character is not itself uncaused, a simple "given" necessarily if inexplicably present in historical life. On the contrary, this warped character — as liberal democracy and Marxism knew well — is a removable, alterable aspect of historical life, or there is no point at all in the effort to ameliorate it. Human creativity has helped to create and fashion these institutions; the estrangement of our creativity accounts, therefore, for the element of distortion and injustice present in all of them.

Thus even the very creativity of each cultural whole is involved in the end in the ultimately oppressive character of its institutions — as the bourgeois democratic culture of the West and its most creative gift to the world, technology, clearly illustrate. How hopefully that culture once viewed the "innocent," "just" and unambiguous future that it dreamed it would create! How evident it is now that the very principles that formed that dream constitute the anatomy of our present problems, dilemmas, and suffering! Each creative moment of history's life rightly rejects and transforms the warped social destiny that it inherits; each believes that thereby it has rid history of its most fundamental problem, the root source of its evil — as liberal democracy and its protestant equivalent viewed feudal aristocracy and authoritarianism and their Catholic justification. However creative, each in turn reenacts in its own forms our common human estrangement, and produces for *its* children and for others its own fated destiny; warped institutions which call for transformation.

A deep spiritual estrangement runs through history and *itself* needs healing. As freedom falls into sin in history, so the creative destiny we seek to bequeath to our children itself falls into fate. The transformation of that social "fate" is a necessary task; but the redemption of the freedom that continually falls, and in falling recreates historical fate, calls for what our creative and even revolutionary action in the world cannot provide.

This truth is seen implicityly by Mao when he speaks of the need for the transformation of the inner person as well as for the transformation of institutions; and when he recognizes the *permanence* of the contradictions of historical life and the continual reappearance of both "proleteriat" and "bourgeois" even in socialism. Social transformation deals with the consequences of estrangement and alienation, not with its deeper causes. Thus estrangement and its consequences will reappear even when the given forms of fate in our time have been radically reduced. An explicit dealing with the problem of sin, as well as with fate, is essential — and this is a social philosophy can never finally either promise or achieve. Our commitment to Christianity, as Augustine argued, is in the end based on the self-understanding that discovers our problem, and so the human problem, to be one of estrangement or sin, and that calls therefore for the answer of a grace beyond cultural possibilities and the possibilities of our own intelligence and will. On this self-understanding the relevance of Christian faith to every cultural situation is based.

Point Three. There is a remarkable sense in Maoism of both the mystery and the meaning of historical process, and the dialectical interrelation of mystery and meaning. For historical process is here viewed as a process of struggle between opposing but interdependent polarities, each dependent on the other but each critical of the other and balancing it. This struggle is seen as necessary in order to preserve justice and harmony; yet risk is also necessary in order to prevent their separation and destruction. Out of the relativity of the parts and the chaos of surface events arises, therefore, a deeper meaning. Here is a picture of a creative process with religious depth, with an intrinsic principle of self-criticism and with hidden but profound telos and meaning latent within it.

From the Christian perspective, this view presents a profound interpretation of the providence of God as it works in history, a hidden purpose working through judgment and new possibilities to create deeper meaning. It is however intrinsic to the Christian perspective that an even deeper dialectic appears in the course of history, a dialectic symbolized not by providence but by the Cross and the Resurrection. For us, as we have seen, the dialectical process of creation, opposition and struggle is at once a process of a human creativity enmeshed in sin, and a process qualified by judgment and grace. The transcendent is present in the process as the ground of creativity and of new possibility, of a dynamic surge through struggle into the new — as Mao recognizes. But the transcendent is also over *against* the process as the principle of judgment, of prophetic criticism of those who rule and even of those who revolt, a principle of judgment of *all* in order that *all* may be rescued. This dialectic, which is the heart of Christianity, can never be present unless the transcendent is recognized as transcendent, unless judgment on even the creative, the wise and the good is made explicit, unless grace appears as powerlessness and suffering as well as victory, and life appears after and through death. The Cross and the Resurrection hover over the creative process as the sole principles of its *continuing* creativity.

Unless even what is most creative knows its mortality and is willing to die, it can hardly live without destruction. Unless life arises in history continually out of the possibility and reality of death, it can hardly live. This Christian principle is dimly foreshadowed in the principle of dialectical opposition, and more clearly seen in the principles of continual revolution and the Mass Line. However, only as explicit, only as internalized, only as appropriated in and through the presence of repentance and of grace can it be real and permanent. Only if the life of the human spirit dwells explicitly in humility, repentance, trust and hope in the presence of the eternal can that life enact this final dialectic and be creative. The Christian symbols, centered on the Cross and Resurrection, do not "save us"; grace does. But they can create for us a self-understanding and an ultimate horizon within which we find ourselves *coram deo*, in the presence of God, reconciled, reoriented and reborn in an inward stance where presence and grace may be received. This gospel must be heard anew, both here and there.

The supreme irony of history — and the supreme illustration of history's *need* for this message! — was that this gospel may be present in all, even on us ourselves, that grace may be present in all, was proclaimed via gunboats, commercial goods, technology and the self-affirming ego of the West, not to mention the power and authority of the triumphant Church! It would be equally ironical if it were to appear once again, in a land now deeply devoted to the masses, in the guise of a new ecclesiastical invasion of the mainland, planned and enacted with all the devotion, resources and ingenuity of the vast ecclesia.

Only a community *itself* under judgment that grace may come to *it*, can give *this* message to a China newly reborn in history out of near death. Only a mission that eschews its own power and glory can communicate this message of judgment on and grace to the culture and religion of the new China. The Church had too long proclaimed justice, reconciliation, repentance, love and unity to the world, and quite forgotten to apply these stern requirements its own life and even to its own mission. The word of God's judgment and grace must first be heard within, acknowledged and appropriated by ourselves, if we are to speak that word in the Spirit to others. If the church merely brings its own culture and its own religion, its Western forms and rites and its ecclesiastical might and power — even if these proclaim the Cross in *our* eyes — it will rightly be rejected again. A mission that dies itself, that sacrifices what it is in the world: in culture, in religion, in theological formulations and in ecclesiastical might, in favor of the transcendent to which it seeks to witness, can be heard — both in China and here. For that alone is the voice, and the commission, that comes to us from the Cross and from beyond the tomb.

CHAPTER THIRTEEN

*Statement of
the Theological Consultation
on Dialogue in Community,
Chiang Mai, Thailand*

Introduction

Dialogue in community was not only the theme of the World Council of Churches consultation held in Chiang Mai, Thailand, in April 1977. The welcome of our hosts, the Church of Christ in Thailand, and of the people of Chiang Mai itself speedily drew us to become a community ourselves, within which a dialogue of different approaches could take place. The context of Bible study and of worship in which we did our work constantly reminded us also of the depths of our communion in spirit and in life as this has been made joyously possible for us by our meeting with God in Christ.

It was also in the Bible study and worship that some of the issues before us became most clear. As we sought again to enter into the thought world of the Old and New Testaments, we all felt, from whatever culture we came, both the strangeness of the Gospel and the wonder of God's self-involvement with his world.

This is the text of the official statement adopted by a Theological Consultation held at Chiang Mai, Thailand, April 18-27, 1977. Authorized by the Central Committee of the World Council of Churches as the priority meeting for 1977, this ecumenical consultation brought together eighty-five people-Protestant, Orthodox and Roman Catholic-from thirty-six countries to discuss ''Dialogue in Community.'' This section was adopted by the whole consultation as an official statement. The subsequent third part of the document, which was more specific, dealing with Christian-Jewish Relations, Christian-Buddhist Relations, Christian-Hindu relations as well as with Christian concern in traditional religions, cultures and ideologies, was received by

In our worship we knew again that the Christian community is one that shares in holy things given by God and is both privileged and obliged to bear witness in a positive way to these undeserved and often unexpected gifts of God.

This newness and given-ness of the Christian message and of the way that God has opened up for us cut across the customary thought and behavior of all our cultures.

To enter again into the mystery of Christian worship, of access to God in his transcendence through our Lord Jesus Christ who came among us, was also a stimulus to take seriously the worship and meditation of others as exemplified in both the ritual and the contemplative life of the Buddhist monks who so helpfully received us as visitors to the Wats of Chiang Mai and its area.

Why the theme "Dialogue in Community"? As the work of the subunit on Dialogue with People of Living Faiths and Ideologies has developed, emphasis has come to be placed not so much on dialogue itself as on dialogue in community. The Christian community within the human community has a common heritage and a distinctive message to share; it needs therefore to reflect on the nature of the community that we as Christians seek and on the relation of dialogue to the life of the churches, as they ask themselves how they can be communities of service and witness without diluting their faith or compromising their commitment to Christ. Such an enquiry needs to be informed both by a knowledge of different religions and societies and by insights gained through actual dialogues with neighbors. The enquiry needs also to take account of the concerns, questions and experiences of the member churches of the WCC.

These needs determined the composition of the consultation, which included historians of religion, sociologists, pastors and those involved in community service as well as biblical scholars and theologians of the various Christian traditions. We came together from many parts of the world, though regrettably some from Eastern Europe, the Middle East, and Latin America who had accepted invitations were not able to come. This was a Christian consultation but the variety of the participants and their regular work in dialogue service, and reflection made sure that we carried on our discussions in plenary and groups with awareness of our neighbors both in the churches and in the communities of living faiths and ideologies. The theme and

the whole consultation as a record of experiences and insights in specific contexts and on particular issues, but was not adopted as an official statement. This last section was presented to the Churches for consideration and evaluation in light of the prior and central statement reproduced here, "Dialogue in Community." This last section can be obtained upon request from the World Council of Churches Program on Dialogue.

The text of the consultation appeared in The International (Occasional) Bulletin of Missionary Research, *April 1977, Vol. 1, 2, pp. 22-25 and is reprinted here by permission of the publisher.*

composition of the consultation also demanded of us, and particularly of the theologians, a reconsideration of traditional models and of the relationship between a deductive theology, evaluating dialogue within a given such systematic framework, and a dialogical theology which is a reflection upon traditional Christian thought in the light of a developing understanding both of human communities and of the communion into which God in Christ calls men and women. As Dr. S. J. Samartha indicated in his introductory remarks, this was "a pause for reflection."

Such a pause for reflection does not justify detachment from the problems of the world today. During our discussions we became deeply aware of the fact that in an age of worldwide struggle of humankind for survival and liberation, the religions have their important contributions to make, which can only be worked out in mutual dialogue. It is a responsibility of Christians to foster such dialogue in a spirit of reconciliation and hope granted to us by Jesus Christ. We came to see how easy it is to discuss religions and even ideologies as though they existed in some realm of calm quite separate from the sharp conflicts and sufferings of humankind. We ask that our statements be read with a recognition that they have a place in a total WCC program which includes major Christian involvement in political and economic stresses and social problems. We ask also that they be evaluated in relation to other WCC concerns and also in their hearing on such discussions as that on the unity of the Church and the unity of humankind.

It will be noted that the words "mission" and "evangelism" are not often used in our statements. This is not because we seek to escape the Christian responsibility, reemphasized in the Nairobi Assembly, to confess Christ today, but in order to explore other ways of making plain the intentions of Christian witness and service, so as to avoid misunderstanding. This was a Christian conference, and Christian integrity includes an integrity of response to the call of the risen Christ to be witnesses to him in all the world.

Part I. On Community
A. Communities and the Community of Humankind

1. As Christians we begin our reflection on community from the acknowledgement that God as we believe him to have come to us in Jesus Christ is the Creator of all things and of all humankind; that from the beginning he willed relationship with himself and between all that he has brought to life; that to that end he has enabled the formation of communities, judges them, and renews them. When we confess him as one Holy Trinity, when we rejoice in his new creation in the resurrection of Christ, we perceive and experience new dimensions of our given humanity. Yet, the very nature and content of our Christian confession draws us to pay the closest attention to the realities of the world as it has developed under God's creative, disciplinary, and redemptive rule. So we are led to attempt a description of communities and the community of humankind, in the light of a basic

Christian confession but in terms which may also find understanding and even agreement among many of other faiths and ideologies.

2. We are all born into relationships with other people. Most immediately there are the members of our families, but quickly we have to explore wider relationships as we go to school or begin work. This may take place in the complexity of relationships within a village society, or within the modern urban centers of town and city which attract ever larger populations. We experience still wider associations within nation, race, religion, and at the same time we may belong to different social classes or castes which condition our ideological outlooks. Then the newspapers we read, the radio and T.V. programs we hear and see give us an awareness of the multitude of ways in which the lives we live are dependent on people in other parts of the world, where ways of life are amazingly varied. From these, and many related contexts, we derive our sense of being part of some communities and apart from others. The sense of identity with some communities and of alienation from others is something we never completely understand but it remains reality for us all at the many levels of our existence.

3. Within each particular community to which we may belong we are held together with others by the values we share in common. At the deepest level these have to do with our identity, which gives us a sense of being "at home" in the groups to which we belong. Identity may be formed within a long historical experience, or in the face of problems newly encountered; it may express itself in communal traditions and rituals shaped through centuries, or in newer forms sometimes less coherent and sometimes more rigid. We are conscious at this point of the formative influence of religions and ideologies which may be closely interrelated; but we recognize that these have themselves been shaped by other elements of the culture of which they are part—language, ethnic loyalty, social strata, caste. Some communities may tend to uniformity in this regard, while others have long traditions of pluralism, and it is not infrequent that individual families may share more than one set of beliefs.

4. We consider the ties between religion and culture to be very influential in community life. An example was readily available for us as visitors to Chiang Mai where we were strongly aware of the cultural identity of Northern Thailand, informed by the Buddhism of the majority population, though we learned also of the distinctive character of Buddhism in Northern Thailand, by contrast to that of, for example, Sri Lanka. During our discussion African participants described the traditional religious patterns on their communities, and demonstrated how these provided resources for their interpreting other religious traditions (notably Christianity and Islam) which have been implanted more recently in many parts of the African continent.

5. Within the experience of the conference of the conference, we were aware that our communities are many and varied. We were conscious also

that they are involved in a constant process of change which evokes their comparison with flowing rivers rather than stable monuments. But if change is always present, there can be no doubt that it has been accelerated in the times in which we live, especially by scientific technology, economic forces, and the mass media. Some participants spoke of changes so rapid and dramatic as to give them the experience of the loss of community, and of the human isolation which follows. Others spoke of the reforming and reshaping of communities: once closed communities being thrown into relationship with others with which they find themselves engaged in the tasks of nation-building; communities formerly of a single cultural identity being opened to a cultural pluralism and plurality of religious systems; communities in which traditional religious systems may undergo far-reaching change, and, re-vitalized, provide renewed identity and continuity with the past. We were conscious that amidst these changes many people are alienated from all community and have either given up the quest for community or are seeking it from many sources.

6. An important aspect of this accelerated change has been brought about by the complex network of relationships which has been created between human communities in recent times. We are conscious, more urgently today than ever in the past, that the traditions of our individual communities are being drawn toward one another, sometimes into a new harmony, sometimes into a destructive whirlpool in the flowing rivers. The interrelatedness of our human communities brings with it many new challenges to mutual concern and pastoral care, our response to which, both individually and collectively as communities, will determine the character of the reality of which we are growing aware—''the community of humankind.''

7. The response is often given in the form of ideologies. In fact, the accelerated change has made us more sensitively aware of the need for conscious social and political action, because we find ourselves in the midst of many ideological projects which attempt in various ways to shape or reshape society. Traditional communities do not escape the impact of ideological thinking and action, and their varied responses may bring conflict as well as renewal.

8. It was to these challenges that we gave our attention in the early part of the conference. While not ignoring the inherent dangers, our experience of human interrelatedness in our different local situations deepened our awareness of the richness of the diversity of the community of humankind which we believe to be created and sustained by God in his love for all people. We marvel and give thanks for this richness, acknowledging that to have experienced it has given many of us an enriched appreciation of the deeper values in our own traditions—and in some cases has enabled us to rediscover them. But at the same time we feel sharply conscious of the way in which diversity can be, and too often has been, abused: the temptation to regard our own community as the best; to attribute to our own religious and cultural identity

an absolute authority; the temptation to exclude from it, and to isolate it from others. In such temptations we recognize that we are liable to spurn and despoil the riches which God has, with such generosity, invested in his human creation...that we are liable to impoverish, divide, and despoil.

9. Because of the divisive role to which all religions and ideologies are so easily prone, we believe that they are each called to look upon themselves anew, so as to contribute from their resources to the good of the community of humankind in its wholeness. Thinking of the challenge to our Christian faith we were reminded both of the danger of saying "peace, peace" where there is no peace, and of Jesus' words in the Sermon on the Mount: "Happy are those who work for peace: God will call them His children" (Matt. 5:9). As workers for peace, liberation, and justice—the way to which often makes conflict necessary and reconciliation costly—we feel ourselves called to share with others in the community of humankind in search for new experiences in the evolution of our communities, where we may affirm our interdependence as much as respect for our distinctive identities. The vision of worldwide "community of communities" commended itself to us a means of seeking community in a pluralistic world. The vision is not one of homogeneous unity or totalitarian uniformity but is for Christians related to the kingly rule of God over all human communities.

B. The Christian Community: The Churches and the Church

10. Scattered within the world of human communities, we as Christians look for signs of God's kingly rule and truly believe in our community with Christians everywhere in the Church, the Body of Christ. Being fully in the world, the Christian community shares in the many distinctions and divisions within and between the communities of humankind. It manifests immense cultural variety within itself, which we are bound to acknowledge as affecting not only the practice but also the interpretation of the faith by different groups of Christians. This was exemplified in our discussions by participants from South Asia who spoke to us of their struggle, within cultures molded by Hinduism, Buddhism, and Islam, to express their Christian faith in a spirit at once obedient to the Gospel and in relation to the cultural context in which they live. From Europe and North America participants were conscious of the degree to which their understanding and practice of the Christian faith has been influenced by Western culture.

11. Our experiences as Christians in this widely scattered community are very varied. There are churches who live in situations of social, cultural, and national suppression, where their identity is threatened and their freedom restricted. There are times and places where Christians may have to stand apart from others in loyalty to Christ but this does not absolve Christians who have indulged in the temptations of cultural arrogance and communal exclusivity, both consciously and unconsciously. Thus we have contributed

156

to the divisions within the community of humankind, and have created antagonisms between different groups within the Christian community itself. As Christians, therefore, we must stand under the judgment of God. We believe that there is a real sense in which our unity with all people lies in our common participation in all that has so tragically created divisions within the world. It is in this way that we relate to our theme the experience of the empirical churches that they constantly need God's forgiveness.

12. But amidst this complex, confusing and humbling situation we believe that the Gospel of our Lord Jesus Christ retains its divine given-ness. Through the inspiration of the Holy Spirit, the Gospel cannot be limited to any particular culture, but sheds its light in them all and upon them all. Nor is the truth of the Gospel distorted by the sinfulness of its Christian adherents. Rather, the Gospel calls us individually and in community to repentance and confession, and invites us into newness of life in the Risen Christ. This reality of renewed Christian community pertains to our very deepest experience as Christians. Different participants spoke of it in different ways:

— our communion in the Church as sacrament of the reconciliation and unity of humankind recreated through the saving activity of God in Jesus Christ;

— our communion with God who, in the fulness of his Trinity, calls humankind into unity with him in his eternal communion with his entire creation;

— our communion in fellowship with all members of the Body of Christ through history, across distinctions of race, sex, caste and culture;

— a sense of communion with all people and everything which is made holy by the work of God in communities of faith and ideology beyond our own.

Though we may express our conviction of the reality of this community in different ways, we hold fast to God in Christ who nourishes his church by Word and Sacraments.

13. We must acknowledge the close relation between our concern for dialogue and our work for visible Church unity. It is not only that the different confessional traditions have been an influence on the different approaches to dialogue and that questions concerning dialogue are seriously discussed within and between churches, but also that the Christian contribution to dialogue is weakened by division among Christians.

14. In the consultation we experienced both the possibility for common confession of the faith and worship together and also some of the obstacles to Christian unity. We were agreed in giving a vital place in our thinking to Bible study and worship; we were able to worship our one Lord in the very different ways of the churches represented among those who led our worship. We were, however, also aware of problems concerning the authority of the Bible remaining unsolved amongst us and of the need for a much closer attention than we had time to give to the problem of relating Christian

worship and the meditative use (rather than simply the intellectual study) of the holy books of other faiths. In one of our acts of Christian worship we were invited by the leader in the course of the service to use responsively a passage of the Bhagavad Gita. This immediately made plain the rejection or deep hesation by some toward any such experience while we discovered in conversation afterwards how meaningful some others find such meditative acts. We recognize the need for further study of the issues thus raised.

15. As Christians, therefore, we are conscious of a tension between the Christian community as we experience it to be in the world of human communities, and as we believe it in essence to be in the promise of God. The tension if fundamental to our Christian identity. We cannot resolve it, nor should we seek to avoid it. In the heart of this tension we discover the character of the Christian Church as a sign at once of people's need for fuller and deeper community, and of God's promise of a restored human community in Christ. Our consciousness of the tension must preclude any trace of triumphalism in the life of the Christian Church in the communities of humankind. It must also preclude any trace of condescension toward our fellow human beings. Rather it should evoke in us an attitude of real humility toward all peoples since we know that we together with all our brothers and sisters have fallen short of the community which God intends.

16. We understand our calling as Christians to be that of participating fully in the mission of God *(missio Dei)*—with the courage of conviction to enable us to be adventurous and take risks. To this end we would humbly share with all our fellow human beings in a compelling pilgrimage. We are specifically disciples of Christ, but we refuse to limit him to the dimensions of our human understanding. In our relationships within the many human communities we believe that we come to know Christ more fully through faith as Son of God and Savior of the world; we grow in his service within the world; and we rejoice in the hope which he gives.

Part II. On Dialogue
C. Reasons for Dialogue

17. We consider the term "dialogue in community" to be useful in that it gives concreteness to our thinking. Moreover it focuses attention on our reasons for being in dialogue, which we identified in two related categories.

Most of us today live out our lives as Christians in actual community with people who may be committed to faiths and ideologies other than our own. We live in families sometimes of mixed faiths and ideologies; we live as neighbors in the same towns and villages; we need to build up our relationships expressing mutual human care and searching for mutual understanding. This sort of dialogue is very practical, concerned with the problems of modern life—the social, political, ecological—and, above all, the ordinary and familiar.

We are conscious also of our concerns beyond the local, and thus feel feel called to engage in dialogue toward the realization of a wider community in which peace and justice may be more fully realized. This leads us in turn to a dialogue between communities, in which we tackle issues of national and international concern for the sake of the vision of a worldwide "community of communities."

18. No more than "community" can "dialogue" be precisely defined. Rather it has to be described, experienced, and developed as a life-style. As human beings we have learned to speak; we talk, chatter, give and receive information, have discussions—all this is not yet dialogue. Now and then it happens that out of our talking and our relationships arises deeper encounter, an opening up, in more than intellectual terms, of each to the concerns of the other. This is experienced by families and friends, and by those who share the same faith or ideology: but we are particularly concerned with the dialogue which reaches across differences of faith, ideology, and culture even where the partners in dialogue do not agree on important central aspects of human life. We recognize dialogue as a welcome way in which we can be more obedient to the commandment of the Decalogue: "You shall not bear false witness against your neighbor." We need dialogue to help us not to disfigure the image of our neighbors of different faiths and ideologies. It has been the experience of many in our consultation that this dialogue is indeed possible on the basis of a mutual trust and a respect for the integrity of each participant's identity.

19. We see dialogue, therefore, as a fundamental part of our Christian service within community. In dialogue we actively respond to the command "to love God and your neighbor as yourself." As an expression of our love, our engagement in dialogue testifies to the love we have experienced in Christ. It is our joyful affirmation of life against chaos, and our participation with all who are allies of life in seeking the provisional goals of a better human community. Thus we soundly reject any idea of "dialogue in community" as a secret weapon in the armory of an aggressive Christian militancy. We adopt it rather as a means of living out our faith in Christ in service of community with our neighbors.

20. In this sense we endorse dialogue as having a distinctive and rightful place within Christian life, in a manner directly comparable to other forms of service. But by "distinctive" we do not mean totally different or separate. In dialogue we seek "to speak the truth in a spirit of love," not naively "to be tossed to and fro, and be carried about with every wind of doctrine" (Eph. 4:14-15). In giving our witness we recognize that in most circumstances today the spirit of dialogue is necessary. For this reason we do not see dialogue and the giving of witness as standing in any contradiction to one another. Indeed, as we enter dialogue with our commitment to Jesus Christ, time and again the relationship of dialogue gives opportunity for authentic witness. Thus, to the member churches of the WCC we feel able with integrity to commend the way of dialogue as one in which Jesus Christ can be

confessed in the world today; at the same time we feel able with integrity to assure our partners in dialogue that we come not as manipulators but as genuine fellow-pilgrims, to speak with them of what we believe God to have done in Jesus Christ who has gone before us, but whom we seek to meet new anew in dialogue.

D. The Theological Significance
of Peoples of Other Faiths and Ideologies

21. As we engage thus in faithful "dialogue in community" with peoples of other faiths and ideologies we cannot avoid asking ourselves penetrating questions about their place in the activity of God in history. We should remind ourselves, however, that we ask this question not in theory, but in terms of what God may be doing in the lives of hundreds of millions of men and women who live in and seek community together with ourselves, but along different ways. So we should think always in terms of people of other faiths and ideologies rather than of theoretical, impersonal systems. We should examine how ther faiths and ideologies have given direction to their daily living and actually affect dialogue on both sides.

22. Approaching the theological questions in this spirit we felt strongly the need to proceed...

—with repentance, because we know how easily we misconstrue God's revelation in Jesus Christ, betraying it in our actions and posturing as the owners of God's truth rather than, as in fact we are, the undeserving recipients of grace;

—with humility, because we so often perceive in people of other faiths and ideologies a spirituality, dedication, compassion, and a wisdom which should forbid our making judgments about them as though from a position of superiority; in particular we should avoid using ideas such as "anonymous Christians," "the Christian presence" "the unknown Christ," in ways not intended by those who proposed them for theological purposes or in ways prejudicial to the self-understanding of Christians and others;

—with joy, because it is not ourselves we preach; it is Jesus Christ, perceived by many peoples of living faiths and ideologies as prophet, holy one, teacher, example; but confessed by us as Lord and Saviour, himself the faithful witness and the coming one (Rev. 1:5-7);

—with integrity, because we do not enter into dialogue with others except in this penitent and humble joyfulness in our Lord Jesus Christ, making clear to others our own experience and witness, even as we seek to hear from them their expressions of deepest conviction and insight.

23. Only in this spirit can we hope to address ourselves creatively to the theological questions posed by other faiths and ideologies. Our theological discussions in the conference aided the growth of understanding between Christian participants from different backgrounds in the following areas in particular:

—that renewed attention must be given to the doctrine of creation, particularly as we may see it illuminated by the Christian understanding of God as one Holy Trinity and by the resurrection and glorification of Christ.

—that fundamental questions about the nature and activity of God and the doctrine of the Spirit arise in dialogue, and the Christological discussion must take place within this comprehensive reference;

—that the Bible, with all the aids to its understanding and appropriation from the Church's tradition and scholarship, is to be used creatively as the basis for our Christian reflection on the issues that arise, giving us both encouragement and warning, through we cannot assume it as a reference point for our partners;

—that the theological problems of church unity also need to be viewed in relation to our concern for dialogue;

—that the search for common ground should not be a reduction of living faiths and ideologies to a lowest common denominator, but a quest for that of spirit and life which is only found at those deepest levels of human experience, variously symbolized and conceptualized in different faiths.

24. We look forward to further fruitful discussions of these issues (among many others) within our Christian circles but also in situations of dialogue. There were other questions where we found agreement more difficult and sometimes impossible, but these also we would commend for further theological attention:

What is the relationship between God's universal action in creation and his redemptive action in Jesus Christ?

Are we to speak of God's work in the lives of all men and women only in tentative terms of hope that they may experience something of him, or more positvely in terms of God's self-disclosure to people of living faiths and in the struggle of human life and ideology?

How are we to find, from the Bible, criteria in our approach to people of other faiths and ideologies, recognizing as we must the authority acccorded to the Bible by Christians of all centuries, particular questions concerning the authority of the Old Testament for the Christian Church, and the fact that our partners in dialogue have other starting points and resources, both in holy books and traditions of teaching?

What is the biblical view and Christian experience of the operation of the Holy Spirit, and is it right and helpful to understand the work of God outside the Church in terms of the doctrine of the Holy Spirit?

E. Syncretism

25. In dialogue we are called to be adventurous, and we must be ready to take risks; but also to be watchful and wide awake for God. Is syncretism a danger for which we must be alert?

26. We first affirm positively the need for a genuine "translation" of the Christian message in every time and place. This need can be recognized as soon as the Bible translators begin their work in a particular language and have to weigh the cultural and philosophical overtones and undertones of its words. But there is also a wider "translation" of the message by expressing it in artistic, dramatic, liturgical, and above all relational terms which are appropriate to convey the authenticity of the message in ways authentically indigenous, often through the theologically tested use of the symbols and concepts of a particular community.

27. We speak here of "translation" where some have spoken of a proper or Christ-centered syncretism. We recognize the intention thus to rescue the word "syncretism," but we believe that after its previous uses in Christian debate by now it necessarily conveys a negative evaluation. This is clearly the case if it means, as the Nairobi Assembly used the word, "conscious or unconscious human attempts to create a new religion composed of elements taken from different religions," in this sense we believe that syncretism is also rejected by our dialogue partners, although we recognize that there may be some who in their alienation are seeking help from many sources and do not regard syncretism negatively.

28. The word "syncretism" is, however, more widely used than at Nairobi and particularly to warn against two other dangers. The first danger is that in attempting to "translate" the Christian message for a cultural setting or in approach to faiths and ideologies with which we are in dialogue partnership, we may go too far and compromise the authenticity of Christian faith and life. We have the Bible to guide us but there is always risk in seeking to express the Gospel in a new setting: for instance, the early Christian struggle against heresy in the debate with Gnosticism; or the compromising of the Gospel in the so-called "civil religions" of the West. It is salutary to examine such examples lest it be supposed that syncretism is a risk endemic only in certain continents.

A second danger is that of interpreting a living faith not in its own terms but in terms of another faith or ideology. This is illegitimate on the principles of both scholarship and dialogue. In this way we may "syncretize" Christianity by seeing it as only a variant of some other approach to God, or we may wrongly "syncretize" another faith by seeing it as only a partial understanding of what we Christians believe that we know in full. There is particular need for further study of the way in which this kind of syncretism can take place between a faith and an ideology.

29. We recognize both that these are real dangers and that there will be differences of judgment among Christians and between churches as to when these dangers are threatening, or have actually overtaken particular Christian enterprises. We may sum up our conclusions on this question of syncretism in terms of the Thai story that the little lizards which climb the house walls in Chiang Mai are saying by their cries both "Welcome" and

"Take Care." We welcome the venture of exploratory faith; we warn each other, "Take Care."

30. This mutual warning developed into a positive attitude as our consultation progressed. Within the ecumenical movement the practice of dialogue and the giving of witness have sometimes evoked mutual suspicion. God is very patient with us, giving us space and time for discovery of his way and its riches (cf. 2 Pet. 3:9). In our discussion we sensed afresh the need to give one another space and time—space and time, for instance, in India or Ghana to explore the richness of the Gospel in a setting very different from that of "Hellenized" Europe; space and time, for instance, in Korea to develop the present striking evangelistic work of the churches; space and time, for instance, in Europe to adjust to a new situation in which secularity is now being changed by a new religious interest, not expressed in traditional terms. We need to recognize the diversity of dialogue itself in its particular contexts and in relation to specific discussions, which formed the third main section of our consultation.

Index

Index

Index

Index

Index

Index